D0782588

MUSCLE ON WHEELS

MUSCLE
on
WHEELS

LOUISE ARMAINDO

AND THE

HIGH-WHEEL RACERS

OF

NINETEENTH-CENTURY AMERICA

M. ANN HALL

McGill-Queen's University Press

Montreal & Kingston • London • Chicago

© McGill-Queen's University Press 2018

ISBN 978-0-7735-5465-8 (cloth)
ISBN 978-0-7735-5532-7 (ePDF)
ISBN 978-0-7735-5533-4 (ePUB)

Legal deposit third quarter 2018
Bibliothèque nationale du Québec

Printed in Canada on acid-free paper that is 100% ancient forest free
(100% post-consumer recycled), processed chlorine free

This book has been published with the help of a grant from the Canadian
Federation for the Humanities and Social Sciences, through the Awards
to Scholarly Publications Program, using funds provided by the Social
Sciences and Humanities Research Council of Canada. Funding has also
been provided by the Faculty of Kinesiology, Sport, and Recreation at the
University of Alberta.

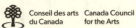

Funded by the   Financé par le
Government   gouvernement   Canada   Conseil des arts   Canada Council
of Canada   du Canada   du Canada   for the Arts

We acknowledge the support of the Canada Council for the Arts, which
last year invested $153 million to bring the arts to Canadians throughout
the country.

Nous remercions le Conseil des arts du Canada de son soutien. L'an dernier,
le Conseil a investi 153 millions de dollars pour mettre de l'art dans la vie des
Canadiennes et des Canadiens de tout le pays.

Library and Archives Canada Cataloguing in Publication

Hall, M. Ann (Margaret Ann), 1942–, author
Muscle on wheels : Louise Armaindo and the high-wheel racers of nineteenth-
century America / M. Ann Hall.

Includes bibliographical references and index.
Issued in print and electronic formats.
ISBN 978-0-7735-5465-8 (hardcover).–ISBN 978-0-7735-5532-7 (ePDF).
ISBN 978-0-7735-5533-4 (ePUB)

1. Bicycle racing – History – 19th century. 2. Bicycles – History – 19th
century. 3. Armaindo, Louise, 1857–1900. 4. Women cyclists – Canada –
Biography. 5. Cyclists – Canada – Biography. 6. Women cyclists –
History – 19th century. 7. Bicycles – Social aspects – 19th century. I. Title.

GV1049.H35 2018   796.6'209034   C2018-901661-2
                                                C2018-901662-0

This book was designed and typeset by studio oneonone in Sabon 10.3/13.5

And the women were there, what a price they had paid
To be at that table so finely displayed
And now I can see at last
The past is before me and the women are there

From Judy Fjell's song "The Dinner Party"

CONTENTS

ACKNOWLEDGMENTS

This book took a long time to research and write. I worked on it steadily for several years, and during that time encountered many people who were not only enthusiastic supporters of the project, but also willing helpers in the search for information. Most I have never met in person, but our email and phone conversations were often exhilarating and always helpful. April Streeter, who is writing a novel about Louise Armaindo, shared interesting tidbits from her research. I owe much to Gherardo Bonini at the European University Institute in Italy, and to Dag Hammar, a cycling historian in Sweden, for their support and willingness to provide me with newspaper articles and photos, and best of all, for their helpful advice.

I did meet Lorne Shields, who became a friend. He has amassed one of the finest collections of all things related to the bicycle, and his knowledge of bicycle history is unsurpassed. I sought his advice countless times. Along with cycling historian John Weiss, he was always on the lookout for interesting bicycle ephemera and archival photos, some of which are included in this book. One of their finds was the delightful poster used on the book's cover. It was painstakingly scanned and digitally restored by Paula Aurini-Onderwater.

A project like this depends on the many archivists and reference librarians who kindly and expediently answer inquiries. I am in debt to those who assisted me at the following institutions: American Antiquarian Society; Bancroft Library, University of California Berkeley;

Benson Ford Research Center, The Henry Ford; Bibliothèque et Archives nationales du Québec; Bibliothèque nationale de France; Brooklyn Public Library; Canada Science and Technology Museum; Granger Historical Picture Archive; Heinz History Center, Pittsburgh; Kentucky Historical Society; Library of Congress; Maine Historical Society; Minnesota Historical Society; Nevada Historical Society; Stephen H. Hart Library, History Colorado. A special thank-you goes to François Campagna at the Cimetière Notre-Dame-des-Neiges in Montreal, who searched in vain for Louise Armaindo's grave, and also to Jim Brown, operation manager at the Folsom Prison Museum, for Fred Rollinson's record and information about prison conditions in the mid-1880s.

There are also other individuals who, in one way or another, have contributed to this project even though they may not have realized it at the time. They are Constance Beaulieu, Susanne Bloomfield, Gerald Gems, Roger Gilles, Sheila Hanlon, Tammy Haley, Michael Heine, Gilles Janson, Alain Lachapelle, Patrick Leroux, Pierre Massue, Buck Peacock, Anne Ptolemy, Andrew Ritchie, Alice Roepke, Debra Shattuck, Clare Simpson, Darlene Slack, Mary Soom, and Jacqueline Stuart.

I am grateful to the Faculty of Kinesiology, Sport, and Recreation at the University of Alberta, my intellectual home for more than fifty years, for their ongoing support of my research, and especially for providing a grant to the publisher for this book. It has been a pleasure to work with the team at McGill-Queen's University Press, and in particular editor Kyla Madden.

Finally, there are two members of my family to whom I owe a huge debt. My sister, Nancy Mitchell, used her unsurpassed genealogical skills to hunt down background information about many of the individuals in this story. Where I gave up the search, she persisted until we had a verifiable account. Jane Haslett, my partner for more than thirty years, is used to sharing our life with my latest research project, and she does so willingly. She is also a superb editor, and as always, this is a better book because of her suggestions.

Muscle on Wheels

INTRODUCTION

The girl was small and compact. Her legs were rather thicker than
beauty demanded, and if you had touched them you would have
found their sheaths of muscle as hard as steel. Though she was the
greatest woman athlete that ever lived, there was nothing masculine
about Louise Armaindo except the toughness of her body. Her smile
was alluringly white toothed and her dark eyes full of sex-appeal ...
though that was a day before feminine fascination had so obvious a
label attached to it.

   In Louise Armaindo's business sex-appeal was of assistance in the
box-office, but was of no help in her actual work. She doubled in
brass, so to speak, as a weight-lifter, bicycle rider and long-distance
walker ... and was better than most men at any of those jobs.
Jack Kofoed, *Thrills in Sport*

In a 1931 syndicated column, "Thrills in Sports," sportswriter Jack
Kofoed wrote admiringly about Louise Armaindo and wondered what
happened to her.[1] Kofoed was following in the footsteps of sports journalist and historian Frank G. Menke, who was the first to claim Louise
Armaindo as the greatest woman athlete who ever lived. Few men, he
argued, could match her in all-around physical powers. In a syndicated
column in 1922, published in over three hundred newspapers throughout

North America, Menke sketched her accomplishments as circus acrobat, pedestrienne, and high-wheel bicycle racer. "Fear," he wrote, "was entirely foreign to her. She did not know its meaning. And she was forever trying something new and novel in the way of athletics."[2] By the mid-1880s Louise was at the height of her athletic career, but by the beginning of the new century she had disappeared from public view. Few realized she was no longer alive, nor did anyone seem to care. When Menke's column appeared, she had long since been forgotten, and he too seemed unaware that she had died more than two decades ago. By the time Kofoed got around to writing about her, likely no one reading had heard about her. In his comprehensive *Encyclopedia of Sports*, first published in 1939, Menke did not mention Louise, nor did he in subsequent editions.[3]

Occasionally, an enterprising sports reporter would remember Louise, such as the one who wondered how the "greatest all-around female woman athlete of all time" – namely, Mildred "Babe" Didrickson – would stack up against Louise Armaindo in her prime.[4] It was difficult to judge how Louise would have fared in modern competition, argued the writer, because there were no Olympic Games for women in her day; moreover, golf and tennis were much too tame for the rugged tastes of the "little French-Canadian lass." Rather, he suggested, Louise might have preferred a backfield berth with a "big-league" professional football club.

Today, nearly 140 years after Louise became a marvel of athletic strength, talent, and endurance, she continues to be ignored not only by cycling historians but also by those who write about women's sport history. There are scattered, though often inaccurate, references to Louise, but nothing of substance.[5] As a French Canadian, she has not been included among the histories of famous, sometimes forgotten, athletes from Quebec. In 1909, Montreal journalist and archivist Édouard-Zotique Massicotte published a book containing the biographies of over fifty French Canadian athletes and sportsmen since the eighteenth century. Among them was only one woman: Marie-Louise Sirois (1867–1920), a strongwoman, who married fellow Quebec strongman Henri Cloutier.[6] The more recently published *Dictionnaire des grands oubliés du sport au Québec 1850–1950*, which contains 283 biographies of forgotten individuals in Quebec sport – athletes, journalists, physical educators, administrators, and promoters – makes no mention of Louise Armaindo.[7]

I became interested in Louise Armaindo because she was Canadian, and certainly among Canada's first women professional athletes. For more than fifteen years, beginning in the late 1870s, she travelled extensively throughout the United States, rarely returning to Canada, even though press reports usually noted that she was French Canadian and from Montreal. She received a brief mention in two of my previous books about the history of women's sport in Canada.[8] With frustratingly little information to go on, I decided that she deserved a book of her own.

Tracking Louise Armaindo throughout the last two decades of the nineteenth century led me to examine the high-wheel era more closely; as a result, I discovered many more women who raced. Like her, several began their racing careers as professional endurance walkers or pedestriennes. They had already experienced the rigours of incessant travel, poor living conditions, and men who claimed to be agents or trainers, yet more often than not took their hard earned money, or worse still abused them physically, even sexually. There were probably about twenty women in the United States who were professional high-wheel bicycle racers during the 1880s and 1890s. Of these, approximately eight also raced safety bicycles from 1895 onwards until their competitive careers ended. We have little information about these women racers or how gender (and to a lesser extent social class) operated in the high-wheel era. By and large these women athletes have not been taken seriously by cycling historians, and they are often dismissed as the "kind of low-class show-business chicanery that amateur organizations sought to purge from sport."[9]

In his social history of the bicycle, Robert Smith begins each of his thirteen chapters with the reproduction of an advertising card depicting a female on a bicycle, more than half of whom were atop a high wheel.[10] These scantily clad women portrayed trick riders in titillating poses designed to appeal to men. The twenty-five cards were issued by the American Tobacco Company in the early 1890s to advertise their chewing and smoking tobacco.[11] Smith also included the famous Waverley Belle Cycles advertisement depicting a woman from behind, naked except for shoes and knee-length stockings, her left arm behind her head with her right arm holding a "Kangaroo" bicycle, a geared safety version of a high wheel. There is no mention of women who raced the high wheel, though he does include an unidentified photo of Elsa von Blumen, a racing contemporary of Louise Armaindo. To be fair, his book contains a wide variety of illustrations depicting bicycle history, including various outfits worn by women when safety bicycles first became popular in the mid-1890s. Nonetheless, those reading the book today would be left with the impression that women who rode high wheels were nothing more than exhibitionist trick riders or circus performers. Some indeed were, but many more were serious, professional athletes.

Only recently have sport historians turned their attention to in-depth explorations of women's professional sports in nineteenth-century North America – what sport historian Roberta Park called "contesting the norm."[12] Mostly, these athletes were pedestriennes, high-wheel and safety bicycle racers, wrestlers, boxers, shooters, and baseball players. This research allows us to examine similarities and differences between sports and the women who competed in them.

In *Bloomer Girls*, for example, Debra Shattuck meticulously reconstructs a forgotten era of women's professional baseball in the United States from the 1860s into the 1890s. The earliest spectacles of women's baseball were best described as "burlesque al fresco," a form of satirical, theatrical comedy performed outdoors by players who lacked the athletic skills to play the game properly. Audiences were primarily working-class men, although women and children were encouraged to attend to provide an air of respectability. Promoters and sports reporters emphasized the femininity of the players with performances advertised as wholesome family entertainment. Despite condemnation, especially from the male baseball fraternity, women's professional teams continued to multiply in the 1880s and 1890s because scores of young, working-class women saw an opportunity to earn a living away from the drudgery of waitressing, laundering, sewing, or domestic servitude. Unfortunately, they were routinely exploited by unscrupulous managers whose sole purpose was to make money off their young charges.[13]

In this respect, they were no different to the strongwomen, pedestriennes, bicycliennes, and boxers, but those athletes, unlike the baseball players, required serious athletic talent, perseverance, and endurance to be successful. Through their performances they contested and challenged the prevailing gender norms in late nineteenth-century America, and as a result they helped to encourage a more assertive Victorian physicality, especially among women.[14]

Were these women athletes competing in sport, or were their efforts strictly for the entertainment of a primarily male audience? To bicycle historians, these events were nothing more than risqué, exploitative commercial spectacles, rather than meaningful athletic events. Certainly novel, they lacked genuine competition, and it was the promoter who benefitted and not necessarily the athlete. This may be true, but the occurrence of these events should be placed within the larger context of the burgeoning entertainment industry of nineteenth-century America, which began to employ more and more women. The circus created the first truly national depiction of women at work as seen by an audience of women, men, and children.[15] Circuses celebrated female power, especially physical strength, risk, and sexuality, and they also expanded notions about Victorian women's capabilities and appropriate work. Louise Armaindo began her professional athletic career in the circus as a strongwoman and trapeze artist in the 1870s. Pedestrianism, which she took up next, provided more opportunities for working-class women to perform before large audiences and earn a living, precarious as it was, through their athleticism.[16]

A common misperception is that women first took up cycling in the mid- to late 1880s with the advent of the chain-driven safety bicycle, made even more comfortable with the invention of pneumatic tires. In fact, women have been riding, and occasionally racing, some form of the bicycle since the first *vélocipèdes* (literally "quick foot") appeared in Europe early in the nineteenth century. Also called *draisines* (after inventor Karl von Drais) or hobbyhorses, velocipedes were similar to present-day bicycles except that they were propelled by pushing off the ground with one foot and then the other. Balance was an issue, but young ice skaters took to them easily. A special model for ladies was marketed, though unsuccessfully, with a lower horizontal bar to accommodate flowing dresses. These early bicycles were impractical for daily use because they were expensive and it was impossible to ride them safely on rough roads or carriageways already occupied by horses. Since sidewalks were the only other option, magistrates and city officials were forced to ban them to protect pedestrians. Although velocipedes had arrived in the United States by 1819, they were soon prohibited in larger cities like New York and Philadelphia. For the next forty years, these early velocipedes and their three- and four-wheeled cousins remained largely a British preoccupation, and only occasionally were there reports of their use in North America.[17]

A pedal-powered velocipede propelled by a crank attached to the front axle was developed in France in the 1860s. International visitors to the 1867 Paris Exhibition saw these velocipedes in action and were sufficiently impressed to bring home glowing reports, perhaps even a few velocipedes. Aptly called "boneshakers," the original versions had wooden wheels with iron hoop tires, but later models had rubber or leather coverings over the metal. Still, they were a rough ride, especially over hard, uneven surfaces. They too were expensive, costing anywhere between $75 and $150, which meant that only the well-off could afford the new-fangled machine.[18]

By 1869 major American cities experienced velocipede mania, and riding schools, often in converted ice or roller skating rinks, sprung up everywhere. Handbooks appeared describing the varieties of velocipedes, their history, how to ride and manage them, and often a section addressed to "ladies." Velocipedes for females – at least some can be identified as earlier versions of a "women's bicycle" – were invented and patented. One developed by a New York company had a frame following the curve of the front wheel and running horizontally to the rear axle. The two wheels were close together and between them was a spiral spring, on top of which was a comfortable, willow-backed chair-seat.[19] Although most women wanted "a little risk and dash which attends the riding of the two-wheeled velocipede," some preferred a three-wheeled velocipede tricycle because it was more stable and did not require a special costume.[20]

In Canada, velocipede rinks and riding academies were established in Toronto, Kingston, Montreal, and Halifax, but there was less enthusiasm for this new machine.[21] An editorial in the *Globe* called it a rich man's toy that would never become popular: "In Toronto, we fancy that few people would care to run a velocipede over the rough and dirty macadamized streets, and the machines will be driven off the side-walks if by their number they should prove a nuisance."[22] A month later, a clearly peeved editorialist complained, "We object very strongly to being ridden down by inexperienced and inebriated youths, who appear to select the most crowded thoroughfares in which to exhibit their want of proficiency."[23] Cities and towns, not just in Canada but also throughout North America, introduced bylaws prohibiting the riding of velocipedes on sidewalks. Unsuitable for rough roads and banned from pedestrian routes, velocipedes were relegated to a few indoor rinks, which were increasingly dependent on riders performing tricks and stunts to stay in business.

Did women race velocipedes? On 1 November 1868, in a local park in the French city of Bordeaux, four women known only as Mlles Louise, Julie, Louisa, and Amélie took part in a five-hundred-metre velocipede race attended by thousands of curious onlookers. In a sketch published in *Le Monde illustré*, the women were "coquettishly" dressed in short skirts or puffy shorts with their stocking-covered legs visible.[24] Mlle Julie won the close race and a gold watch for her efforts. A few weeks later, when the same race was reported by the American publication *Harper's Weekly*, the women's legs were mysteriously covered up.[25] Clearly, what to wear while riding a velocipede, especially where speed was important, was a fraught issue. Many people, mostly male, offered an opinion. The French journalist Richard Lesclide, who published a velocipede manual under the pseudonym of Le Grand Jacques, recommended a peaked cap, short blouse, belt, and pants tucked into half-high boots even though it might give the wearer an air of "hooliganism." Short skirts without crinolines would be more suitable, and on the question of whether to "show leg," the journalist equivocated but made it clear that exposed legs should be shapely.[26]

Women's velocipede races in France began as novel events, and it was sometimes difficult to attract contestants, but soon there was a small coterie of adept riders who enlivened the French racing circuit as part of the growing sports-entertainment industry. Female velocipedists also performed in the Hippodrome, a wooden stadium holding up to 15,000 spectators, in the Bois de Boulogne in Paris. On 7 November 1869, a

I.1 *Top* Women's velocipede race in Bordeaux, France, *Le Monde illustré*,
21 November 1868 (Bibliothèque nationale de France)

I.2 *Bottom* Women's legs were covered when reprinted in *Harper's Weekly*,
19 December 1868 (Granger)

"Miss America," who was the wife of Rowley B. Turner, the Paris agent for a British manufacturer of velocipedes, became the only woman to complete the 123-kilometre long-distance race between Paris and Rouen. With a reputation as a fierce competitor, she came twenty-ninth among a field of more than a hundred starters.[27]

There is less evidence of women's velocipede races in North America during this period, and if they occurred, it was usually as part of an entertainment spectacle created by a promoter to make money. Carrie Augusta Moore, a well-known and accomplished ice and roller skater, and widely publicized "Skatorial Queen," also gained a reputation as the "Velocipede Queen." On one occasion in the Jersey City Veloci-pedrome, Moore was complimented on her exhibition of graceful roller skating, but when she demonstrated her velocipede racing skills against W.H. Darling, a male competitor, the *New York Times* pronounced that "velocipede races for lady riders are out of place and anything but attractive."[28] As far as public opinion was concerned, Moore fared much better when she demonstrated her ability to perform a gymnastic routine while riding her bicycle.[29] Incredibly, she would pick up two chairs, one in each hand, and carry them around the room; make figure eights and curves without using her hands; circumvent the room without using her hands or feet; and stand with one foot on the saddle while passing a hoop over her head. Similar performances by Edith Shuler of Chicago enthralled audiences in Milwaukee, Wisconsin, with the added attraction of riding double with a male velocipedist.[30]

These infrequent accounts of women racing and performing on velocipedes, in the open air or in the urban skating rinks and veloci-pede halls of major European and American cities, can be viewed as progressive and genuine athletic contests. Spectators, both male and female, flocked to these indoor shows not only for thrilling entertainment, but also because they provided an opportunity to see the much talked-about velocipede in action. These performances, considered to be risqué and sensational by some, showcased women's skill, athletic prowess, and exertion, something usual at the time. They were also the forerunner to the high-wheel bicycle races that followed.

The majestic high-wheel bicycle with spider wheels and rubber tires emerged in the mid-1870s as the standard bicycle. Popularly nicknamed a "penny-farthing" in Britain because of the relative sizes of the large front and small back wheels, it was also called an "ordinary" to distinguish it from other types of bicycles. First introduced to an American audience in 1876 at Philadelphia's world fair, it was soon imported and then manufactured by Albert Pope of Boston, and his Columbia brand became the most popular. The new configuration went considerably faster than the clumsy velocipede because it was lighter and had a larger front wheel that covered more ground for every pedal stroke. Since it proved fairly roadworthy, the high wheel also became recreationally popular, especially among athletic, well-off young men. The large-circumference front wheel, padded with a rubber tire, effectively absorbed shocks while suspending the rider above the dust of unpaved roads. Unfortunately, it was also susceptible to cross winds, and an unseen bump could throw a rider flying. The difficulties of mounting and dismounting, especially as the front wheel became larger, were made somewhat easier by a small step to the left side of the frame just over the rear wheel. Mounting was accomplished by the rider putting his or her foot on the step and vaulting into the saddle from behind.

Cycling historians often characterize the high-wheel era as masculinized and the safety era as feminized.[31] The social impact of the high wheel, they argue, was unequivocally in favour of men because women were effectively excluded from high-wheeling activities, except in the most marginal sense of participating in bicycle club social functions. Indeed, Charles Pratt, the founder of the League of American Wheelmen, wrote in his 1879 manual for club cyclists, "As a sport, bicycling is manly, innocent, humane, and rational ... It is pre-eminently a gentlemanly recreation, a refined sport. It is pursued by noblemen and right honorables abroad, and by nature's nobility in our own untitled land." Professional high-wheel racing, he maintained, is ungentlemanly with all the "excesses and cruelties, which are so often objectionably attended upon boxing, billiards, trotting, pedestrian races, and other public exhibitions of physical training or endurance."[32]

Cycling historians also insist that Victorian women, and by this they usually mean bourgeois women, did not ride the high wheel "partly because Victorian dress and behaviour codes made it virtually impossible for a woman to ride one, and partly because the men engaged in the sport constructed activities as acts of male bonding, often surrounded by militaristic trappings."[33] There were, according to them, very few exceptions and if there were, they were to be found in the circus and theatre, where the normal codes of Victorian conduct were waived. In a book about how the bicycle reshaped American life, the author writes that women on high wheels were "acrobats, hussies, or freaks," and that one early performer was seen as a "sort of semi-monster."[34] In a curious footnote, bicycle historian Glen Norcliffe states, "For instance, Mlle Louise Armaino [*sic*] of Montreal is depicted in the *Wheelmen's Gazette* of 1885 racing a high bicycle as part of what seems to be an 'entertainment.'"[35]

Although some women enjoyed riding an adult-size tricycle, the introduction of the rear-driven safety bicycle in the late 1880s brought about the so-called feminization of the bicycle as more and more women took to riding. The problem with this dichotomization of "masculinist" versus "feminized" in terms of the social history of the bicycle is that it does not make a distinction between a bicycling era and the bicycle itself. As we have seen, bicycling from the early days of the velocipede was not necessarily a gendered activity. However, the bicycle itself was a gendered object, and unless otherwise stated, bicycles were effectively male.[36] Since their invention, bicycles have been gendered in order to accommodate women riders with long skirts. The problem with the high wheel was that it was almost impossible to mount and ride wearing a long skirt. It simply was not safe. As one commentator of the day argued,

If any daring person inquires why ladies cannot ride the bicycle, he must address the inquiry not to Nature, which has interposed no objection, but to the same irrational conventionalism which has decreed to the female equestrian an ungraceful, inconvenient side-saddle and a trailing robe that make her helpless while in her seat and endanger her life as soon as unseated ... Give her – or, rather let her dare to take – for the occasion, not that terrible Bloomer, but some modification of sensible gymnasium or short dress, and she will quickly adapt it to satisfy all requirements of

delicacy and grace, and will thus be able to mount this swift steed
now awaiting her – a steed which fits well enough the Nature-
woman, but cannot unmake itself to fit skirt-civilization.[37]

Some manufacturers tried to create a women's version of the high wheel
where the rider sat lower, further back, and side-saddle, but the model
was quickly abandoned.[38] It was not until the rear-driven safety bicycle
came on the market, especially the diamond-frame design, that the high
crossbar designated a male bicycle, whereas a dropped bar signalled a
female machine. The point is that there was nothing other than clothing
restrictions preventing women from riding the high wheel, and if their
costumes were suitable, like those of the women high-wheel racers, then
it was entirely possible.

Even feminist historians of cycling often assume that the high-wheel
era was masculine and the safety era was feminine. For example, Sarah
Hallenbeck in *Claiming the Bicycle* considers the role of women's rhetor-
ical activities (ranging from bicycle seats to bloomers to short stories) in
the transformation of bicycle culture and the bicycle itself. Although she
makes a brief mention of Louise Armaindo and also her contemporary
Elsa von Blumen, who, according to Hallenbeck, "gained notoriety,"
she also states that they received little attention outside the cycling press
and they raced primarily before male audiences.[39] As I demonstrate in
this book, neither of these assumptions is true. Moreover, the continuing
characterization of the high-wheel era as masculine and the safety era as
feminine ignores obvious class divisions and renders women's incredible
athletic activity in the high-wheel era invisible.

The tale told here is but a small slice of cycling history. Louise Armaindo was the first highly successful woman high-wheel racer, and as
a result, she raced primarily against men (and occasionally horses).
She became one of the guys, so to speak, because they were her constant
companions wherever she travelled, raced, and lived. As more women
entered the sport and female-only races became possible, Louise was
challenged by younger girls and women. Ignored by the male racing
fraternity, who no longer wished to race against her, she was more
often than not beaten on the track by these female upstarts. Late in
her career, the professional cycling racing culture that Louise helped to

create evolved as new technology took hold in the form of the more stable and ultimately faster safety bicycle. Proud of her skill on the high wheel and scornful of the chain-driven safety, Louise never raced one. By the mid-1890s, the high-wheel era of cycling history had come to an end, and so too had the racing career of Louise Armaindo.

The story emerges chronologically beginning with what little is known about Louise's background as a French Canadian from a small community near Montreal, and how, as a young woman seeking employment, she ended up in Chicago in the late 1870s. Initially, she performed as a strongwoman and trapeze artist, possibly in a circus, until she discovered the sport of pedestrianism, the earliest form of endurance race walking. Louise became a pedestrienne, and along with fellow Canadian Thomas Eck, she set out to earn a living by travelling and giving pedestrian exhibitions in small American towns. Chapter 2 explores the world of female pedestrianism in more depth as dozens of working-class women, including Canadians Mary Marshall, Exilda Lachapelle, Louise Armaindo, and others, took to walking for money throughout the United States.

In the late 1870s several pedestriennes, including Louise, learned to ride the high-wheel bicycle and began to race (chapter 3). Among her contemporaries was Elsa von Blumen, who raced trotting horses, and initially was not interested in competing against Louise. The next three chapters (4, 5, and 6) explore Louise's adventures as a high-wheel racer from 1883 until the end of 1888, when she raced primarily male professionals such as Tom Eck, John Prince, William Woodside, William Morgan, and Henry Higham. Although she was the preeminent female racer in the United States, she was in essence one of the fellows, living and travelling with them as they performed throughout the country.

Sports promoters realized that women's high-wheel races could be popular and lucrative if only there were riders skilled enough to race. Chapter 7 describes the entrance of many more women into the world of high-wheel racing such as Lulu Gordon (who became Frankie Nelson), Lottie Stanley, Jessie Oakes, May Allen, Helen Baldwin, and others. Louise, still determined to race men, initially ignored these women, but eventually it was worth her while to race and travel with them, although by the late 1880s she was considerably older than these young newcomers. The 1890s brought the pneumatic-tire safety bicycles and the end of the high-wheel era. Thousands of women took to riding the newer bicycles. Chapter 8 explores the problems the bicycle craze posed for women racers as they struggled to find opportunities to compete against a tide of criticism. Louise refused to switch to racing a safety; her career dwindled, and then was brought to a halt by personal tragedy. The epilogue provides a brief summary of women's cycle racing in the United States after Louise Armaindo involuntarily retired from the track. The reader also learns what eventually happened to the two central characters in this story, namely, Armaindo and Tom Eck.

This book is also about gender and the history of cycling. By this I mean a history of cycling that takes gender and gender relations centrally into account. Often, this translates into a singular focus on women, but bringing men more fully into the story of women's sport is intended "to prompt more careful discussion of gendered collaboration in how sport has been performed."[40] Louise's story, as well as those of other women high-wheel racers, cannot be told without reference to the many men who controlled this sport during the latter part of the nineteenth century, especially in the United States. They were the racers, managers, trainers, agents, and bookmakers. They were also the administrators in amateur sport organizations like the League of American Wheelmen (LAW), and the editors and reporters of influential cycling magazines such as the Boston-based *Bicycling World*. The lives of these women, at least while they raced, were controlled almost entirely by men, some caring and responsible, and others not so much.

Issues of race, gender, and race relations, although important, are not discussed here for several reasons. There is little evidence that people of colour, specifically blacks, participated in cycling during the high-wheel era.[41] As discussed previously, it was white, middle-class, young men in major urban centres who rode the high-wheel, primarily for recreation, through their bicycle clubs. Those who raced were typically amateurs, and as the sport developed a few professionals earned a living through impromptu races, exhibitions, and eventually an organized racing circuit. There is no evidence at all that women of colour in the United States or Canada raced a high-wheel bicycle. Moreover, in the 1880s these machines were expensive and beyond the reach of anyone without means, though professional racers were often supplied with bicycles.

It was not until the safety bicycle era in the 1890s that race became a contentious issue in cycling. The cheaper, often second-hand, easier to ride safeties opened the sport to thousands more enthusiasts, including women and blacks. Cycling clubs sprang up across the continent, some exclusively for women, and in the segregated United States, all-black and by implication all-white clubs emerged. Professional cyclists were already denied any form of membership in the LAW, although determining a professional as opposed to an amateur was always a prickly issue. As more women took up cycling, the LAW slowly welcomed them into its ranks. In 1892 a mere 2.6 per cent of the total LAW membership was female.[42] It was also forced to grapple with two additional issues: whether to accept "colored" cyclists and all-black cycling clubs as members, and whether to allow black racers in races sponsored or sanctioned by the LAW.[43] In February 1894, after much debate and several aborted attempts, primarily because of opposition from more northern states, the LAW instituted a ban on "colored" membership.[44] The Canadian Wheelmen's Association, established in 1882, though it often followed the LAW's lead on many issues, did not introduce a similar colour ban.

Kittie Knox was a twenty-year-old biracial cyclist associated with the Riverside Cycle Club, the major "colored" cycling organization in Boston. She was also a member in good standing of the LAW, and had a membership card to prove it. In July 1895, along with other Boston cyclists, Knox travelled to Asbury Park, New Jersey, to take part in the LAW's annual week-long meet. When she registered at the meet, she was refused due to the LAW's recently approved "color line." Sadly, a few of the leading women cyclists threaten to leave the LAW should Knox remain a member. In the end, Knox was not ousted from the meet, nor did she withdraw. However, despite considerable controversy and publicity over the incident, the LAW did not change its racist policy.[45] At the same time, Marshall "Major" Taylor, a superbly talented black racer from Indianapolis, began to dominate his white rivals, first as an amateur and then a professional, on the cycle racing tracks of America and Europe. Although the LAW banned black membership, Taylor could still race in LAW-sanctioned meets, and in 1896 he received his professional licence from the Racing Board. However, this did not mean his struggle for the right to race was over; in fact, it intensified.

Although some white racers accepted Taylor with good grace, there were many who did not by conspiring to exclude him from victory through physical intimidation, verbal insults, and harassment both on and off the track. Taylor persevered and became one of the most successful cyclists of all time.[46]

Kittie Knox and Marshall Taylor had probably never heard of Louise Armaindo because her racing career was over by the time they were just starting. Unquestionably, however, she was *la mère du cyclisme féminin*, the mother of women's cycling.[47] She rode only a high wheel, well before the Victorian women safety racers appeared in North America and Europe in the mid-1890s. Her legacy goes back almost 140 years. Early in her career, she raced primarily men, and later increasingly more women, on either crude indoor or rough outdoor tracks. Her racing accomplishments are astounding. Most surprising is the fact that she is rarely recognized for her pioneering role in women's cycling, in Quebec, in Canada, and generally in the world of women's professional cycling. My hope is that this book will change all that.

CHAPTER ONE

CIRCUSES AND WALKING TRACKS, 1870s

Who was Louise Armaindo? Her real name was Louise or Louisa Brisbois (also spelled as Brisebois). We know this for certain because when Louise married, she was identified as "Louisa Brisbois" on the marriage record.[1] Discovering her origins has not been easy, and what we know is not definitive. Given the very few clues provided through interviews Louise gave during her athletic career, and the fact that she frequently lied about her age, we may never be certain of her background. One of the problems with historical research related to circus performers and other athlete-entertainers is that not only did they adopt stage names; they also created stage biographies that often embellished the truth about their backgrounds. Why Louise chose the name Armaindo is a complete mystery, but tracking her digital footprints some 140 years later became a little easier because it was such an unusual one.

There are some consistencies in the information provided in these interviews and other articles about Louise's background.[2] Most important is the fact that she was French Canadian, and that she spoke both French and English, the latter with an accent. According to one article, she was born on 12 October 1860 in Ste-Anne-de-Bellevue, Jacques Cartier County, on the westernmost tip of the Island of Montreal, Quebec.[3] She also claimed never to have been an amateur athlete, and at fourteen years of age decided to become a professional by following in the footsteps of her mother, a professional strongwoman. Louise was proud of stating that when her mother was twenty-one, she lifted 900 pounds dead weight. By the time Louise herself was eighteen and performing as a strongwoman, she could lift 760 pounds. She also trained as a trapeze artist before she took up pedestrianism (endurance walking), and finally high-wheel bicycle racing. "It will be a matter of wonder to many how this girl can endure so much fatigue," wrote a Chicago newspaper reporter, "but it should be taken into account that she is a trained athlete and gymnast, being a trapeze performer and capable of putting up a ninety-pound dumbbell many times in succession."[4] He also explained that Louise also had "a regular stage training, or rather circus schooling," and that she could ride a horse longer than any of the other lady riders of note.

One thing we know for certain about Louise's background is that she was descended from René Dubois dit Brisebois, who immigrated to New France as a French habitant in the seventeenth century, probably around 1658. A few years later he married Anne-Julienne Dumont, who, along with other young, healthy *filles du roi* (king's daughters), had been recruited by the French Crown and sent across the ocean to help populate New France. Together René and Anne-Julienne had nine children, including two sons whose descendants eventually settled in the west end of the Island of Montreal. Louise would be among these offspring, but unfortunately there are several Louises, all of whom are cousins of some sort, among a complicated and convoluted web of family interrelationships.[5]

Identifying the Louise Brisbois who became Louise Armaindo is speculative and probably no better than a best guess. Until a relative or descendant can be found, we may never know for certain the true origin of Louise Brisbois/Armaindo. However, there are a few more clues that help to narrow the genealogical search. One is that Louise's mother supposedly died at a relatively young age, information that comes from a brief article about Louise published in a German newspaper.[6] According to this report, it was after her mother's death that Louise was sent to a girls' school in Chicago, which seems improbable given the distance and expense. Another clue is that her father lived to a relatively old age because in an interview in 1889 the reporter made reference to how Louise had made considerable sacrifices to help her "old father" in business. At the same time, Louise mentioned a brother, who, according to her, was one of the most successful divers in the world.[7]

Louise continually lied about her age and, as she grew older, she was determined to make herself appear younger. As mentioned previously, the only birthdate found in print was 12 October 1860. An intensive genealogical search has turned up no Louise or Louisa Bris(e)bois born in either Ste-Anne-de-Bellevue or Montreal in that year. When she was married in 1888, her age on the church record was listed as twenty-four, which would mean that she was born in 1864. In court records relating to a hotel fire in 1896, in which Louise was seriously injured, she claimed that she was twenty-seven years of age. This would mean that she was born in 1869. Finally, when Louise died on 2 September 1900 and was supposedly buried a few days later in Montreal's Notre-Dame-des-Neiges cemetery, her age on the burial record was stated as forty-two, which implies that she was born in 1857 or 1858.[8] Was this her true age?

Given these bits of information, where does this leave us? My best guess is that Louise is the daughter of Charles Brisebois, born in 1830 and a descendant of Jean-Baptiste, son of René Dubois dit Brisebois. In February 1857, Charles married Hélène Brunet in the Ste-Anne-de-Bellevue parish. A baptismal record dated 14 October 1857 shows that Marie Louise Brisebois was the daughter of Charles and Hélène.[9] It is possible, therefore, that her birthdate could be 12 October 1857 because baptism usually occurred shortly after birth. In the 1861 census, Charles (confusingly listed as "Pierre") was living with his wife Hélène and their children Louise, aged four, and Hélène, aged two. His occupation is noted as *voyageur*, normally an expert woodsman and boatman employed by a fur trading company to transport goods and supplies. He was also a *journalier*, which means labourer.[10] In 1867 tragedy struck when Charles's wife died at the age of thirty-two. He immediately married again, this time to Julia Brennan, who was of Irish descent and considerably younger than Charles. Their family eventually consisted of Louise, her younger sister, Hélène (listed as Ellen), and four half-brothers, Charles, William, Samuel, and Ferdinand. Louise appears in the 1871 census living with her family in Ste-Anne-de-Bellevue.[11] She is not listed on the 1881 census because she is no longer in Canada. This is confirmed by her appearance in Chicago in March 1879, where she was competing in a pedestrian contest under the name of Louise Armando (likely a misspelling).[12]

Louise was fond of bragging about her *Oncle* Joe: "He one gr-r-r-r-r-and Frenchman! He so strong it take seex poleesmen to hold hees hat!"[13] Joe was not her real uncle, but rather Joseph Montferrand, a larger-than-life *Canadien* folk hero from Montreal. A giant of a man with legendary strength and agility, he fought in taverns on principle and in the ring for money. He travelled the fur trade routes as a *voyageur* with the North West Company, but for most of his life he ran rafts and booms as a lumberman on the Ottawa River. Joe Mufferaw or Mufraw were the English versions of his name, and his reputation still resonates in the Ottawa Valley today.[14] Although he died in 1864, when Louise was still a child, she no doubt heard stories about him and perhaps idolized him as a champion of *Les Canadiens*. More importantly, Montferrand had a sister whose name was Hélène. Since Louise's mother was possibly named Hélène, it made sense for her to imagine that Montferrand could actually have been her uncle.

We know nothing of Louise's childhood, except that "she was always throwing big stones, and seeing how far she could run and jump."[15] If I have found the correct Louise, she would have been ten years old when her mother died in 1867. Four years later, she decided to follow the life of a professional athlete by going into training in a gymnasium. What is unclear is whether she began this training in Ste-Anne-de-Bellevue, or in Montreal, or possibly in Chicago. Her father had married again and was enlarging his family so possibly sending his eldest daughter away either to school or to follow her dream of becoming a professional athlete made sense. Why Chicago?

There has been a French Canadian presence in Chicago for most of its history. It was Quebec-born Louis Joliet and Jesuit missionary Jacques Marquette, who in 1673 were sent by Jean Talon, the intendant of New France, on an expedition to explore and map the area where Chicago eventually emerged on Lake Michigan. The waterways between Lake Michigan and the Mississippi River were essential to fur traders who ventured southwest from Montreal and Quebec City, and the Midwest was a vital component of the French empire in North America. All this changed after the Seven Years' War in 1763 when France surrendered its territories between the Atlantic and the Mississippi to Britain. By the mid-nineteenth century, the city of Chicago had been transformed from a fur-trading outpost to a capitalist town.

People streamed to Chicago, called "America's city," from all parts of the country seeking employment and a better life. With rail lines coming from every direction, Chicago was a national transportation hub. It was also a bustling metropolis, having been mostly rebuilt after the devastating fire of 1871 that destroyed a third of the city, including the downtown. As it rose again quickly from ashes, the city was grander and statelier than ever.[16] Facing intense economic pressure at home, French Canadians began migrating to nearby Kankakee area, where they founded the town of Bourbonnais, and in the 1870s a large number of French Canadian families settled in the Brighton Park area of Chicago.[17]

Alfred Brisbois, a distant cousin of Louise Brisebois, who became a well-known photographer, was born in Chicago in 1853. His parents moved between Canada and the United States several times, but young Brisbois finished his education in old Sandwich, located along the Canadian border of the Detroit River and now part of the city of Windsor. Although Brisbois tried his hand at several occupations, he finally chose photography, travelling extensively until settling in Leadville, Colorado, where he established his own business. His photographs of American cultural icons Annie Oakley and Buffalo Bill Cody are well known. Brisbois eventually returned to Chicago, where he managed a photographic studio between 1891 and 1900. Whether he was aware of the athletic feats of Louise Brisbois/Armaindo is unknown, and no photographs of Louise taken by him have been unearthed.

By 1880 Chicago's rapidly growing population had reached half a million, and among these were thousands of young women from small towns. They left home primarily to find work, although some sought anonymity in a large city where no one knew them. Over four million women were gainfully employed in the United States by 1880, some 15 per cent of all workers.[18] Roughly one in five of these working women lived apart from family and relatives. They were, in the parlance of the day, "women adrift," a term used to describe Victorian women who were wage earners and did not live with kin or their employers. These women challenged and undermined the Victorian "separation

of spheres" ethos that segregated women from men and relegated them
to the domestic world of the home. When they mingled freely with men
in rooming houses, at work, and at places of recreation, they also challenged the perception that all women, single or married, needed the
economic and moral protection of family life.[19] Canadian women like
Louise represented over 10 per cent of foreign-born women adrift, and
they were overrepresented in terms of the proportion of Canadians in
Chicago in general. Most of these women worked in the needle trades,
such as dressmaker or seamstress, and many held service jobs in domestic day work or laundering.

Louise presumably escaped these humdrum occupations through her
employment in the entertainment world, which, though a rapidly growing
industry, provided few opportunities for women. In the late 1870s and
into the 1880s, this kind of female employment was minimal because in
the 1890 United States census, "actresses, professional show-women,
etc.," accounted for only 4,491 gainfully employed women, a mere 0.12
per cent of all female workers.[20] Louise's trapeze days did not last long,
mainly because the pay was meagre and certainly not enough to keep
her in the fancy outfits required for performing. Flying high on a trapeze
was hard on the nerves and certainly dangerous, so that every week
newspapers reported at least one accident resulting in serious injuries
and an occasional death.

Louise supplemented her small income by performing as a strongwoman, following in her mother's footsteps. She may have heard of another Canadian strongwoman, Millie De Granville, whose real name
was Alma Hayes. Little is known about Hayes's background other than
that she was born in Montreal on 31 May 1852 to parents who came to
Quebec from Europe. She worked professionally as a circus performer
beginning around 1874, and for the next fifteen years toured with a
variety of circuses throughout the United States, even venturing into
Mexico and Cuba. Known as the "lady with the jaws of steel," De
Granville was among the first iron jaw artists who performed in North
America.[21] During her performances she would throw chairs around
with her bare teeth, and then daringly twirl on a rope up to the top of
the tent supported only by a piece of leather held in her teeth.[22] One
newspaper commentator was in awe of her feats of strength, but also

noted that they were "rather indelicate even for the circus."[23] De Granville's performances and those of other circus strongwomen generated a female physicality that was fearless, brazen, outrageous, and often broke social taboos.[24] Performing as a strongwoman also provided a means to earn a living. No doubt Louise weighed her prospects in this promising line of work, and she had the strength and talent to do so.

At the Chicago Athenæum in the spring of 1878, and before a large audience, Louise lifted 760 pounds and had records to prove it. On another occasion a witness saw her lift 750 pounds without a harness or shoulder straps.[25] According to yet another report, she could also handle Indian clubs and dumbbells "with a skill that would make some of the sterner sex blush."[26] She is said to have "pressed" a 105-pound dumbbell five times in succession with her right arm and three with her left.[27] Many years later, there was a report that at one time she had considerable notoriety as Zoe, the "Human Cannonball."[28] However, all we have now are tidbits of information about Louise's exploits as a strongwoman, and possible circus performer, because no mention of her name as either Brisbois or Armaindo has been found in the well-documented histories of early North American circuses.

The Chicago Athenæum, where Louise performed, was a brand new, four-storey building on Dearborn Street. Created as a philanthropic society to provide relief for victims of the 1871 fire, the Athenæum soon became a community educational centre offering day and evening classes in a wide range of subjects. The new building included commercial stores on the first floor; reading rooms, classrooms, and a library on the second; and on the third and fourth floor was a spacious, well-lit, and ventilated gymnasium alongside splendidly equipped dressing rooms, showers, and baths. The gymnasium was the chief attraction of the new facilities allowing the Athenæum to offer courses in physical culture to both sexes and to organize athletic exhibitions. Another important feature of the Athenæum gymnasium was a four-foot wide, oval track, measuring a little over sixteen laps to the mile and designed specifically for pedestrian matches.[29] Walking around a flat track, usually indoors, may have seemed easier to Louise than flying around on a trapeze, being shot from a cannon, or even lifting heavy weights. It was certainly more enticing provided the money was better.

As a spectator sport, pedestrianism was familiar to Chicagoans and they enthusiastically supported their hometown hero, Daniel O'Leary, an Irish immigrant who made his living as a door-to-door book salesman. After the Great Fire, his downtown business dried up and he was forced to walk daily out to the suburbs, which put him in great shape to walk around a pedestrian track. O'Leary's goal was to challenge the reigning pedestrian star Edward Payson Weston, another door-to-door book salesman with a flair for self-promotion. His walking exhibitions, held mostly in roller rinks, were a commercial success. O'Leary and Weston finally went head-to-head in November 1875 in a five-hundred-mile race held in Chicago's Inter-State Exposition Building, a huge barn of a building with standing room only for spectators around a make-shift tanbark (mulch) track. O'Leary, who was several years younger than Weston, won handily, earning widespread approval as Chicago's favourite son. More importantly, the match was a commercial success that launched O'Leary's career as a promoter.

In the years following the Civil War, pedestrianism had a substantial following even though it was competing for spectators among sports like baseball, pool, rowing, and prizefighting. There was no league as in baseball, nor was there an organized circuit of signed performers. Instead, a comparative handful of walkers travelled about the country seeking a marathon contest, or they went alone by walking X number of miles in X number of days, often in an attempt to break a record. Indoor six-day marathons were the creation of promoters eager to cash in on the public's interest in long, cross-country treks by walkers. For the athlete to make money, there had to be a way to attract it, and that was through gambling. Bookmaking was legal, and bookies hauled portable booths from one sporting event to another. The athletes them-selves rarely saw much of this money. It might be announced, for ex-ample, that one pedestrian would race another for two hundred dollars a side, which did not mean that the winner would emerge two hundred dollars richer. Pedestrians were generally underpaid hired athletes, employed by a backer who would put up the wager and gave the athlete a cut of the winnings. Long-distance walking was, in the words of one commentator, for stouthearted members of the working class.[30]

In early February 1876 Chicagoans witnessed their first walking match between two female pedestrians, or *pedestriennes* as they were called, when Bertha von Hillern and Mary Marshall competed on a track laid out in the Second Regiment Armoury building at the corner of Jackson and Carroll Streets. The race was managed by Daniel O'Leary, who realized there was money to be made in a novel event featuring two women. Bertha, a nineteen-year-old German immigrant, had arrived in the United States around 1875 and settled in Chicago amongst its large Germanic community. She brought with her a reputation as a pedestrienne, and although she had aspirations to become an artist, she lacked the money to study and paint. Thirty-four-year-old Mary Marshall was a Canadian from eastern Ontario, whose real name was Mary Tryphena Curtis. She appeared to be supporting herself and possibly a teenage son selling books door-to-door, which is where O'Leary probably found her.

The women's goal was to walk three hundred miles over six days, going round and round on a sawdust track measuring one-tenth of a mile in length. The typical six-day format was from Monday to Saturday to avoid disrupting the Christian Sabbath on Sunday. An indoor setting allowed for the supervision of contestants from start to finish, providing proof they did not cheat. Each contestant supposedly put up a five-hundred-dollar stake with the winner receiving the total purse, and O'Leary kept the gate receipts after paying his expenses. Though a sudden cold snap in February made for frigid conditions inside the armoury until the heat from several stoves warmed the air, attendance during the day was respectable and brought out a noticeable number of "ladies." The armoury was filled to capacity in the evenings, especially during the last day of the race when the outcome was in doubt. By the end of the fifth day, Bertha von Hillern was five miles ahead of her opponent and victory seemed assured. Poor Mary suffered from painfully sore and swollen feet, but still boasted that "she would win the race or die in her tracks." On the sixth and final day, Mary began walking at nine o'clock in the morning and did not stop until the race ended at ten o'clock that night. Part way through the morning she threw off her shoes and completed the race in stocking feet. In the end she won the race, accomplishing nearly 234 miles to Bertha's 231½, but she was

1.1 Poster advertising Bertha von Hillern's endurance walk in Louisville, Kentucky, in 1878. She completed one hundred miles in less than twenty-five hours, averaging a mile every fourteen to fifteen minutes (Kentucky Historical Society)

exhausted and delirious. Bertha complained bitterly that it was against the rules of pedestrianism to walk in one's stocking feet, and this flagrant violation, along with the bad air and tobacco smoke in the armoury, were the causes of her loss.[31]

A rematch between Bertha von Hillern and Mary Marshall took place a month later at the Chicago West Side rink. The six-day event was going smoothly, though attendance was only fair, when Bertha withdrew from the contest on the grounds that the rules were unfair. Whenever one woman left the track, the other had to leave also. Bertha claimed she was at a disadvantage because she was counting on her superior endurance to win. If Daniel O'Leary was managing this event, he likely made little money.[32] Also, pedestrian races among men occurred regularly at this time and Chicagoans were becoming more blasé towards the sport.

Louise Brisbois was possibly a spectator at these pedestrienne matches in Chicago. Perhaps she thought that because of her extensive circus training she was just as strong and determined as either Bertha von Hillern or Mary Marshall. Superbly athletic and pleasantly attractive, Louise saw no reason why she should not give pedestrianism a try to bring in more money than she could earn as a strongwoman and circus performer. What she needed to get started was a manager and promoter. She found this person in Tom Eck, a fellow Canadian.

Thomas William Eck was born on 10 April 1856 in the small village of Prince Albert in Reach Township in Canada West (today's province of Ontario) and located north of Lake Ontario, about twenty miles northeast of Whitby. In Tom's youth, about six hundred people lived in Prince Albert, a busy grain and timber centre. As a "general agent" Tom's father was likely involved in several local businesses to support his wife, Margaret, and four children, which included Tom (age fourteen) along with siblings Sarah, Edwin, and Calvin.

All we know of Tom's early life was that he was a versatile athlete with a love of horses. He became a jockey in his teens, and by the time he was twenty, he had a good reputation as a harness racing driver, sometimes winning a share of the purse.[33] He also played cricket and lacrosse and was a capable ice skater but settled on athletics as his route to stardom. He was a good quarter-miler for his day, posting a time of

1.2 Poster advertising a walk by Mary Marshall in Worcester, Massachusetts. She completed the fifty miles in less than twelve hours (Courtesy American Antiquarian Society)

52.4 seconds at a meet in Toronto in 1875.[34] His favourite event was the standing long jump (also called the broad jump). In those days, the jumper's momentum was facilitated by dumbbells or small weights carried in each hand and swung forward during the jump, not unlike the stone *halteres* used by jumpers in the Olympics of Ancient Greece. In 1876 Tom purportedly established a world record at a track meet in Woodbine Park in Toronto by jumping thirteen feet and two inches, using twelve-pound dumbbells.

Now a young man of twenty, Tom was living in Oshawa, a manufacturing town on the shore of Lake Ontario about thirty miles east of Toronto.[35] Perhaps he went there to find work in one of the town's many manufacturing concerns such as the famous Joseph Hall Works, which employed as many as three hundred workers and had an excellent apprenticeship program. As the oldest son, he would be expected to earn his own living and, by 1876, his parents had two additional mouths to feed because sisters Margaret and Cara had joined Tom's three younger siblings. Two more children, John and Niala, would come along later making Tom the oldest of eight children.[36] Throughout this time, Cyrus Eck moved his family several times from Prince Albert in Reach Township, to Aurora in York North, to Newmarket in Ontario West, and finally to Whitchurch also in Ontario West. He died in Whitchurch in 1909 at the age of seventy-five.

A few days after his twenty-first birthday in April 1877, Tom Eck travelled to the United States, entering at Port Huron, Michigan, and then made his way to Chicago.[37] Why he went to the United States then and why he chose Chicago is unclear. Did he think there was a better chance to earn a living through his athletic skills than was possible in Canada? Was it his intent to become a trainer and manager of other athletes? Tom was inventive, smart, wily, and determined, and no doubt soon found a way to earn a living. In Chicago, Tom met Louise Brisbois, although under precisely what circumstances is unknown. Most likely it was at some sort of athletic venue or event. She was probably attracted to this athletic and handsome fellow with clear, penetrating eyes and a bushy moustache. For his part, Tom saw something in the gutsy French Canadian that convinced him she was serious about becoming an athletic star, and it soon became obvious that he was attracted to her too.

Louise quickly became a pedestrienne and was known as Mlle Louise Armaindo or Madame Armaindo. We can only speculate as to why she chose this particular name.[38] Louise decided herself, or was advised by others, to choose a stage name, just like the many singers, actresses, chorus girls, circus entertainers, and performers of athletic feats who made their living in the growing American entertainment industry. The use of a pseudonym was also common among bourgeois women wishing to conceal their real family name, though this was not something that concerned Louise whose background was working class. The first time "Louise Armando" (likely a misspelling) appeared in a press report was at a pedestrienne contest in Chicago in 1879. On the evening of 18 March in the Exposition Building, following a day of men's races, a ten-mile walk was held for women. A dozen contestants, including Louise, were entered in the race before some 1,500 spectators, described in the newspaper as a "howling, crazy, free and easy mob," but a good-natured one that came primarily to encourage their friends on the track.[39] After a little more than two hours, Mary Ackerly, a flower girl who sold bouquets about the hotels, came first; a Mary Miller came second and Louise was third.

By October 1879, Louise claimed to have been engaged in the pedestrienne business for two years, and although she called herself the "champion female pedestrienne of Canada" not a single report of her racing in Canada during this time has been unearthed.[40] Indeed, she does not show up again in a newspaper account or at least one accessible through a digitized search until early August 1879 when she (and presumably Tom too) was in St Louis, Missouri. Louise was giving five-mile exhibition walks during a men's six-day go-as-you-please pedestrian contest at St George's Hall. "Go-as-you-please" meant that competitors were permitted to walk, trot, jog, run, sprint, or crawl as opposed to the more traditional "fair heel and toe" method, where one part of the foot must always be in contact with the ground.[41] According to the report, she was training for an upcoming thirty-six-hour walk.[42] This may have been a walking match against Carrie Reynolds (or Howard) and Nellie Worrell, who each walked fifteen-hour stretches, held in Union Park Hall in St Louis, although no report was found.[43]

By the first week of October 1879, Louise and Tom were in Sedalia, Missouri. The previous week saw them in Kansas City, where Louise competed in a walking contest of some sort. They had been secured as entertainment by the *Sedalia Weekly Bazoo*, and soon after they arrived in town, the paper sent a reporter to find out more about Mlle Armaindo. She claimed that she had engaged in some fifteen professional pedestrienne contests and had given over one hundred exhibition walks in various cities and towns in the United States (there was no mention of Canada). She boasted that she had only been beaten once, in St Louis, in the thirty-six-hour walk against Reynolds and Worrell, during which she claimed to have walked eighteen hours and fifteen minutes without stopping.[44] Therefore, it seems strange that no record or report could be found to verify at least some of these events, but while researching Louise and her exploits I soon came to accept that she was prone to exaggeration, if not outright lies. Besides, Tom Eck was present during this particular interview, and as her manager he would be keen to embellish the growing reputation of his protégé. They had brought along Louise's numerous medals and trophies, which were exhibited while she walked.

The *Bazoo* reporter provided one of the first descriptions of Louise, especially her physical appearance. At five feet three inches, she was small, muscular but shapely, and weighed 132 pounds. "It was duly impressed upon the mind of the reporter," noted the scribe, "that she was amply able to take care of herself at any place and under any circumstances."[45] She was also described as a brunette, the possessor of a very healthy complexion, and about twenty years of age. So confident was Louise of her pedestrienne talent that she issued a challenge to any woman in the world to walk or run any distance from one to one hundred miles. She was not yet among the notables in the pedestrienne world, having to make her reputation mostly through exhibitions or as a sideshow in a men's race. This was the case in Sedalia, a small Missouri railroad town founded in 1860.

The location for the Sedalia race was in Smith's Hall on a makeshift sawdust track, twenty-seven laps to the mile. Except for some side betting among the almost five hundred patrons in attendance, no money was involved. The trifling prizes were an elegant French clock, a pair of English walking shoes, and a gold pen with a cigar and a supply of peanuts offered as the consolation prizes. A handsome bouquet would go to the most graceful walker, to be decided by the ladies in the audience. The eight male competitors began walking promptly at eight o'clock in the evening. The rules for this particular match were heel-and-toe (as opposed to go-as-you-please) with the winner covering the most distance in four hours. These rules did not apply to Louise, who appeared about half-past eight in her street clothes, accompanied by manager Tom Eck, to enthusiastic applause from the crowd. She reappeared a half hour later in her walking costume, a short dress exposing a good set of calves, and on her feet a pair of low-heeled English walking shoes laced up to the ankles.

After a suitable introduction, Louise stepped onto the track and took off at breakneck speed amid cheers from the audience, many rising and straining to see her in action among the male racers. She completed her first mile in exactly ten minutes at which point she requested that the band in attendance play some music while she continued her second mile, completing it in twenty-one minutes. She kept up this pace completing a mile about every ten minutes and the audience cheered wildly whenever she passed one of the male walkers. Occasionally, Eck would jump onto the track and accompany her for a few laps. At ten minutes to midnight, Louise completed her requisite fifteen miles (her time was just under three hours) and she left the track, seemingly not fatigued in the least. Only three men were left in the official race with the winner, Lou Hughey, completing twenty miles and fourteen laps in four hours, although he was so tired he could not come up on the stage to accept his prize. Afterwards, everyone involved in the contest – scorers, umpires, contestants, reporters, and others – were invited to Kaiser's, a local restaurant, for an oyster feast.

Tom and Louise remained in Sedalia for most of October, taking part in several exhibition walks with side trips to similar events in local railway towns such as Boonville and Moberly. Again, she did not compete for any of the prizes, which were items donated by local merchants and suitable for men (a case of Anheuser beer, silk handkerchiefs, silver tobacco box, and the like). She was an interesting sideshow to the main event, just like child pedestrian Harry Johnson, only eight years old and suited up in white tights handsomely trimmed with blue, who walked a few miles in the middle of the race. Louise was fitter and more experienced than most of these local athletes, and when she was allowed to go head-to-head against a man, for example in a five-mile heel-and-toe walk, she usually won. Even when she entered the track in the middle of a race, she inevitably overtook the leader much to the delight of the audience. In one match she walked for five miles, completing it in fifty-four minutes, and shortly after came back to show off her running style. She completed seven laps, equal to a quarter of a mile, in one minute and 48½ seconds, certainly slow by today's standards. For her efforts that night, Louise received a silver cup and a bottle of French perfume. One evening Louise promised to show off her trapeze skills to an excited audience, but a rowdy in the crowd began spouting insulting language, whereby all the "ladies" among the spectators left the building and Louise refused to perform. Pedestrianism in those days was sometimes farcical, but it was also sufficiently respectable to draw hundreds of spectators.

Tracking Louise's pedestrienne career is challenging because there are so few sightings available to us today. After their month-long stay in Sedalia, Missouri, Tom and Louise headed north to Palmyra, where the local paper reported that a "Canadian woman of very masculine form, named Armaindo, has been making a show of her dexterity here by walking and running long distances very fast, and the sight has attracted large crowds of both sexes nightly."[46] Tom left Louise in Palmyra while he headed to Quincy, Illinois, where as an "advance agent" he was able to arrange exhibition matches for his protégé.[47] By the end of December, they were in Burlington, Iowa, preparing for a tour of the state.[48] For much of 1880, they were based in Springfield and travelled to smaller centres in Illinois – Cairo, Jacksonville, Lincoln, Peoria, and Pekin – giving exhibitions of their walking prowess. Louise usually walked a longer distance and Tom gave an exhibition of "fast walking." Where she was billed as the "champion pedestrienne of Canada," he was the noted "champion fast walker of Toronto." One of their favourite races was to walk five miles against five local men each of whom covered one mile. In Springfield in May, Louise walked twenty-five miles in four hours and

one minute, supposedly the fastest time ever by a woman.[49] She was immediately challenged by a Madam LaFayette, "Champion of the West,"
to a walking race in Springfield, but there is no trace of this contest.

By late fall of 1880, Louise and Tom were in Ontario, one of the few
times they returned to Canada. Tom's family lived in Aurora, so perhaps
he took Louise home to meet them and at the same time engage in a few
walking exhibitions. An announcement in the *Aurora Banner* made an
outrageous claim: "M'lle Louise Armaindo, champion pedestrienne of
the world, gives an exhibition walk of five miles in the Town Hall tonight
(Friday), commencing at eight o'clock sharp. This is the first appearance
of this lady in Canada, and no doubt there will be a large attendance."[50]
Tom took on his younger brother Calvin in a two-and-a-half-mile race.
The couple also appeared in nearby Uxbridge where Louise walked five
miles in just over forty-three minutes, beating five men walking one mile
each.[51] The two soon headed back south of the border to revitalize their
careers as athlete-entertainers.

Pedestrianism in Canada, and more accurately eastern Canada, was
neither as popular nor as developed as it was in the United States.
Besides, as discussed in the next chapter, the peak year for pedestriennes
was 1879, and from then on interest in the sport began to wane. Louise
never did become a star on the women's pedestrian circuit, but before
we leave the pedestriennes it's important to understand how the sport
laid the groundwork for the high-wheel bicycle era that followed. Along
the way, we will meet other luminaries in this sport who, like Louise,
exchanged their walking shoes for a bicycle.

CHAPTER TWO

PEDESTRIENNES, 1878–1880

Miss Von Blumen is called the Queen of Lady Pedestriennes, and has
won an enviable reputation. She comes with the very highest recommenda-
tions from all over the country, and we have no doubt she is just what she
is represented ... and she has never failed to accomplish what she
has undertaken.

"Miss Elsa Von Blumen," *Highland (OH) News*, 10 July 1879

Miss von Blumen – not her real name – was a contemporary of Louise
Armaindo in the pedestrienne world. Her story is as astonishing as
Louise's but somewhat easier to document. Caroline Wilhelmina Kiner
was born in Kansas on 6 October 1859 to George and Anna Kiner. Both
were German immigrants from Prussia, probably as young children,
since George had been a soldier and fought in the American Civil War.
By 1870 the family was living in Oswego, New York, on the southern
shore of Lake Ontario. Caroline, or more familiarly Carrie, was ten years
old with three younger sisters. Never a robust child, her health continued
to decline until her now widowed mother took the family to Rochester,
hoping the dryer climate would improve her daughter's delicate condition. On the advice of her doctor, Carrie began to exercise with dumbbells and clubs, and walked regularly until she could manage five to six
miles a day. Realizing that walking for a living was possible, she sought

out Bert Miller, who trained and managed several other pedestrians. Carrie took the stage name of Elsa von Blumen, an obvious salute to her German heritage, and with Miller as her manager, she began her pedestrian career in early 1879.[1]

Albert "Bert" Miller (sometimes "Burt") was an alias for William H. Rosevelt.[2] Born around 1843 in Albany, New York, he came to Utica as a young man, and in 1862 enlisted in the New York 165th Infantry Regiment, fighting for the duration of the Civil War. In the 1870s he settled in Rochester, where he became involved with pedestrian matches and other entertainment, especially those involving women. He was an unsavoury character, and when he died of heart disease at age forty-nine in 1892, it was said that he "always managed to lead a lazy life at the expense of female endurance in sporting circles."[3]

Margaret "Maggie" Gangross, whose stage name was Bertha von Berg, was likely the first female pedestrienne managed by Bert.[4] A Rochester seamstress with a fondness for walking, she came to Bert's attention after completing the twelve miles between Rochester and Fairport in just over two hours. She began her pedestrian career in August 1877, and under Bert's tutelage completed several exhibition walks. Muscular, tall, and "possessed of wonderful pluck, nerve, and Spartan-like grit," von Berg often competed against an amateur male pedestrian usually over a distance of one hundred miles on an inside track.[5] Within a year there were growing concerns about the cruel and unreasonable way Bert treated his protégé, and by the end of 1879 he and Bertha had parted company.

Meanwhile, Bert and his wife accompanied Elsa von Blumen as they made their way from one pedestrian venue to another. Again there were instances of Bert's bad-tempered and predatory behaviour with one particularly unflattering early report. Bert apparently got drunk and called Elsa vile names. Even more revealing was his financial arrangement with his young pedestrienne. She received twenty-five dollars for each one hundred miles she completed, with the rest of the proceeds going to Miller and his wife, who normally stayed in a fancy hotel while Elsa was put up in a cheap room.[6] On another occasion, Bert forced Elsa to ride in an open carryall just after she had walked those one hundred miles. Rumours circulated that Elsa would soon leave her manager, but she was likely more compliant than Bertha von Berg, and bad publicity was harmful for securing exhibitions and contests at which to make money. Later, the seemingly reformed manager was advertised as the "distinguished master of physical culture, Prof. Burt Miller."[7] Whether or not he also shared more of the profits with his pedestriennes is not known.

Elsa's specialty was walking one hundred miles in twenty-seven hours or less, usually competing against a local male pedestrian walking 120 miles, or against two of them, each walking sixty miles. Her exhibitions often took place in an opera house or music hall where a special sawdust track, usually three feet wide, had been laid, with spectators seated inside facing the track. Since these were small facilities, one circuit of the miniature track would measure only a fraction of a mile. In one hall, located in Wheeling, West Virginia, the track was exactly 187 feet in circumference. Since there are 5,280 feet in a mile, it required twenty-eight laps and forty-four feet to make one mile. Therefore, in a one-hundred-mile walk, Elsa would need to complete 2,823 laps. Allowing for two feet to a step, this would make 264,000 steps altogether.[8]

In this particular walk, Elsa was matched with amateur pedestrian and prominent Bellaire jeweller Newton L. Marsh, who would attempt to walk 120 miles in twenty-seven hours or less against Elsa's one hundred miles. The event began at eight o'clock in the evening, continued throughout the night and all next day, and finished just after ten o'clock at night. Carrying a light whip, Elsa wore a short, grey, poplin dress trimmed with pink satin. They walked almost continuously averaging between eleven and twelve minutes per mile, taking periodic short breaks with longer ones for breakfast and supper on the second day. Spectators came and went, and were sparse in the middle of the night, but by eight o'clock on the evening of the second day, there was standing room only. Just after ten o'clock that night Marsh completed one hundred miles and decided to call it quits. Elsa was not far behind and during her final mile kept up a furious pace to the music of "Yankee Doodle." Amid deafening cheers she closed her one hundredth mile in exactly eleven minutes, her quickest of the race.

At just over five feet four inches, Elsa was a little taller than Louise Armaindo but weighed about the same (130 pounds). Often described as retiring and lady-like in her deportment, her walking outfit was always a grey suit covered by a dress that fell to just above her shoes. As her reputation grew, Elsa became known as the "White Fawn" of Rochester, a name given to her by the governor of New York, Lucius Robinson, who was smitten by her petite form and child-like, innocent face. She also collected testimonials from respected men in the community, which were duly printed in the local paper to publicize her walks. A special appeal was often directed at women to attend, with the assurance that the exhibition would be one of refinement and nothing would happen to offend the most fastidious of ladies. If women were in attendance, the entertainment was also suitable for the best and most refined circles of society, unlike some pedestrian events where rowdiness, betting, and gambling were tolerated.

Elsa von Blumen modelled herself after one of the first pedestrienne celebrities in the United States, Bertha von Hillern, the young German immigrant introduced in the previous chapter. A German paper published in Cincinnati even went so far as to suggest that Elsa might be von Hillern's successor.[9] During Bertha's short but successful career, due to her extraordinary endurance and her agent's business connections, her efforts made a significant impact, especially among middle- and upper-class women. After match-ups with Mary Marshall, first in Chicago early in 1876 and later in November in New York's Central Park Garden, von Hillern never again walked in competition except against herself.

Her first solo exhibition took place just before Christmas in 1876. At the invitation of physicians in Boston, she completed 350 miles over six days on a temporary track (twenty laps to a mile) laid out in the city's music hall.[10] During the next year and a half, she travelled throughout the eastern United States giving solo exhibitions where she would walk eighty-eight miles in twenty-six hours or one hundred miles in twenty-eight hours. Walking consecutive hours meant that she went without sleep and with very little food during the time she was on the track. She was cleverly promoted by her manager, David Thomas, a press agent with the Barnum circus organization, who ensured that von Hillern's walks were well publicized, and that she was made available for enlightening interviews. Under Thomas's guidance, Bertha saw herself as an example to be emulated by proving to "my sex that correct diet,

2.1 Elsa von Blumen, the "White Fawn" of Rochester, New York, c. 1883 (Author's collection)

strict temperance and systematic exercise have much to do in securing perfect health."[11] Some women took her advice to heart and formed walking clubs, where members pledged "to eat oatmeal for breakfast, put on a loose, light Bloomer walking dress and take a long walk in the country at least three times a week."[12] Others attended her lectures on the benefits of exercise and healthy eating.

By the mid-1880s there was increasing interest among physicians, physical culturists, and entrepreneurs in regimens of vigorous physical exercise for both women and men to encourage greater strength, enhanced muscularity, and increased body size. Gymnasiums were established and equipped, and home exercise equipment, such as the lift machine – the precursor of the modern weightlifting machine – was invented and sold by enterprising agents. Many reform-minded Americans embraced the notion of a larger, stronger female body.[13] When pedestrienne Bertha von Hillern came to prominence in the late 1870s, the movement towards bigger, stronger, more active women, directed primarily at those who had time and money, was fully recognized. Bertha might well have been the first female athletic personality to endorse fitness products, such as a special liniment to relax tired muscles. She was also the subject of lectures titled "Physical Culture and Bertha Von Hillern" given by Leroy J. Cherrington, whose main objective was to sell the Dr Butler Health Lift.[14] By the summer of 1878 von Hillern had left the sawdust track to pursue a career as a landscape artist, although she continued to promote exercise for women, especially walking, hiking, and mountain climbing, through her articles and talks.[15]

The two Berthas – von Berg and von Hillern – along with Mary Marshall likely influenced Louise and Elsa to try earning a living through pedestrianism. Louise probably didn't realize that Mary Marshall (Mary Tryphena Curtis Lipsey) was a fellow Canadian, but had she known about her background, she would certainly have empathized with her. Born on 5 July 1841 in Soperton, Leeds, Ontario, Tryphena Curtis (as she was called) was the oldest sibling of eventually four brothers and two sisters. At nineteen, she married Irishman Thomas Lipsey, an ironworker, and they soon moved to Dunkirk, New York. A son, James, was born in 1862.

2.2 Poster advertising a walk of eighty-eight miles in twenty-six consecutive hours by Bertha von Hillern in Portland, Maine, 1877 (Collections of Maine Historical Society)

When Tryphena began her pedestrian career in 1876 in Chicago, under the name of Mary Marshall, newspaper reports indicated she was a widow, when in reality she had a husband and a teenage son. Whether she and her husband were still together is unclear because rumours circulated about a rocky marriage due to Lipsey's drinking and abuse. By the spring of 1877, with Bertha von Hillern refusing to walk against her, Marshall was forced to go solo as well. From April till July she travelled throughout New England putting on exhibitions of fifty or one hundred miles. She also became pregnant again, which forced her to disappear after the summer. Her son Allen (the father was Lipsey) was born in Soperton, Ontario, in February 1878.[16] After nearly a year, Mary, who now preferred to be called May, resumed her pedestrian career. Making up for lost time, she kept up a furious pace by travelling and performing extensively. By early 1879 she had amassed, according to her, an astonishing record of one hundred 50-mile, twenty-three 100-mile, six 225-mile, and four six-day walks, which was the equivalent of 9,000 miles. She had also defeated twenty-two men and a number of female walkers.[17] Confident and boastful, Marshall proclaimed that she was the "best human walker in the country" and bragged that as a "woman of iron heart" she could accomplish anything she undertook.[18] Her immediate goal was to exceed the achievement of the English pedestrienne Ada Anderson, who had recently walked a quarter mile every fifteen minutes for a month.

Madame Anderson, as she preferred to be called, had worked as an actress, circus clown, singer, and theatre proprietor in London before taking up pedestrianism in 1877. She had been trained by William Gale, a well-known and successful endurance pedestrian, who encouraged her to specialize in walks covering hundreds of miles over several weeks without sleep. Seeking greater challenges, she and her husband arrived in the United States in October 1878 and immediately sought out a New York venue for a twenty-eight-day walk. They attempted to rent Gilmore's Garden (later renamed Madison Square Garden) but had to settle for Mozart Garden, a smaller variety hall in Brooklyn. Anderson's goal was to walk a seemingly impossible 2,700 quarter miles in 2,700 quarter hours, a total of 675 miles in twenty-eight days. Night and day, commencing every fifteen minutes, she made seven

2.3 Madame Ada Anderson, the great 2,700 quarter-mile walker, *Frank Leslie's Illustrated Newspaper*, 1 February 1879 (Brooklyn Public Library)

circuits around the track, which on average took between three and four minutes. She then retired to her dressing room for the remaining eleven or twelve minutes, during which time she either ate, slept, changed her costume, or had a quick bath before the bell went again. Officials made certain she stuck to the rules, and curious spectators, including many women, came and went at all hours. Betting was plentiful and heavy, the odds being against the pedestrienne.

Anderson, thirty-five years of age, was variously described as robust, rosy, hearty, strong, and muscular; her walking style was admired for its graceful, swaying movements, and even, steady tread. She suffered badly blistered feet in the first couple of weeks, but overcame the problem with treatment. Since she managed to sleep only about an hour during each twenty-four, sleep deprivation was her biggest enemy. Increasingly, she suffered "sleepy spells," which meant that she walked around the track with her eyes closed and sound asleep. Occasionally, she walked an extra lap by mistake, and sometimes an assistant had to wake her and guide her back to the dressing room. To relieve the monotony and boredom she would jump onto the stage and, seated at a piano, serenade the crowd for a few minutes before resuming her walk. Anderson began her walk on 16 December 1878 and completed it on 12 January 1879 with reports that she earned between seven and eight thousand dollars for her efforts.[19]

Madame Anderson was now a celebrity, and her success in Brooklyn set off a pedestrian mania as dozens of working-class women throughout the United States took to walking for money with some trying to better her feats. Most were untrained and they failed miserably, never to be heard from again.[20] Among those succeeding were established pedestriennes like May Marshall, who completed 2,796 quarter miles in 2,796 consecutive quarter hours in a Washington gymnasium in mid-February. Unfortunately, the event was a financial failure and the audience was asked to contribute to a collection for the exhausted pedestrienne.[21]

At the same time Marshall walked in Washington, the exotically named Exilda Lachapelle was completing 2,700 quarter miles in 2,700 quarter hours in Chicago. Lachapelle was one of several celebrated pedestriennes depicted in a book published in 1878, titled *Practical Training for Running, Walking, Rowing, Wrestling, Jumping and All Kinds of Athletic Feats*.[22] In a later interview, she claimed to have been born in Marseilles, France. When she was very young, her doctor father moved to Canada, but both parents died soon after, leaving her in the care of an uncle. As a young child she loved to walk and run fast, which led to her walking professionally, first in Marseilles, and then as she travelled with her uncle.[23] Like many early athlete-entertainers, Lachapelle created a stage biography that only partially resembled the truth. Surprisingly, Exilda Lachapelle, like May Marshall and Louise Armaindo, was Canadian.

Born on 15 February 1859 in Montreal, Exilda was baptized Marie Ezilda Langlois dit Chapelle (her last name was Langlois, but the family also went by Chapelle). Her parents were Louis Langlois dit Chapelle and Herméline (Herminie) Daniel.[24] It's unlikely that Louis was a doctor, but his occupation is not known. The young family was beset by tragedy. Their first child, Louis Charles, born in 1857, died nine months later; then came Marie Ezilda in 1859, followed by Josephine in 1861, who died at age two; Jeremiah, born in 1864, survived, but Joseph Louis, born in 1865, died shortly thereafter. Even more tragically, Herméline died in 1868 at age thirty-two, leaving Louis with two young children, one of whom was Exilda. Nothing further is known about Louis, but Exilda and perhaps her brother Jeremiah may have been sent to a relative or a friend of the family. In 1874 and only fifteen, Exilda was married in Montreal to William Ross Derose, who was also French Canadian, eight years older and a bailiff. William, their son, was born on 7 May 1876, but he died three days later.

The facts of Exilda Lachapelle's life make it clear that she was a gritty survivor, which probably accounts for her success as an endurance walker. She was physically slim, petite, compact, and, according to one observer, "every muscle is serviceable."[25] Unlike some of her fellow pedestriennes, she did not lope around the ring or skip in a half run; her gait was even and graceful. Her attire was a light silk dress with little adornment that came just below the knee, and on her feet she wore high, lace-up shoes. Exilda always insisted that her pedestrienne career began when she was thirteen (in 1872), but where she performed is unknown. It was not in taverns and small theatres in Montreal and environs, as some have suggested, because there is no evidence that pedestrianism as a sport, let alone for women participants, took place there at that time.[26] However, we know little about the origins of pedestrianism in eastern Canada. I suspect that Exilda's walking career really began when she and her husband immigrated to the United States, probably to Wisconsin, likely sometime in the fall of 1877.[27]

Early in 1878, in a brief note in the *Chicago Daily Tribune*, Exilda complained that she had found no one willing to walk a long tramp against her; therefore, she challenged anyone to one hundred miles to be walked in the city. "She is by no means a novice," explained the article,

2.4 French Canadian pedestrienne Exilda Lachapelle, c. 1878 (Houseworth's celebrities [graphic] theater portraits collection, Lachapelle Exilda—POR 2, The Bancroft Library, University of California, Berkeley)

and "having a good Canadian reputation, she will make it lively for any contestant."[28] Exilda and her husband travelled throughout Wisconsin and Illinois seeking walking matches, though mostly she walked solo attempting to complete one hundred miles in twenty-six hours or less. In Madison, Wisconsin, for example, she accomplished this with more than half an hour to spare on an indoor sawdust track that required thirty laps to make one mile.[29] Occasionally, she went up against a male pedestrian in a ten-mile race; for instance, in Rockford, Illinois, she raced against a fellow who beat her by less than two minutes. The press report was entirely complimentary of Exilda's efforts, noting that though the male pedestrian strode out with a long and quick step, the "willing little French woman held him to the work with pertinacity, and beat him on the last mile." When the difference in the length of their limbs was considered, Lachapelle's feat was the more extraordinary of the two.[30]

All this was excellent training for Exilda's severest test of endurance early in 1879, which was 2,700 quarter miles in 2,700 consecutive quarter minutes round and round on a track laid out in the Folly Theatre on Desplaines Street in downtown Chicago. Built in 1870, the Folly was the only theatre to survive the Great Chicago Fire of 1871. Exilda walked for a month and suffered sore feet, stiff limbs, and sleep deprivation. Towards the end of her weary march, a physician was in daily attendance and an assistant accompanied her on the track.[31] Even so, after completing the 2,700 quarter miles, Lachapelle walked another 300 quarter miles over the next fifty hours by completing one quarter every ten minutes. The *Chicago Tribune* editors were not amused: "Somebody is making money out of this half-dead woman, whose sufferings and privations would excite the keenest pity if imposed upon her by some savage taskmaster in the heart of Africa."[32] It was time, according to the critics, to stop this distressing torture.

Did Louise Armaindo observe Exilda Lachapelle's month-long walk in Chicago? It is entirely possible because Louise took part in a ten-mile walking race in Chicago's Exposition Building in March 1879, and there is a good possibility she was in Chicago during January and February. What did she think? Was she tempted to join the ranks of the many women seeking fame and money as endurance walkers? One problem was a scarcity of halls and venues to accommodate them all. By the fall of 1879, Louise and Tom Eck were travelling further south in Kansas and Missouri before making their way back north to Illinois. They were an attractive twosome with Louise giving walking exhibitions, mostly at shorter distances and sometimes against local male pedestrians, while Tom went ahead to arrange the next event. Louise was clearly not one of the luminaries of the pedestrienne world, but she was earning a living, just like countless other women tramping around the sawdust tracks.

As the walkers grew in numbers, and endurance matches increased in frequency, the sport of pedestrianism attracted the inevitable critics, along with an emerging backlash. These attacks, many originating from the pulpit, were not specifically against women walkers but against pedestrianism as a sport.[33] It was, argued these moral crusaders, especially wasteful of money, happiness, and physical exertion, and a magnet for gambling, intemperance, and profanity. It was also cruel, dangerous (even deadly), unbecoming of a Christian nation, and no better than cockfighting, dogfighting, and prizefighting. Highly negative editorials appeared in major newspapers, some asking why these brutal exhibitions were allowed in a civilized community. "It is nothing more or less than a public trial by slow torture," argued the *Chicago Tribune*, "which does not advance athletic sports in the least; for the actual walking done in these sawdust rings is not, as walking, good for anything."[34]

Pedestriennes had a special drawing power. Victorian women were considered "weaker vessels," who attracted mostly male spectators wishing to see them strain their bodies against time; whereas women spectators came to honour their sex and take pride in their physical accomplishments.[35] Conversely, commentators argued that pedestrienne exhibitions, especially the six-day variety, were degrading to women because they preyed upon a vulgar curiosity and were certainly injurious to their health. Women walking for money in public were no different to those singing, dancing, swinging from a trapeze, or playing the piano. In a six-day pedestrian contest, women were pitted against each other, not to see who could walk the best, but who could be deprived of sleep the longest and then forced back on the track by merciless trainers. Therefore, it was not the walking itself that was objectionable, but walking under such conditions that the spectacle became one of competitive brutality.[36] Again, an editorial in the *Chicago Tribune* best summed up the critique against women pedestrians:

> In almost all sports there is some rivalry, some struggle, or an exhibition of the human form brought to a high pitch of muscular perfection: in this there is nothing but a woman, dressed in short skirts, her legs encased in some kind of worsted hose, walking monotonously around a sawdust ellipse, about which sit a number of stolid spectators, who every now and then break out, apparently without rhyme or reason, into frantic applause. After walking round a certain number of times she goes off into a room, where she falls asleep. After a certain number of days of this her feet begin to swell and become painful; later on she begins, it is said, to see visions, and walks around in a sort of dream, like those which people dying of hunger and thirst have; at any rate, she can hardly stand upright, and has to be forced up to her work. When she finally leaves the track, she is in a condition which makes continuous medical attendance a necessity to save her life.[37]

Provoking much of this outrage was a disastrous women's walking match held in Gilmore's Garden in New York from 26 to 31 March 1879. Walking professionally on a Sunday was not allowed, so the walkers began at 11 p.m. on Wednesday and quit at midnight on Saturday; then returned to the track just after midnight on Monday for the final day. Billed as an international six-day championship, eighteen pedestriennes, supposedly from nine different countries, lined up at the start of the go-as-you-please race. Among the starters were well-known walkers Exilda Lachapelle, Bertha von Berg, Bella Kilbury, and Sarah Tobias, and others who were inexperienced and poorly trained. Two of the best performers did not compete: May Marshall was performing elsewhere in Brooklyn, and Ada Anderson was taking time off in Chicago. Several of the least experienced walkers dropped out after a couple of days, and when the race started again on the Monday, only seven remained. Lachapelle, who was the pre-race favourite, withdrew early on. She was embarrassed by her inebriated husband who was flirting with women in the stands, and she was fed up having to work while he drank. She eventually returned to finish the race but was not allowed. In the end, only five walkers finished with Bertha von Berg accomplishing the most miles.[38]

Among the fallout from this calamitous event, the normally supportive *National Police Gazette* summed up the state of women's pedestrianism best: "Fortunately it is probable that the thing has been killed by its own absurdity, and it is not likely that it will pay any one soon again to ask the patronage of the public for such an exhibition, but should the cupidity of any manager attempt to coin money out of the sufferings of necessitated women, it is to be devoutly hoped that the authorities may see their way clear to prevent such a disgrace upon our city and our century."[39] Medical authorities also condemned female pedestrianism. After witnessing an attempt by two pedestriennes to walk four thousand quarter miles in four thousand quarter minutes, the Philadelphia County Medical Society passed a resolution expressing their condemnation of the "barbarities now being inflicted upon women in this city under the falsely assumed name of exemplification of physical culture and pedestrianism, but which simply consist in the deprivation of natural sleep for long periods of time, a form of torture not surpassed in the annals of the Inquisition."[40] These doctors presented their resolution to the mayor of Philadelphia asking him to stop the exhibition, but he declined, lacking the authority. When the pedestriennes learned of this resolution, they called it absurd and continued walking.

Nonetheless, there was sufficient criticism of female pedestrianism in the eastern United States that promoters opted to try the West Coast, especially San Francisco. Some pedestriennes agreed to go west – Exilda Lachapelle among them. For a weekly salary, Exilda and relative newcomer Fannie Edwards walked over several weeks in Platt's Hall in San Francisco. Both accomplished three thousand quarter miles but no winner was declared. At the same time and on the same track, Bertha von Berg gave exhibition walks for several hours a day, alongside local pedestrian John Armstrong, walking a half-mile every quarter hour for twenty hours a day. A women's six-day race was scheduled for mid-July with Lachapelle and Edwards competing along with three others, but von Berg backed out over money issues. Exilda won handily, and when she and Bertha went head-to-head in a six-day match in September, Exilda won

2.5 Pedestrienne star Fannie Edwards, c. 1879 (Houseworth's celebrities [graphic] theater portraits collection, Edwards, Fannie—POR 4, The Bancroft Library, University of California, Berkeley)

again.[41] Now the darling of San Francisco, Lachapelle went east to re-cuperate, and did not return for six months. Women's races were orga-nized without her, mostly among local contestants, and although well received, the sport continued to struggle.

In mid-December 1879, Madison Square Garden was yet again the venue for a women's six-day go-as-you-please international walking race. There were twenty-five starters and among them were some of the top stars – Exilda Lachapelle, May Marshall, Ada Anderson, Fannie Edwards, Madame Tobias, and Bella Kilbury – and also a relative un-known, Amy Howard, a slight, seventeen-year-old blonde from Brook-lyn.[42] First prize was one thousand dollars and a championship belt valued at five hundred dollars. Rules stipulated that contestants agree to "engage in no quarreling, loud talking, profane or obscene language, either upon the track or in their tents."[43] Furthermore, they could not talk to anyone in the audience while on the track; they must at all times keep perfectly neat and clean; and they were not to appear on the track in tights without a dress overtop and hair neatly arranged. However, no smoking signs were totally ignored, and as the race progressed, the air was blue with cigar smoke.

Amy Howard surprised everyone and from the third day onwards, she kept the lead. While many others were limping along, she "strode around the circle with a strong, elastic step and jaunty air, and was about the only woman of them all who showed any of the genuine qualities of a pedestrian."[44] Before 5,000 cheering spectators, Howard won the race after completing 393 miles. She was immediately challenged by Madame Tobias, who came second with 387 miles. However, before the challenge race could take place, New York City aldermen passed a resolution to draft an act to suppress and prevent female pedestrian exhibitions on the grounds they were "offensive to the sense of propriety and decency, demoralizing in their influence on the community, and cruel and inhuman to the participants."[45] Anyone promoting or holding such an exhibition would be punished.

Female pedestrian contests were now effectively banned in New York City, which meant that other jurisdictions in the eastern United States might follow suit. At the very least, there would be no more events in Madison Square Garden. San Francisco, on the other hand, was willing

2.6 Amy Howard, standing beside her championship belt, *National Police Gazette*, 6 August 1881 (Library of Congress)

to host such events, and several pedestrienne stars – Howard, Lachapelle, Tobias, and von Berg among them – crossed the country seeking opportunities to compete. The first race, a go-as-you-please six-day event, took place in early May 1880 in the Mechanics' Institute Pavilion, a large wooden structure used primarily for industrial exhibitions, at the corner of Eighth and Mission Streets. Twenty walkers lined up at the start, but by the fourth day almost half had quit, including Lachapelle, who was sick from the long journey west.[46] Howard and Tobias were the winners with 409 and 400 miles, respectively, more than any female pedestrian

had accomplished before.[47] Amy Howard was the best of all pedestriennes. When she was in a race, the result was never in doubt, and her
records lasted for years.[48] Although the sport continued for several more
years with a coterie of devoted participants and reports of occasional
races, the glory days of women's pedestrianism had ended.

Louise Armaindo and Elsa von Blumen were personally unaffected
by the criticism directed at female pedestrianism because they were neither star pedestriennes, nor did they participate in any of the controversial six-day races. Besides, they were a long way from New York
and San Francisco when these events took place. As pedestriennes, Elsa
and Louise did not compete against each other; in fact, they probably
never met. Elsa did most of her walking exhibitions throughout various
communities in Ohio, sometimes venturing into Wheeling, West Virginia, just across the Ohio River. During the spring and summer of
1880, she slowed down considerably, and a report in *Bicycling World*
in late November 1880 suggested she had been living in retirement in
Rochester for some time. Louise, on the other hand, was based primarily in Illinois for much of 1880, travelling throughout the state with
Tom Eck, and demonstrating her ability to walk twenty-five miles in
less than four hours. Then she disappeared until late in 1881.

Aside from the criticism directed at women's marathon walks, pedestrianism as a sport was in decline due to an inevitable conflict between
promoters and athletes. On the track, promoters wanted athletes to put
out 100 per cent effort all the time, whereas the athletes knew the best
strategy was to conserve energy for the finish and hang back with the
pack. This made for a boring contest except for the final sprint. Rules
were introduced stipulating that walkers had to cover a set number of
miles or there would be no prize. Nonetheless, with higher admission
prices and walkers who plodded along, interest in the sport waned and
promoters turned to the more exciting six-day bicycle and roller skating
races.[49] A more controlled environment and different formats, with racers on the track for a set number of hours a day, alleviated many of the
problems plaguing pedestrianism. Financially, both men's and women's
pedestrianism depended on gambling to keep it going, and without heavy
betting, it could no longer generate enough money or media attention to
remain viable.

No longer able to make much money, some pedestriennes simply quit the sport; others returned to the theatres and saloons as burlesque singers, actresses, or chorus girls. A few decided to continue as athlete-entertainers in a new spectator sport – high-wheel bicycle racing. Both Elsa von Blumen and Louise Armaindo made the choice to reinvent themselves as bicycliennes. Eventually, they would meet when one challenged the other. Another pedestrienne who turned to the high wheel for fame and fortune was Lizzie Baymer.

CHAPTER THREE

EARLY BICYCLIENNES, 1879–1882

Lizzie Baymer, described as a handsome young woman with well-cut features, black hair, large brown eyes, and a clear complexion, was an eighteen-year-old seamstress living in a boarding house in San Francisco. On the evening of 8 October 1879, Lizzie was on a track set out in the Mechanics' Institute Pavilion along with fifteen other contestants at the start of a six-day walking race. She had no previous experience as a pedestrienne. Most of the others were local amateurs with little pedestrian knowledge, but among them were more skilled walkers, including the well-known Bertha von Berg (Maggie Gangross). Also walking was Canadian Lillie Denman from Montreal, who had been successful at shorter distances, but was making her debut at a six-day continuous walk. The contestant walking the greatest number of miles in 144 hours would win the first prize money (25 per cent of the net proceeds) and a gold and diamond medal valued at $175.[1]

It was clear from the start that Lizzie Baymer was out of her depth. The news reports were not kind and she was variously described as the "heavy-weight coryphée" or "stately and eminently staid" or "slow and sorrowful." She was well behind the leaders, and after completing only eighty-eight miles by the third day, Lizzie withdrew. She was totally out of the prize money and there was simply no point in continuing. The favourite, Bertha von Berg, suffered from pneumonia and also had to withdraw.[2] Only half of the original contestants finished the six-day race, and the winner was May Belle Sherman of San Francisco with 337 miles to her credit.

This was an inauspicious beginning for a woman who some six weeks later took part in the first high-wheel cycling race for women held in the United States. The date was 29 November 1879. Lizzie Baymer had learned to ride a high wheel at a San Francisco bicycle school run by Fred T. Merrill, a popular trick rider. Held in the same Mechanics' Pavilion, the women's race was a preliminary two-hour match to a men's three-day race. Lizzie's opponents were Addie Lee and a Mrs Martin, both of San Francisco. At five foot six, Lizzie was the tallest of the three and by far the fastest. She rode with grace and confidence on a fifty-inch Coventry bicycle, imported from England, wearing a black velvet Turkish vest over a blouse, matching velvet trunks, flesh-coloured tights, with her long black hair tied up in a turban affair.[3]

Before some 1,500 spectators, the women raced on four consecutive nights, and Lizzie won each event. There were no prizes, but Lizzie's admirers gave her a gold medal with the inscription, "Lizzie Baymer, the champion lady bicycle rider of California." More importantly, her fame spread and she was engaged by Messrs Starling and Bailey to perform in Eureka, a bustling mining town in central Nevada, in May of 1880. "Champion Lady Bicyclist of the Pacific Coast! A Great Novelty!" exclaimed the advertisement in the *Eureka Daily Sentinel*. The paper advised, "every reader of the *Sentinel* who admires the muscular development of the female sex to see Miss Baymer in the coming exhibitions."[4] Since there were no other high-wheel riders in Eureka, and certainly no women, Lizzie performed either by herself or against local male pedestrians. A small track had been laid out in the Eureka Hall, a newly built, two-storey theatre on the main street. At thirty-six laps to a mile, the track made for very tight turns, especially on a high-wheel bicycle. In one race, Lizzie crashed into the stage, broke her bicycle, and ended up with a cut lip and bruised knee. The pedestrians in these races were given a head start. For example, in a one-hundred-mile race against a Joseph O'Brien, he was allowed a forty-mile head start. Lizzie still beat him by riding a hundred miles in ten hours and twenty-five

3.1 Lizzie Baymer of San Francisco, first high-wheel woman racer in North America, 1880 (Nevada Historical Society)

minutes to O'Brien's walk of 57¾ miles in ten hours and forty-four minutes. Both rested periodically, but not for much more than a total of one and a half hours.

After ten days of exhibitions and races, Lizzie returned to California and travelled to towns including Grass Valley, Chico, and Marysville giving trick riding and racing exhibitions. On several occasions, she was slated to race against a trotting horse, which did not happen until early in August 1880, when Lizzie appeared at the Agricultural Park in Sacramento. The race started as planned but the backers of the horse changed animals on the second mile, and Lizzie, even with a good lead, withdrew from the contest because the agreement was that she would ride against only one horse.[5] Instead, Lizzie gave a riding exhibition in the blazing sun with the temperature in the nineties, and received this commentary in the *Sacramento Daily Union*: "There are young gentlemen here who can ride better and faster than Miss Baymer. She does not know how to hold her hands, and while graceful enough and decidedly handsome and muscular, her bicycle riding is not of a character to warrant anyone in paying a half dollar to see her wheel about a racetrack. As an entertainment the exhibition was a failure."[6] Nonetheless, Lizzie Baymer gained some attention through New York's *National Police Gazette*, when it published a lithograph of the "champion velocipedist of the Pacific coast."[7]

Meanwhile, the pedestrienne Elsa von Blumen was emerging again, this time as a high-wheel racer. In the fall of 1880, when Elsa first began practising on a high wheel, she used a beautiful nickel-plated machine, thirty-four inches in diameter and made by the Pope Manufacturing Company of Boston. Her cycling costume usually consisted of an attractive steel grey suit. The long-sleeved jacket had a gold fringe and opened in front. She wore matching leggings to just below the knee met by long socks and lace-up boots. On her head was a high-plumed hat that resembled a helmet. She soon exchanged her practice bicycle for one more suitable for racing, which was a forty-eight-inch Special Columbia cut to measure with rat-trap pedals (ones with toe clips) to match her small feet. As soon as she felt ready, Elsa gave bicycle exhibitions in Rochester, announcing these events through neat circulars replete with tasteful commendations. "When she does take a header," noted *Bicycling World*, "she lands on her feet very prettily."[8]

Elsa's manager and promoter was Bert Miller, who had overseen her pedestrian career. Just as he had cleverly crafted her pedestrienne image as a highly respectable entertainer, and one endorsed by upstanding and influential citizens, he did the same for her high-wheel racing career. This was good business practice because his livelihood depended on the money brought in by his cycling protégé. Since Elsa was one of the first women in the United States to race the high wheel, Bert decided that pitting her against running and trotting horses was more profitable.

The notion of racing bicycles against horses was nearly as old as the bicycle itself. In 1868, during a highly publicized event in France, a velocipedist raced against a horse and buggy from Castres to Toulouse for forty-five miles over rough roads. He cycled for six hours and was beaten by the horse, but only by twenty-five minutes. Despite the loss, his gutsy performance was widely heralded as a "stirring moral victory" for the mechanical horse and its imminent rise as the carriage of the future.[9] At London's Alexandria Palace in 1875, a large crowd watched the trotting mare Lady Flora barely edge out cyclist David Stanton, who was riding a high wheel, over a ten-mile course. Also in 1875, a member of the Vélo-Club d'Angers rode a fifty-four-inch high wheel from Paris to Vienna. He covered the seven hundred miles in twelve days and apparently beat the performance of a noted horseman by a few days. In each of these examples, the cyclist was male. However, a few years later, Ernestine Bernard from the Hippodrome in Paris, a highly celebrated expert cyclist, was matched against a local running horse in Toronto, Ontario. The race was a three-mile heat won by the French athlete, but since the horse stumbled and fell on a short turn, it was hardly a fair contest. A reporter from the *National Police Gazette* commented on Ernestine's remarkable speed and skill, although he was doubtful she would beat a horse of respectable quality doing its best. The *Gazette* also published a racy illustration of the event with Ernestine "clad in the scant garments appropriate to the occasion."[10] The bicycle depicted looks like a cross between a boneshaker and a high wheel, or what might have been a transitional machine of some sort.

3.2 Elsa von Blumen as a high-wheel racer, 1882 (Collection of Lorne Shields, Toronto, Canada)

Elsa and Bert travelled throughout the summer of 1881 to the fair-grounds and driving parks around New York cities and towns like Syracuse, Binghamton, Potsdam, Brockport, Chatham, Watertown, Hudson, and Utica. Usually she rode one mile around the track while the horse went a mile and a half, or she rode three-quarters of a mile to the horse's mile, with the winner determined by the best of three heats. Often she won two heats outright and therefore the race, a feat made even more impressive given the rough condition of many racetracks. Elsa had visited some of these places as a pedestrienne, so that she was already known and admired, which served to bring out the spectators often in the thousands. The crowds loved her. They greeted her with tremendous applause when she entered the track, and cheered her loudly during the races. As her reputation grew, she earned the title of "America's first and only lady bicyclist."[11] More importantly, the purses offered at Elsa's races were increasingly handsome with most set at $200 (about $4,500 today).

In a time of limited opportunities for women to participate in vigorous physical activity, Elsa saw herself as an example for other women to follow. Again, it was likely her manager Bert Miller who saw an opportunity to promote Elsa as a leading proponent of women's physical emancipation, willing to be associated with women's suffrage. In a well-publicized statement, Elsa explained why she rode and raced the high wheel:

> In presenting myself to the public in my bicycle exercises, I feel that I am not only offering the most novel and fascinating entertainment now before the people, but I am demonstrating the great need on the part of American young ladies, especially, of physical culture and bodily exercise. Success in life depends as much upon a vigorous and healthy body as upon a clear and active mind. In my travels I daily see hundreds of ladies, and even gentlemen, with flat chests and narrow shoulders, and a shuffling gait – the result of neglecting the needs of the body. My experience as a bicycle athlete has beyond question saved me from a consumptive decline.[12]

She went on in her statement to evoke the name of her friend Mary A. Livermore, a well-known American suffragist and social reformer, who

3.3 Elsa von Blumen racing the trotting horse Hattie R in Rochester, New York, *Frank Leslie's Illustrated Newspaper*, 18 June 1881 (Author's collection)

had encouraged Elsa in her work and, at the same time, advocated physical training for all young women. Elsa reminded the public that she would compete in friendly rivalry against both gentlemen and horses, but would countenance no wagering or gambling at her performances; and the respectability of her past exhibitions would be maintained throughout the present ones. Elsa, and certainly Bert Miller, firmly believed these conditions were sufficient to ensure that "all lovers of health and physical vigor will award me their approbation and patronage."[13]

By the fall of 1881 there were rumours of a race between Elsa von Blumen and a "Chicago bicyclienne" to be held as a winter attraction at the Chicago bicycle rink.[14] Louise Armaindo was surfacing again, but this time on a high-wheel bicycle. We last saw Louise in late 1880 when she and Tom Eck were in Canada performing as pedestrians. By spring of the following year they had returned to Chicago. Tom showed up in the spring exhibition of the Athenæum gymnasium and distinguished

3.4 A rare photo of Louise Armaindo taken by the photographer John Wood of 208 Bowery, New York City, c. 1883 (Author's collection)

himself by performing backward jumps with weights, jumping to records of nine feet eight inches and ten feet two inches.[15] There was silence around Louise until November 1881 when a series of entertaining exhibitions took place at Wilkinson's Bicycle School and Gymnasium. These included Louise, the only woman rider, showing off her new skills by riding a mile against time. Her instructor, "Professor" Frederick S. Rollinson, wrote, "The lady rider, Mlle. Louise Armaindo, is by fame a pedestrienne. This same rider has accomplished the feat of walking seventy-five miles without getting off the track. She rides a forty-eight-inch wheel; is very muscular in upper and lower limbs; can lift steadily a dumb-bell weighing eighty-five pounds above her head; was one of my first pupils on the opening of the school; learnt very quickly; rides in a very fine form – by far more graceful than Eliza [*sic*] Von Blumen; will make a stayer, if not a fast rider."[16]

Fred Rollinson entered Louise's life at just the right time. Public support for pedestrianism, especially in Chicago, was waning, but interest in high-wheel racing was on the rise. Rollinson had arrived in the United States in 1879 from Derbyshire, England, when he joined a European team of riders giving exhibitions in various American cities. His speciality was trick riding, where he rode a high wheel in every conceivable position by standing on the saddle or lying on the machine with his feet over the handles and his head resting near the saddle. He had also perfected an amusing routine, "The Dude Learning to Ride." More seriously, he participated in professional races, but his aim was to settle somewhere permanently and open a bicycle riding school. Rollinson became associated with John Wilkinson, the Chicago agent for Columbia bicycles, who opened a riding school connected with the Chicago Bicycle Club located in the south side Natatorium at the corner of Michigan Avenue and Jackson Street.[17] The Natatorium had a summer season from mid-April until mid-October when it functioned as a swimming bath, followed by a winter season when it was transformed into a gymnasium as well as bicycle riding school. After the spring of 1882, the Chicago Bicycle Club used the Exposition Building (right opposite the Natatorium and on the lake front) for their meeting rooms and training. Rollinson was hired to manage the riding school, and he became Louise's instructor and trainer.

So confident was Louise of her riding skills that she immediately challenged Elsa von Blumen, or any other lady bicycle rider in the world "to ride the bicycle twenty-five to 100 miles for $100 to $250 a side, or for a medal showing an emblem of the championship of the world for lady bicycle riders."[18] The race would take place in Chicago, or wherever mutually agreed upon by the contestants. The personalities of the two riders were remarkably different. Where Louise was brash and boastful, Elsa was modest and demure; where Louise was outgoing and flashy, Elsa was conservative, even staid. No doubt advised by her manager Bert Miller, Elsa was in no hurry to take up Louise's challenge.

She would prove that she was the better rider without going head-to-head with this new rival.

In late November 1881, Elsa was in Pittsburgh, Pennsylvania, where it was announced that she would attempt to ride 1,000 miles in six days. A track was laid out in Old City Hall, one-sixteenth of a mile in circumference, which meant that Elsa needed to make 16,000 circuits to accomplish her goal. By the end of the fifth day, she had ridden 849 miles but was stiff and sore, had lost several pounds, and her hands were so badly blistered they had to be plastered. With the help of stimulants, she completed the 1,000 miles on the sixth day with eight minutes to spare. There was some controversy over the scorer, who happened to be Bert Miller's brother-in-law. Overall, the event was a financial success and certainly a victory for Elsa in her quest to show that she was capable of more than just racing horses.[19]

Early in 1882 Louise began travelling with Fred Rollinson and Tom Eck to perform in a series of bicycle tournaments designed to entertain audiences in western American cities. They started in Louisville, Kentucky, where Louise raced against her two male companions but was given a handicap. For instance, in a twenty-five mile race against Rollinson, she had a four-mile head start. She won by one and half miles in a time of one hour and thirty-four minutes.[20] She did the same thing in Cincinnati, Ohio, a couple of weeks later. In St Louis, Missouri, early in March, she rode over six hundred miles in seventy-two hours, twelve hours each day, the best long-distance record in America at the time. Demands were immediate that Elsa von Blumen should take on Louise and settle once and for all who the better rider was, but there was continuing silence from Elsa's camp.

With Louise's growing reputation, other male riders were beginning to take notice. John S. Prince, a young Englishman with an established racing record, had been in the United States only a few months but he called himself "Champion of America." Issuing a challenge to Louise, he offered her a five-mile head start in a fifty-mile race. Louise countered with six miles, arguing it was still a small handicap for a woman in a long a race. Prince accepted Louise's proposition with the race slated for Boston in a few weeks.[21]

Meanwhile, Louise and her two male companions headed north to Canada. They put on their usual show at the Horticultural Gardens Pavilion in Toronto, but the track was very tight at eighteen laps to the mile, which prevented much speed on the part of the cyclists. Nonetheless, Louise was complimented as an "exceedingly graceful rider" and her exhibition was much admired by the audience.[22] From Toronto they travelled to Montreal, which was possibly the first time Louise was back in home territory since she left Canada. The Montreal Bicycle Club sponsored a three-day exhibition at the Crystal Rink. Among the feature events was a one-hundred-mile race between Armaindo, Eck, and Rollinson, which did not go exactly as planned. Tom dropped out after forty-one miles. Fred ran into a spectator attempting to cross the track, which caused a severe fall that made it impossible for him to finish the race with much speed. Louise also took a header because her attendant carelessly removed a coat she was wearing after a rest break. Luckily, she was not hurt and was able to finish the race in just under eight hours, two laps ahead of Rollinson.[23]

Louise was clearly in a class of her own, at least as far as women racers were concerned. An untested rider, Ida Blackwell, was busily training in Boston under the watchful eye of John Prince, and she was eager to take on Louise. On 29 April 1882 she met Louise at the huge New England Manufacturers' and Mechanics' Institute (also called the Casino) building in Boston before a thousand spectators. Ida was given a lap head start in a five-mile race. Louise burst out from the standing start, covering the first mile in a blistering three minutes and fifty-two seconds, the fastest time yet by a woman. Ida didn't stand a chance, and she finished her four miles and three laps almost two minutes behind Louise. Ida was never heard from again.[24]

Louise followed up this victory a month later with her promised contest against John Prince. The fifty-mile race was held at the Casino in Boston before a large crowd. Louise had conceded to a five-mile handicap (instead of six), and she was confident of maintaining the lead. Prince dug in, and by the forty-second mile, he had made up his handicap and was just behind Louise. He held this position until the last mile for an exciting finish when both riders went all out with Prince beating Louise

3.5 Thomas W. Eck beside his high-wheel bicycle, taken by a photographer in Quincy, Illinois, 1884. Tom signed the photo "Champion of Canada" (Collection of Lorne Shields, Toronto, Canada)

by only half a lap. "She rides just like a man," was heard throughout the audience, although, as one commentator pointed out, few men ride with the same grace and ease.[25]

Those clamouring for a matchup between Elsa von Blumen and Louise Armaindo were soon to get their wish. Elsa spent the first six months of 1882 mostly racing horses. Although she disliked long-distance racing, she managed to net 850 miles during six days in Detroit in April, but it was 150 miles less than she wished to accomplish.[26] There was also a curious report of her jumping into the Mississippi River to rescue a young woman from drowning. The girl's father was so grateful that he presented Elsa with a thousand dollars in gold, which would have been considerably more than her earnings through racing.[27]

The long-awaited showdown between Louise and Elsa took place in July 1882 at Ridgeway Park in Philadelphia. Over the course of six days, they raced ten miles daily in two-mile heats. Riding a fifty-inch wheel to Elsa's forty-eight-inch, Louise won twenty-one of the thirty heats. In the evenings, they raced together against horses – twenty-one miles to the horses' twenty-five miles – but the horses found the track too narrow and they were withdrawn after losing to the cyclists.[28]

A week later at the Sea Beach Palace Hotel on New York's Coney Island, Elsa and Louise teamed up against William J. Morgan in a six-day race. A Welshman by birth, Morgan had immigrated to the United States a few years earlier and begun to establish his reputation as an endurance cyclist. A track made of heavy pine planking, measuring nine laps to the mile, was laid out in the garden adjoining the hotel. Seats were provided for spectators on the turf outside the course, although one could see the race from any part of the grounds. Over six days, the two bicycliennes alternated every half hour for six hours, whereas Morgan rode continuously for six hours each day. There was a noticeable difference in their riding skills. Morgan was very steady and sat firmly in the saddle, upright except if sprinting, and then he bent well forward. Von Blumen, as always, carried herself gracefully; she always sat upright in the saddle, but her machine (a forty-eight-inch Columbian) wobbled, and it was noted that she would do better if she used a larger wheel. Most agreed that Armaindo was the best rider of the three. She was in perfect control of her bicycle (a fifty-inch Yale roadster), and most of the time she was bent well forward from the hips.[29]

After the first day the women were in the lead with seventy-seven miles and four laps to Morgan's seventy-one miles and four laps. They maintained their lead for four days, despite a stiff breeze and heavy rain on the third day, which rendered the track slow and dangerous. Both women took a header on this day. Louise landed on her face with such force they thought she had broken her nose. Luckily, she hadn't, but her face was swollen and sore, and when she left the track that day she was heartily cheered. Morgan prevailed in the end, but just barely, with a winning score of 467 miles and eight laps. The women's combined total was 466 miles and one lap. Louise had ridden slightly more miles than Elsa, who had switched to a new forty-nine-inch Yale bicycle that suited her better.[30] As the race went on the crowds increased steadily, which paid off handsomely for the contestants. As the winner, Morgan received 50 per cent of the gate, and the two women 20 per cent, although no actual amounts were reported.[31]

The day after the six-day race in Coney Island finished, Louise and Elsa went head-to-head over fifty miles on the same track. It was hardly a contest because Louise set a very fast pace, completing fifty miles in just over three hours and thirty-one minutes. She left the saddle only once at the fifteen-mile mark to have her machine oiled. When she finished, Elsa was eleven miles behind.[32] It would be another seven years before Louise and Elsa would race against each other again.

Elsa von Blumen temporarily retired from high-wheel racing for the remainder of 1882 and most of 1883, purportedly to study art. However, the real reason was likely a disastrous personal life. Early in 1883 Elsa went with friends on a three-week visit to Hannibal in Oswego County, New York. There she met Emery E. Beardsley, a farmer, who at twenty-five was only a couple of years older than Elsa. After a ridiculously brief courtship they were married in Hannibal on 31 January 1883 under her real name of Caroline (Carrie) Kiner. Elsa's recollection of this marriage was very vague since it was obviously hasty, and she firmly believed that she was "under some influence" at the time.[33] The couple lived in a small dwelling in Hannibal near her parents-in-law. After about three months, Elsa went to her parents in Rochester for a brief visit. Upon her return to Hannibal she discovered that several trunks containing her clothing, jewellery, and cycling medals had been broken into with items missing. A search warrant revealed some of the stolen items in a haystack behind Beardsley's father's house. Elsa immediately returned to her parents' home, where she stayed until she decided to resume her racing career, and what to do about her husband.

What of Lizzie Baymer? After 1880 she disappeared from the high-wheel racing scene. The *New York Clipper* reported that she was a proprietress of a coffee saloon in Santa Rosa, California.[34] What we also know is that, for a while at least, she was still paying attention to women's cycle racing. In a tattered scrapbook, a copy of which resides with the Nevada Historical Society, Lizzie kept track of her adventures and, in one of the last pages, she pasted in a few articles about Louise Armaindo.[35] No doubt Lizzie wondered if she could have beaten the legendary Armaindo, but she never got the chance. Lizzie had no agent or promoter on her side, which was an absolute necessity if a female racer was to find competition.

CHAPTER FOUR

CHAMPION BICYCLIENNE, 1883

Louise Armaindo continued to pit her skills against a handful of professional riders. Although the rewards were primarily financial, she was a competitor who enjoyed beating her male rivals, especially when the stakes were for the "Championship of America."[1] In September 1882 she again met John Prince at the Polo Grounds in New York where she received a three-mile handicap in a twenty-five-mile race. Prince wore white tights, his arms bare, and on his head was a black jockey cap. Louise was dressed in a crimson jacket trimmed with silver lace, red trunks, red and white stockings, heavy walking shoes, and a scarlet silk cap. A diamond crescent glittered at her throat. There were some five hundred spectators in the grandstand, many of whom were women wearing Louise's crimson colours.[2]

Prince rode a fifty-four-inch Yale machine; Armaindo's was the same, but it had a fifty-one-inch wheel. Prince took the lead from the start and steadily increased the distance between them, slowly making up the three-mile handicap. Louise worked her pedals "like the cranks of a locomotive" and, with perspiration running down her face, it was clear she was overdressed for the occasion. Near the end, the crowd cheered enthusiastically in support of Louise and the women waved their handkerchiefs. It was all to no avail because Prince passed her on the second lap of the last mile, winning the race by eighty-four seconds. It was a slow race since they were some eighteen minutes behind the record.

Tom Eck was not only Louise's official manager and agent, but also her partner and probable lover. In press reports as early as 1879, Tom was often referred to as Louise's husband.[3] However, no record was found of an official marriage between the two. It is also clear that they were business partners because they needed each other to earn money. It was Tom's job to find her opponents and races, and to promote her growing reputation. He was also in charge of her training. Occasionally, when no challenger could be found, he was forced to go up against Louise himself to his inevitable defeat, which brought about charges of "hippodroming" or predetermining the outcome. After watching Tom and Louise race at a meet in Springfield, Massachusetts, one commentator complained, "If it is necessary to exhibit female riders to please a certain element in a crowd a half-mile dash is enough to serve the purpose."[4] When there were no human riders available to challenge, Tom pitted Louise against a horse. All this put her in superb condition for the first serious test of her racing career. She would race against the leading male professionals without the advantage of a handicap.

A reporter was watching Louise train and ride at the Chicago Natatorium in preparation for these races. Suddenly wheeling up to the visitor, Louise stopped, dismounted, and inquired, "How do you like me for ze expert bicyclienne?" "Oh, pretty well," said the reporter, "but you are almost too fat to be in good racing condition." "Too fat! Too fat!" Louise screamed. "You of my leg feel! You ze muscle find and not ze fat!"[5] She was an incredibly strong and superbly fit young woman, and she was about to prove it.

For six days in May 1883, William M. Woodside, William J. Morgan, and Louise Armaindo took part in the first real long-distance race for the US championship. On a makeshift track laid out in the Battery D Armory on Chicago's lakefront, with thirteen laps to the mile, they raced twelve hours a day, beginning at eleven in the morning and ending at eleven at night. They took breaks whenever they wished, but to do so meant that someone else would move ahead. At the end of the first day, there was little separating the three riders. After the fourth day, Armaindo had moved ahead slightly after completing 561 miles to Morgan's 559 and Woodside's 558. "For persistent attention to the

business and continuous staying qualities," wrote an awed reporter,
"Louise Armaindo, the French girl, takes the souvenir."[6] Louise increased her lead over the last two days and closed the seventy-two-hour
race at 843 miles. Morgan came second after 820 miles, whereas
Woodside had seriously fallen back finishing at only 723 miles.[7] Her
post-race commentary was interesting: "No one can have any idea how
I had to punish myself to hold to the end; but I had determined to beat
those two men, and I did it."[8] She also commented on the presence of
a great many women in the audience, who encouraged her with kind
words and rapt attention. For Louise, that was one of the best things
about the race.

The contest was a huge success with some two thousand people visit-
ing the armory nightly to watch the exciting action. Newspapers praised
Louise's win against the best riders of Ireland and Canada, often failing
to mention that she too was from Canada. An editorial in an Arizona
paper, willing to concede bigger hearts and clearer brains than men to
the "gentler sex," said it would also have to accept their stronger limbs
and greater endurance. "Don't let us glorify the males any more at the
expense of the females," said the writer, but "let us place them in the
same niche to which their virtues and their limb power entitles them."[9]
In addition to her share of the gate, Louise was awarded two valuable
badges for her victory. One represented professional honours and was
valued at three hundred dollars. It was in the shape of a wheel suspended
by chains from two bars that were appropriately engraved. The other,
given to her by admirers, was a magnificent five-point gold star valued
at five hundred dollars. In the centre was an engraving of a woman cyclist
surrounded by five diamonds.[10]

Woodside was crushed. Admitting to a "breakdown" towards the
end of the race, he was far from convinced that the "plucky little"
Louise was the better rider, and he wanted another chance to prove it.
He immediately issued a challenge: "I therefore hereby challenge her to
ride a similar contest for $100 to $1000 a side, and the championship of
America, the race to be open to all comers who will deposit a similar
amount. If Mademoiselle does not care to ride so long a distance again,
I will give her five miles start in fifty, or ten in one hundred, and race for
$100 to $500 on any track not less than eight laps to the mile."[11] Louise

4.1 John S. Prince, taken by photographer John Wood, 208 Bowery, New York, c. 1883 (Author's collection)

did not ignore Woodside's challenge, but she had her own agenda and was not about to get sidetracked. A week after the race in Chicago, she again defeated Morgan and Woodside during a 120-mile race in Janesville, Wisconsin, riding forty miles each evening on a track of twenty-three laps to the mile. Louise took the lead from the beginning and won by three laps.[12]

Who were these male professional riders who raced against Louise and how good were they? John Shillington Prince was born in 1858 in Langley Green, Worcester, England. At age seventeen he became a professional cricketer. He played all over England and distinguished himself as an excellent bowler. In the fall of 1879, at age twenty, he quit cricket and took up racing the high wheel. Over the next two years he raced extensively, defeating many of the best riders in England, including John Keen, the English champion. Prince came to the United States in September 1881 and settled in Boston, immediately resuming his high-wheel racing career. He defeated Fred Rollinson five times to claim the Championship of America, and so far he had beaten Woodside and Morgan three times each. He held the best records in America over one, five, ten, and fifty miles. At five feet nine and a half inches, he was reasonably tall and weighed a healthy 170 pounds.[13]

William J. Morgan (see Figure 6.4) was born around 1860 in Monmouthshire, which over the years has been claimed by both England and Wales. Morgan, however, was always described as a Welshman arriving in the United States as a young man of about twenty.[14] He began his high-wheel racing career around the same time as Louise. In that sense they were contemporaries; like her, he was only getting started. For some reason, he was billed as the "Champion of Canada," though how he obtained this title is a mystery. A relatively small man at five feet and seven inches, he weighed 130 pounds.

William M. Woodside was born in Philadelphia on 30 October 1860. He grew up in Ireland because his father retired from business and purchased an estate in the northern part of the country. Woodside returned to the United States in 1878, where he took up the high wheel, making his first appearance on a track in the summer of 1880. He was most successful at shorter distances such as the one-, two-, and five-mile races. In 1881 he went back to Ireland, where he frequently came first in the Irish championships at the ten and fifty miles. He returned to America in December 1882 and raced since then, billed as the "Irish Champion." In all, he had completed sixty-seven races, winning sixty medals. Tall and slender at six feet and one inch, his riding weight was 168 pounds, and he rode a fifty-six-inch machine.[15]

Prince, Morgan, and Woodside were among the best professional high-wheel racers in the United States, and perhaps elsewhere. Physically they were considerably bigger and taller than Louise, whose height was variously reported at between five feet one and four inches. Shorter in stature, she was well-muscled, with her weight usually stated as around 130 pounds. Taller racers obviously had an advantage because

4.2 William M. Woodside, the "Irish Champion," 1888 (From the collections of The Henry Ford)

they could use a high wheel with a larger front wheel, but a shorter rival could nullify this advantage with quicker, more efficient pedalling. In an interview early in her career, Louise described her body: "I am not very large up here" (placing her hands on her breasts) "but I am large down here" (pointing to her thighs).[16] She also reminded the reporter that when she was eighteen she had lifted 760 pounds dead weight. Of her French Canadian heritage, she said, "I come of a race of people that are strong."[17]

The Armaindo-Morgan-Woodside racing trio was a remarkably popular entertainment attraction, the more so because of Louise. There was no question that more "ladies" attended the races than would be the case if only males were racing. It was also important to keep these contests as exciting and close as possible, and Woodside, probably the speedier racer, agreed to give the other two a handicap. Their next race was in Milwaukee's Exposition Building, where a new board track had been constructed. Tom Eck declared it to be the fastest track in America – faster than the one in the Boston Casino or the Chicago Exposition – and also the safest at eight laps to the mile with easier turns and smoother floor surface.[18] Over the six-day, three-hours-per-night race, Woodside agreed to give Morgan a twelve-mile start and Louise thirty miles, both to be distributed over the six days.

The event turned out to be the best and most exciting racing so far witnessed in the Northwest. Louise declared she was planning to go for speed rather than endurance because of only a three-hour ride each night. Increasingly boastful and supremely confident, she was also going to try and break all short-distance records. By the second day, Louise was in front, but Morgan and Woodside were catching up. Some five thousand free tickets were made available to children, who began filling up the building, along with an increasing number of women spectators. Louise was tireless and clearly the crowd favourite: "when the plucky little woman would urge her noiseless steed and flash past either of her male competitors, the spectators loudly testified their appreciation."[19] They were even more appreciative when she changed her costume to a gaudy ensemble of pink silk tights, bronze boots, white undervest, wine-coloured jacket, and red-white-blue jockey cap. On the last day, Morgan and Woodside were hampered with problems with their bicycles, leaving

Louise the clear winner with 294 miles to Morgan's 285 and Woodside's 277.[20] However, none beat any of the short-distance records. Louise seemed unbeatable until a three-day event in Milwaukee, where the trio rode two hours each evening. She had been ill before the race, and even with a ten-mile start, was overtaken by the other two, though only by a couple of miles.[21]

In the early 1880s there were few women high-wheel racers willing to subject themselves to disappointment, even ridicule, by going up against Louise Armaindo in a race. Elsa von Blumen had supposedly retired from competition and it was several years before she reappeared. Early in July 1883, a race was organized between Louise and Maggie Wallace at the Battery D Armory in Chicago. Little is known about Maggie other than that she was trained by her brother and was a native of Washington, DC. Described as a "pretty dark-haired lady, whose eyes sparkle with ambition and pluck," she was a novice rider but had made rapid progress.[22] The scheduled race was for twenty-four hours, twelve hours a day for two days. Louise generously offered to give Maggie a twenty-mile head start, but her manager refused: "Granting Madam the credit of being the champion, I am willing Miss Wallace should compete on equal terms; and should Miss Wallace win, there will be so much more credit due her."[23] When the two competitors arrived on the track they were resplendent in close fitting, scarlet velvet jackets with white sleeves and trimmed with lace and silver braid. Louise wore her pink tights and usual jockey cap. Maggie's tights were blue, and she had wound a blue and white silk handkerchief around her head.

It was clear from the start that Maggie was no match for Louise, and she was badly outclassed. Louise got away rapidly gaining three laps on her rival in the first mile. While Louise rode steadily without a break, Maggie's bicycle wobbled badly, and she frequently left the track. Later on during the first day, Maggie returned from a break but took a header when she was started off too suddenly by her trainer. Louise collided with Maggie's wheel and was thrown to the ground. Maggie wasn't hurt but Louise had a badly lacerated arm. After it was dressed and bandaged, she got back on her machine and continued at the same furious pace. Maggie quit after the first day. During the second day, at manager Eck's urging, Louise passed the known record for twelve hours with five minutes to spare completing the race with a 247 total mileage.[24] She had left the track only six times and only for a few minutes each time.

"The performance of Louise Armaindo," proclaimed the *Chicago Inter Ocean*, "is deserving of the highest praise."[25] Since Maggie Wallace had withdrawn, Louise felt that it was up to her to give patrons their money's worth, and she resolved to beat the twelve-hour record, which had recently been established by a male racer named W.C. Young in New York City. The article also pointed out that Young had made his record on a smooth asphalt track of nine laps to the mile on the first day of the race. Louise, on the other hand, established her record on the second day of the race on a rough board track at fifteen laps to the mile. Besides, she was still suffering from a fall taken on the first day.

Louise and Tom spent the summer of 1883 performing in major centres throughout Illinois. She was often the main attraction. In Springfield, for example, at an exhibition in Oak Ridge Park, anticipation concerning Louse was high, if not a little overblown: "the lady wonder, Mlle. Armaindo, who has proven herself to be without a peer, male or female, as a bicyclist in America and it is possible she stands without a superior in the world."[26] The Springfield *Monitor* pointed out that "Mlle. Armaindo's record has now traversed the world as the best ever made by man or woman, and Springfield is indeed fortunate in having an opportunity to witness the wonderful exhibition of this renowned lady."[27] One of the largest crowds to gather at Oak Ridge Park witnessed Louise fly around the track completing five miles in twenty-one minutes, not her best time but certainly a respectable one. This was followed by an "exciting" race between Louise and Tom, although it's unclear who won. Unfortunately, on the second night, Tom's bicycle was broken, leaving Louise to do the performing. She again rode five miles around the track, bettering her time to nineteen minutes and five seconds, and after a fifteen-minute rest, she completed ten miles in forty minutes and twenty seconds, again a good effort by averaging around fifteen miles per hour.[28] Tom and Louise closed out their engagement in Springfield with a couple of additional performances, and they were sent on their way with "kindly wishes for their success wherever they go."[29]

Their next stop was Peoria, Illinois, but sadly all was not well between the couple. A report in the *Peoria Journal* indicated a serious strain in their relationship: "they had several quarrels and on Monday evening Eck pounded his wife at the room in the Merchants' Hotel here so that it was necessary to call in a doctor."[30] The couple separated with Louise heading to Jacksonville for more bicycle exhibitions. It was reported that she had "gone to browse in other fields, as it where, and her 'mash' in this city seems to be quite inconsolable."[31] The slang term "mash" was often used in and around the theatre. It referred to a dandy or the object of one's affections; it could also mean an infatuation or crush.

The estrangement did not last long. Louise was too valuable a commodity for Tom, and she needed him as a foil for their races together. Within a few weeks there was a report that Captain W.P. Emery, a Springfield attorney, was making arrangements in Quincy, Illinois, for several appearances by Louise, who would be accompanied by Tom Eck.[32] Indeed, for several days in late August and early September, the couple had a successful run before large crowds in both Quincy and Mount Sterling. They also appeared together at the Western National Fair held in Bismark Grove in Lawrence, Kansas. Louise was the fair's novelty attraction, and she raced Tom over five miles around a well-maintained track. According to the *Leavenworth Times*, it was not much of a race (Louise won as usual) and it would not have attracted much attention at all "had it not been for the scanty attire worn by Miss Armaindo."[33] The *Lawrence Gazette*, on the other hand, described the race quite differently and proclaimed it a marvellous success. It was watched with intense interest by more than twenty thousand spectators, who filled the grandstand and completely surrounded the racetrack. Tom kept ahead the first mile when Louise passed him keeping a fair distance between them until the last quarter. With a sudden burst of speed, Tom closed the gap between them, and came within a foot of beating Louise.[34] What is certain is that the race drama was orchestrated. We will never know which account is the more accurate!

By mid-September Tom and Louise were headed back to Chicago performing along the way mostly at local fairs. About seven hundred people witnessed Louise beat Tom in a twenty-mile race in Topeka, Kansas, held at a local rink. About a hundred miles west of Chicago, in Sterling, Illinois, the couple performed at an agricultural fair, where Louise raced against local ponies ridden by their owner's daughter.[35] They were a

4.3 *Top and bottom* Advertising card for the Bushnell Fair, Illinois,
2–5 October 1883 (Author's collection)

special attraction at the "big 25 cent fair" in Bushnell, Illinois, performing in a "grand" bicycle tournament. Whatever the difficulties in their relationship, they seemed to have at least resumed their working partnership. *Bicycling World* reported that while away the couple had "heaps of fun besides making loads of money."[36] Tom also renewed his proposition to match Louise against anyone, male or female, in a six-day race for which he was prepared to post a forfeit at any time.

At this time, six-day bicycle racing in the United States was just beginning to come into its own.[37] Originally a spin-off from six-day pedestrian matches (see chapters 1 and 2), they became the most popular form of bicycle racing in Europe and North America. By bringing these races indoors, promoters were able to sell tickets and bookmakers could set up gambling outlets. Spectators could see for themselves that the races were authentic and the competitors did not cheat. For those concerned about preserving the Sabbath, races were held from Monday until Saturday. We will see how Tom Eck played a major role in the development of six-day bicycle racing in the United States, originally as a competitor, but more importantly as a trainer and promoter.

Louise Armaindo's well-earned reputation continued to grow. The *New York Clipper*, the influential entertainment and sports newspaper, published a biographical sketch, including a summary of her important races.[38] It was accompanied by a woodcut illustration of Louise based on the photograph (see Figure 3.4) taken by John Wood of the Bowery in New York, who specialized in creating cabinet cards of athletes and performers. These were photographs, approximately four by six inches, mounted on cardstock (similar to cardboard). They were just the right size to be displayed on a cabinet or shelf, hence their name. It was popular to mail them to friends and relatives, or for athletes and performers to sign them and distribute them for promotional purposes. Louise stood beside her high wheel staring resolutely off to the side. Her racing costume was a curious mix of valour and femininity, with several medals adorning her chest, bracelets around both wrists, and lace trim on her jacket. In 1883 she was reported to have cleared $4,000 (about $100,000 today) through her bicycling.[39] Louise Armaindo was in a class of her own.

CHAPTER FIVE

MUSCLE ON WHEELS, 1884

As the preeminent female racer in the United States, Louise caught the attention of Fred J. Engelhardt, a Chicago-based promoter of sporting events and an agent for sporting and other celebrities.[1] Engelhardt formed an alliance called the League of Bicycling Champions with John Prince, Fred Rollinson, Tom Eck, and Louise. Joining the tour was Henry W. Higham, an Englishman, born in Sheffield, Yorkshire, in 1851.[2] He had done well in long-distance professional cycling races in the United Kingdom since 1878, and became the Champion of Scotland.[3] Trick riding was also one of his specialities and he often performed at racing venues. In 1882 he emigrated from Nottingham, England, to the United States with his wife, Harriet, and their five children, taking up residence in Washington, DC.

The group planned to perform in cities west of Chicago, and then in San Francisco with the possibility of a tour to Australia and England. Engelhardt's role was to travel ahead making the necessary arrangements. He enthused about Louise, the "brightest planet of this constellation," and the only woman ever to have won a championship race against men at any athletic game.[4] He also reminded potential audiences that similar events in the east were well attended by ladies, which he ascribed to the fact that Armaindo "had vindicated the right of her sex to claim physical equality with man."[5] The financial arrangements of the League of Bicycling Champions were interesting, if not complicated. All earnings were to be pooled. After expenses, 10 per cent would be set aside in a racing

5.1 Englishman Henry W. Higham wearing his Champion of Scotland belt, 1880 (Courtesy of the Higham Family)

fund to be used for training and equipment. The fund would also be available for stake money in matches with outside challengers. If no external challenges were received within a reasonable time, the accumulated fund would be used as a stake for Prince, Armaindo, and Higham in a six-day race. The amount of the fund was to be made public. Any outside rider desiring to start the six-day race was required to add a *prorata* amount to the main stake. In other words, if the racing fund amounted to six thousand dollars, each outside rider entering the race would pay two thousand dollars as an entrance fee.[6]

Members of the League left Chicago by train on 16 November 1883 and headed to Kansas City, their first stop on the tour. They were in Denver by late November, Salt Lake City over the Christmas season, and in San Francisco by early January. Advance publicity was substantial due to the efforts of manager and promoter Fred Engelhardt. Extravagantly billed as the champion bicycle riders of the world, Louise Armaindo was "Queen of the Wheel"; John Prince and Henry Higham champions of America and Scotland, respectively; Fred Rollinson was the champion burlesque rider, and Tom Eck the professional expert.[7] Their performances were advertised as extraordinary displays of fancy and burlesque riding, double trick riding, and exhibition races. Admission was fifty cents. Billed as the "star event of the year," the League attracted some five thousand spectators to their show at Jewell Park in Denver by competing in exhibition races among themselves and with local wheelmen.[8] In Salt Lake City the *Daily Herald* commented that "Miss Louise Armaindo, the champion lady rider of the world, was of course the centre of attraction, and her magnificent development as well as the ease, grace and force of her movement, were the subject of comment."[9]

When the group finally reached San Francisco, they decided that this "aggregation of muscle on wheels" would not appear in public until all members were well rested and in fit condition. The *Daily Alta California* was particularly taken with Louise: "She is dainty, delicate, and very feminine in her ways and looks as if under favorable circumstances she could carry one end of a flirtation with a good deal of piquancy. But when Louise playfully elevates a brace of fifty-pound dumb-bells, or toys with a single ninety-pounder, one mentally resolves that petite and graceful as she appears, she has not the slightest need for a male protector to keep the dudes from pestering her."[10] The fact that Louise was the only woman travelling with male companions, who indeed did protect her, went unnoticed by the reporter.

At their performances, Louise's riding was a revelation when they saw her "gracefully driving a wheel around about as fast as a first-class road horse."[11] She raced Tom Eck over one mile, winning as usual. She and John Prince then engaged in a two-mile race with the winner uncertain until the finish. The Higham and Rollinson exhibition of double fancy riding far surpassed anything seen so far in California. Prince would usually compete against a local amateur over five miles. Higham gave another exhibition of trick riding astonishing spectators by lifting his hind wheel entirely off the ground and riding around on the large front wheel. Rollinson's imitation of a dude learning to ride a high wheel elicited the most laughter and applause. Dressed in tight pants, swallow-tail coat, plug hat, shirt bosom, and kid gloves, with a monocle jammed into his right eye, he fell forward and backwards off his bicycle, ran into railings, tripped over his hat, and jammed his head through the spokes of the wheel. Every mishap was accompanied by feigned disgust on Rollinson's part to the noisy delight of the audience.

The League's performances came to a sudden halt in mid-February when Rollinson disappeared. A week later, he appeared in a Sacramento court alongside pedestrian C.J. Barry, both of whom were charged with grand larceny for "appropriating property from the residence of May Lambert."[12] Apparently, Miss Lambert, a public woman (prostitute), was intoxicated along with Rollinson and Barry when some of her jewels were stolen. Bail was set at two thousand dollars for each man, but no one came to Rollinson's rescue, clearly not any of his companions. A few weeks later, when the case came before a higher court judge, both men pleaded guilty and were sentenced to terms of one year for Rollinson and three years for Barry in the notorious Folsom State Prison located just north of Sacramento.[13] Despite his plea, Rollinson maintained his innocence and bitterly condemned the conduct of his fellow cyclists, claiming that they had deserted him and stolen his property. Both men began serving their sentences immediately.

Without Rollinson, the League collapsed, although Armaindo, Eck, Prince, and Higham continued to perform in a series of exhibition races in and around San Francisco. One twenty-six-hour race also included the African American pedestrian Frank "Black Dan" Hart, whose racing career was managed and financed by sports promoter and pedestrian Daniel O'Leary. Among the six racers, Hart came in last, Louise placed third behind Higham and Prince, and all three beat the existing record of 257 miles. The gate was divided among the winners and Louise took home 25 per cent.[14] By the end of March, Higham had left the group and returned to Chicago; the others were supposed to travel to Mexico, but this did not happen. Eck too appeared to have left for Illinois.

The unfortunate Rollinson was released from prison in March 1885.[15] Later, it was confirmed through the confession of a dying man that Rollinson was not guilty of the crime for which he was imprisoned. Upon his release, he went about meeting challenges, racing trotting horses, and performing his "dude" act on a bicycle until he was committed to the Napa State Hospital, a psychiatric facility, where he spent almost a year before setting out on his travels again.[16]

The old Mechanics' Institute Pavilion in San Francisco had been demolished, and a new building on the corner of Grove and Larkin streets opened in 1882. Considered the Madison Square Garden of the west, it was a large barn-like structure with a seating capacity of nearly eleven thousand spectators.[17] The pavilion was the perfect venue for Louise's next racing accomplishments. Over six days, from noon to midnight each day, she teamed up with John Prince to compete against horses – tough, small half-breeds, commonly known as scrub mustangs – ridden by Charles M. Anderson, the "prince of frontier equitation."[18] Armaindo and Prince relieved each other every hour, whereas Anderson changed his horses whenever he wished on the condition he use the same fifteen animals throughout the race. Pavilion seats were moved to accommodate a clay and loam track on the outside for the horses, seven laps to the mile, while on the inside a line was chalked out on the bare floor marking the track for the bicyclists.

The race began on 14 April 1884. Anderson's half-wild mustangs, new to an indoor track, would sometimes buck, rear, or charge the fence, and run the "whole gamut of equine cussedness."[19] Clad in a white frilled shirt, black velvet pants with gold lace trim, kid gloves, and a small velvet cap, Anderson sat well back in the saddle, clasped his legs to the horse's sides, took a firm grip on the reins, and used his spurs and whip for control and speed. Prince, in blue tights and red trunks, started with him and soon was more than a mile ahead. Anderson's horse startled and stared wide-eyed as the bicycle whizzed past. During Armaindo's turn, she completed a mile in just over three minutes, acknowledging a hearty cheer from the crowd by doffing her cap and riding with hands free. Anderson changed his horses every hour to test them and therefore lost time mounting and dismounting. After the first day, and with only nine hours of riding due to a late start, the score stood at 78 for Prince and 75 for Armaindo (for a combined total of 153 miles) and just over 143 miles for Anderson.

There was much praise for Louise and her riding: "She is a marvellous woman, never seems to tire, and rides her machine as though it were mere play."[20] And there was also skepticism: "Of course, such a pace cannot fail to tell, and the Madame will find woe for all her pluck and endurance before she gets through."[21] As the race went on, the cyclists fared better than the horses, some of whom were clearly not up to the task and had to be rested, which left Anderson with fewer mounts. By the end of the third day, halfway through the race, Louise and Prince had a combined score of 474 miles to Anderson's 466. The horseman suffered another setback on the fifth day when he dropped his whip and on the next lap tried to pick it up without dismounting. His saddle slipped and he was thrown against the fence striking his head and ended up with a large wooden sliver embedded just above his eye. He lost over twenty minutes while a doctor attended to his injury.

In the end, after seventy-two hours of racing, the two cyclists prevailed and beat Anderson by a mile and a half with a combined total of 1,073 miles. Prince and Armaindo each bested the previous record for thirty-six hours, twelve hours a day by several miles. As for the prediction that Louise would suffer in the end, she seemed fine the next day though slightly paler.

Their feat was big news. The *National Police Gazette*, for example, by then one of the leading sports journals in America, ran a full-page article titled "The Wonderful Riders of the Flying Wheels Who Have Beaten Man and Beast."[22] The updated information about Louise was similar to what had appeared a few months earlier in the *New York*

Clipper. Woodcut illustrations of the racers standing by their bicycles accompanied the article. A handsome John Prince was wearing tights, a singlet, and a sash around his waist. Louise wore a buttoned, short dress with long sleeves. It came to her mid-thigh with tights covering her legs. Decorating the dress was a wide, lace collar and two rows of lace around the skirt. Several medals were pinned to her chest, and on her head was an attractive jockey cap.

By 1877 the *National Police Gazette* was owned and published by Richard K. Fox, an Irish immigrant whose goal was to make his paper the greatest journal of sport, the stage, crime, and romance in the United States. Fox expanded the *Gazette* to sixteen pages, included many more illustrations, and printed it on pink-tinted paper to attract attention. Available at newsstands for a dime, it was provided free in barbershops, hotels, pool halls, saloons, and taverns, all places where men congregated. By 1880 the paper had a sports department and sports editor, and invited submissions from athletes and their managers. It was aimed at, and read almost entirely by men. During its heyday in the 1880s and 1890s subscriptions exceeded 150,000 and a few special issues required printings of 400,000. An estimated half million more men read the paper free when they went to the barbershop for a haircut or the pub for a drink.[23]

The *Gazette* was overwhelmingly supportive of working-class women, many of whom worked in burlesque, vaudeville, and the theatre. *Gazette* girls, as one writer has suggested, were not offered merely as sex objects: "Their activities – sometimes portrayed as deviant, sometimes not – ranged from smoking, drinking and dancing to more mundane endeavours such as cycling, skating, bowling, or walking."[24] The paper also celebrated independent and accomplished women, including professional athletes. Pedestrienne Amy Howard, in addition to cyclists Elsa von Blumen, Louise Armaindo, and later star Lottie Stanley, received special coverage in the paper.[25] Fox also enhanced the paper's visibility by sponsoring various athletic contests and offering "diamond" belts and cash prizes to contest winners. For example, Amy Howard was backed by the *Gazette* when she issued a challenge to any female walker to compete in a six-day go-as-you-please race for $1,000 to $5,000 a side. Lottie Stanley was awarded the *Police Gazette* diamond

5.2 Lithograph of Louise Armaindo, *National Police Gazette*,
10 May 1884 (Library of Congress)

medal when she won the six-day (eight hours per day) bicycling "world"
championship for women.

After teaming up with Prince in San Francisco for the gruelling but
successful race against mustangs, Louise decided to head east back
across the country and then north. Both Louise and Tom were in Aurora,
Ontario, over the May twenty-fourth weekend. It's possible that Tom
needed to defend his Canadian professional "championship" title,
which he did in a "walkover," and at the same time visit his family. At

the Aurora Driving Park, the two competed in a couple of exhibition races against horses, although for Louise it was slightly embarrassing because the trotting mare Mayflower beat her in two heats in a one-mile race. Tom led up until the eighth mile in a ten-mile race, when spokes broke on his bicycle wheel and he lost the race by three hundred yards.[26]

Soon after their trip to Canada, Louise announced that she was tired of racing against men, and that she had joined forces with Fred C. Sewell to perform trick riding in circuses. Sewell, based in Boston, had formerly been the double fancy riding partner of "Professor" W.D. Wilmot, but their partnership had come to an end in May 1884. By June the Armaindo bicycle troupe, consisting of Louise, Sewell, and Eck, was performing at the Oak Ridge amusement park in Springfield, Illinois. The three would race against each other over two, three, or five miles followed by Louise and Fred's acrobatic performances on two bicycles or with both of them on one machine.[27] Reports were that Louise had developed into an "exceedingly graceful and expert fancy rider."[28] All in all, the troupe's performance was a great success and presumably financially rewarding. After Springfield they fulfilled engagements in Bloomington and New Haven, Connecticut.

Louise's growing reputation brought opportunities to promote bicycle products, and specifically the Duryea saddle and spring manufactured by the Missouri Wheel Company in St Louis. Presumably she received some remuneration for doing so, or at least a few saddles. "I have used the Duryea Saddle exclusively in all my long-distance riding and racing for the past twelve months, and will say for it that it is the best I have ever used, and would not be without one for its weight in gold."[29] She went on to say that it did not chafe, and it allowed her to ride a wheel two sizes larger than she rode formerly.

By late September the Sewell and Armaindo fancy riding partnership came to an end due to a "misunderstanding."[30] It was probably because Louise could not stay away from the track and her efforts to best male racers, where she truly excelled. She received the most acclaim and recognition, and definitely better pay, for these races. In Chicago in mid-August, Louise and John Prince began another six-day speed and endurance race against Charles Anderson and his fifteen horses. Like the earlier race in San Francisco, Louise and Prince rode alternatively every half hour for twelve hours daily against Anderson, who was allowed to change horses whenever he wished over fifteen hours. However, this race took place for the first time out-of-doors in a baseball park on Chicago's lakefront allowing for some ten thousand paying spectators. Two tracks were laid – an inner one of wood planking for the cyclists and the outer one of dirt for the horses. Louise took a header on the second day of the race, badly spraining her wrist, but she mounted again almost immediately and was heartily cheered by the crowd. It was a close race. With three hours to go on the last day, the bicyclists were ahead by four miles. Anderson rode to win by driving his horses harder and gained steadily after each lap. At eleven o'clock he was declared the winner by two miles and two laps. Anderson's final score was 874 miles and five laps compared to the combined score of 872 miles and three laps for Prince and Armaindo.[31] Since this was the first match of its kind to be held in the open air, the scores went on record.

A couple of weeks later, with Prince racing elsewhere, William Morgan and Louise took on Charles Anderson and his horses at the Union Grounds in St Louis, Missouri. The contest lasted for eight days from four o'clock in the afternoon until eleven at night. The bicyclists alternated every half hour over the seven hours while Anderson rode seven horses as he saw fit. The large crowd, including hundreds of "ladies," certainly got their money's worth on the first day. Morgan took a header when a labourer attempted to cross the track and the bicyclist collided with him. The bicyclist was badly bruised but quickly remounted. A little later, Anderson brushed against Morgan causing his horse to stumble and fall headlong. The rider picked himself up and he too quickly remounted. No further accidents occurred throughout the contest, with the score almost even after each night's race. Fully 3,500 spectators witnessed the exciting finish when Anderson pulled ahead and won by three miles. The net gate receipts (admission was twenty-five cents for adults and ten cents for boys) were split with 75 per cent going to the winner and 25 per cent to the losers.[32]

It was common practice on the high-wheel circuit for top professionals to race under an assumed name or "Unknown" in order to take advantage of unsuspecting betters who were unaware of the real identity of the racers. Such a race took place between Patterson, of Toronto, and

Johnson, of St Joseph, Missouri, at Athletic Park in Kansas City, Missouri. The race was the best of three one-mile heats for $500 aside. Patterson won the first heat, but toward the finish of the second heat, Johnson's saddle slipped and he was thrown to the ground, breaking his wrist. Johnson was convinced his saddle had been tampered with. The race was called off, but the purse of $1,000 was paid to Patterson. Outside bets of $2,500 had been made, but the stakeholders refused to give up the money, resulting in some very angry betters. Johnson was none other than Tom Eck, and Patterson was Fred Westbrook, another professional racer.[33] The story did not end there. Years later, Eck recounted that Louise had put up about $300 of the stake and she was furious. She met with Patterson at the hotel next morning, drew a pistol, forced him to give back the money, and let him go.[34] Louise could certainly take care of herself, especially when a sum of money was at stake.

By mid-November, Louise, Tom, and William Morgan were back at Athletic Park in Kansas City, Missouri, for a three-day bicycle tournament. Each day some two thousand spectators watched a variety of amateur and professional races. Louise raced a horse over five miles and won easily because the poor animal became winded after the third mile and was taken from the track. Against men, she competed in a half-mile handicap race, where she was given a two-hundred-yard head start, and beat them two out of three heats. Louise also tried to lower her own half-mile record of one minute and forty-two seconds, but couldn't quite make it. After the tournament, Louise and Morgan took on Kansas equestrienne Lizzie Williams over a twenty-mile race with the cyclists changing every mile and the horsewoman alternating horses whenever she wished. Again, the horses won but only by a sixth of a mile.[35]

Elsa von Blumen, who had temporarily retired from racing for most of 1883, reappeared on the track the following summer, still managed by Bert Miller and pitting her skill and speed against trotting horses. At a race in Oil City, Pennsylvania, in early September, Elsa was thrown from her bicycle and was injured badly enough to be laid up for a few days. The poor horse broke its leg and had to be put down.[36] In Washington a couple of months later, Elsa took on John Prince in a five-mile race. She was given a two-minute head start, but Prince won the race

5.3 Elsa von Blumen in 1886 (Collection of Lorne Shields, Toronto, Canada)

anyway. Dissatisfied with the result, Elsa challenged Prince to a one-hundred-mile race, which was held in Baltimore. Prince generously gave her nineteen miles at the start, but the indoor track was small at fifteen laps to a mile so that Prince could not properly utilize his usual bursts of speed. Elsa, showing signs of distress near the end, won the race by just over a mile in a time of seven hours and twenty-seven minutes.[37]

The 1884 racing season was not a profitable one for Elsa because she had several falls during various races, resulting in serious injuries that caused her to cancel engagements. She had also bought a new bicycle, a twenty-two-pound Rudge racer, from a company in Rochester. She could not pay for it and eventually the machine was seized. By wintertime Elsa was back in Rochester supposedly learning the trade of dressmaking. Her husband, Emery Beardsley, filed a divorce suit, but Elsa tricked him by appearing at his home in Hannibal, New York, for a day. Emery received her as his wife, and consequently the suit was quashed.[38] She divorced him on her terms several years later. Meantime, Elsa posed no threat to Louise on the racing circuit.

Louise Armaindo was still very much at the top of her game with no one to compete against except male professional racers. She held all the women's racing records, although they were not recorded as such because the League of American Wheelmen paid no attention to them. At the end of December in Chicago's Battery D Armory, a six-day, twelve-hours-per-day race was to take place between two teams: Louise Armaindo and William Morgan versus William Woodside and John Brooks. However, Morgan had a foot problem and could not ride. The race promoter, Tom Eck, tried to convince John Prince to take his place, but Prince was not interested. Between them, Morgan, Prince, and Woodside held the majority of the American professional racing records.[39] Unfortunately, the race was called off, but had it taken place, the money was certainly on Armaindo and her partner.

CHAPTER SIX

JUST ONE OF THE GUYS, 1885–1888

By the mid-1880s there were still no other female racers for Louise to compete against, with the exception of Elsa von Blumen, who seemingly had little interest in testing herself against Louise. She had done so once before and not fared well. Elsa was more genteel than Louise, consistently representing herself as someone other women could emulate in terms of exercise and good health. She preferred exhibition races, mostly at outdoor county fairs, and was uncomfortable in the smelly, jostling, gambling atmosphere of the indoor track. Louise, on the other hand, had become a long-distance, endurance specialist favouring the indoor, six-day races because at least then she had a chance against men, especially if given a reasonable handicap.

Early in 1885 Louise and her usual male companions – Tom Eck, John Prince, William Woodside, and William Morgan – were in Memphis, Tennessee, competing in a six-day, eight-hours-a-day, professional race. It was sponsored by the Memphis Cycle Club and held in the Exposition Building. Louise's costume was a blue velvet jacket handsomely embroidered with silver, crimson knee pants, grey stockings, and half a dozen medals pinned about her neck. "The little lady rides the prettiest wheel in the collection," effused the *Memphis Daily Appeal*, which also commented on the considerable sprinkling of elegantly dressed ladies among the crowd of spectators.[1] On the last day of the race, children were admitted for only ten cents and over a thousand took advantage of the cheap entrance fee. Although it was a bona fide contest, with scores and times being kept by the club, the outcome was never in doubt. For most of the race Morgan held the lead, finishing with 450 miles and nine laps. Louise was third behind Morgan and Eck, making 343 miles and six laps over forty-eight hours of racing. As a result she earned 20 per cent of the net receipts, probably a tidy sum. Prince and Woodside were a distant fourth and fifth, respectively.[2] Again Louise proved that over a long distance she could hold her own against men with or without a handicap.

From Memphis, the group headed to New Orleans with the hope of performing at the World's Industrial and Cotton Centennial Exposition. Unfortunately, no one at the fair had the slightest interest in bicycling, and the group travelled to Galveston, Texas, where they spent "two weeks of work and pleasure."[3] San Antonio was their next stop for several contests against trotting horses and another six-day race. Louise was interviewed by a reporter from the local newspaper, something that rarely occurred. He described her as a "spirited talker, rather too rapid in an interview, and speaks with a slightly foreign accent, being of French Canadian parentage."[4] Louise gave her age as twenty-four years, and said she weighed 135 pounds. When the reporter entered the room, Louise was playing a piano and singing a low, sweet melody, but she stopped to welcome him.

"You play, I see," said the reporter.

"Why not?" asked Louise. "My piano, sewing and pets keep me from having the blues when I am not riding."

"When did you begin to ride?"

"I began in Chicago about five years ago. I was an athlete before that and my mother was an athlete before me. I have lifted 760 pounds dead weight, and my mother lifted 900 pounds."

"Did you start out as a professional the first thing?"

"Yes."

"Never was an amateur?"

"No."

"Then you never had a fall: never took a dive off your cycle?"

"Oh yes, I did. I fell in a race with Elsa von Blumen while going at a two-mile gait, and was insensible for five minutes. I have had plenty of falls, some so hard I thought I should be killed, but in all my experience

I have never broken any bones, or sprained even my little finger. You see I am naturally strong and my muscles are well trained."

"How came you to learn the bicycle?"

"I saw a great deal of them and liked them. Thought they were nice for ladies and I learned. It took me three lessons to learn and it was hard at first but I made up my mind to learn and I did."

Louise went on to explain that her best racing record so far occurred in May 1883 in Chicago when she completed 843 miles in seventy-two hours, beating both Morgan and Woodside. She proudly showed the reporter her large gold medal in the form of a star with an engraved pendant attached to it. She also mentioned the gruelling seventy-two-hour race in San Francisco in April 1884 when she and John Prince beat Charles Anderson and fifteen horses with a combined score of 1,073 miles. Louise continued to brag to the reporter about her athletic prowess and accomplishments.

> Can I spar, run or jump? No, but I used to be a pedestrian. I have walked 18 hours and 15 minutes without a stop. I have lifted dumbbells, and my greatest feat used to be to lift a 92 pound bell. This beats any women's record in the world. Have I any rivals in my sex? Well yes; Elsa von Blumen used to race against me, and Miss Sylvester, of Chicago, was lately brought out and many thought she was to be my conqueror on the wheel. But pshaw, I beat her easily. I love to race, and when I race I work hard. I have drawn blood from my nose many a time by hard racing. I love to ride the bicycle. It is nice for a lady. It is graceful, exciting, and you go fast. I have good health with it, too. How many miles an hour? I can make 16 miles an hour.[5]

Louise and Annie Sylvester certainly knew one another. They were sometimes seen riding together in Chicago's South Park where they drew a large crowd.[6] Despite Louise's claim, there is no evidence they ever officially raced together. Sylvester, often billed as the peerless queen of cyclists and the world's champion trick and fancy rider, could and did race on the straight. At a fair in Montrose, Pennsylvania, for example, she raced against a horse over one mile but was primarily engaged to perform her trick riding.[7] Growing admiration for Sylvester annoyed Louise although Annie had no intention of challenging her to a race. Louise had already tried her hand at fancy riding with Fred Sewell for a few months in 1884, and decided it was not for her. She missed the excitement and thrill of racing, even if it meant competing against men.

Born on 2 March 1864, Sylvester's real name was Annie Elizabeth James. She grew up in a large Catholic family on a farm just outside of St Louis, Missouri. Before she was twenty, Annie James had married, borne a son, buried him a year later, and divorced her husband. Early in 1884 she boarded a train and headed to Chicago to find work. Frank E. Yates, a Chicago sportsman and businessman, was an enthusiastic cycling advocate. Determined to find a new female cycling star, he put an ad in a Chicago paper looking to hire three girls of "fine form and fine physique" to ride bicycles.[8] Annie had never before ridden a bicycle, but reasoned that her good looks and well-proportioned body might get her the job, and she was right. Even though scores of young women applied, Yates winnowed them down to Annie and another young woman called May Arlington. Yates set to work teaching the two aspiring bicycliennes how to ride a high wheel, and they learned quickly. Annie chose the stage name Sylvester, after the Pope and saint of the same name.

After a few weeks of hard work, Sylvester and Arlington made their first appearance in May 1884 as fancy and trick riders at Chicago's Battery D Armory. Dressed in tasteful costumes, the two bicycliennes were watched by a small group of local bicyclists and representative of the press, presumably all men. The show was pronounced an entertainment success and ready for the road. However, it was only Annie who went on tour, and May Arlington was not heard from again. Managed by Fred Yates, Annie toured the country giving exhibitions of fancy and trick riding. Riding a fifty-inch Expert high-wheel bicycle, some of her tricks included placing the machine on two chairs and mounting without help; riding on only one wheel; jumping both wheels clear of the floor; and from a standstill, removing a cloth from the axel of each wheel without dismounting. From roller skating rinks, country fairs, and Grand Army of the Republic reunions, Annie progressed to circuses, then to vaudeville, playing in leading theatres throughout the United States.[9]

6.1 Trick rider Annie Sylvester, c. 1884 (Courtesy of John Weiss)

Meanwhile, Louise continued to be the recipient of positive publicity. The *Springfield Wheelmen's Gazette* provided a full-page feature, almost identical to the earlier piece about Louise in the *National Police Gazette*. It itemized her many racing accomplishments by providing the date, place, distance, time, and whom she defeated. First published in 1883 by the Springfield (Massachusetts) Bicycle Club, primarily to advertise the club's fall tournament at Hampton Park, the *Springfield Wheelmen's Gazette* briefly became the most widely disseminated cycling journal, with circulation exceeding the LAW *Bulletin*, published by the League of American Wheelmen.[10] A fetching woodcut of Louise accompanied the article, which ended with the following comment: "The probability is that Louise Armaindo has ridden more miles on a bicycle than any other person in America, having taken part in nearly all the long distance races, against horses and men."[11] In the picture, Louise is standing beside her high wheel, described as a Royal Mail and weighing about twenty-two pounds. However, in a subsequent issue of *Bicycling World*, someone commented that "anyone with an eye could tell you that the machine depicted is a Yale of the 1881 or 1882 pattern."[12] Readers of *Bicycling World* and other cycling journals certainly knew the difference between the various makes of bicycles.

After their visit to San Antonio, the cyclists split up. Tom and Louise stayed in Texas and travelled to other towns, mainly Waco, Sherman, and Fort Worth, racing against themselves or against horses. By spring, Louise was in Washington, DC, where she teamed up with Henry Higham, who had been with the group travelling to California the previous year, to perform in a series of races involving a tricycle and a bicycle.[13] Higham rode a Humber tricycle geared to sixty inches, which was really just a high wheel with the addition of a second wheel. The rider mounted the tricycle like a high wheel, but powered the front wheel through a drive chain. Although the Humber tricycle was prone to headers, just like the high-wheel bicycle, the extra front wheel added lateral stability. It proved very fast and was a favourite with racers.[14] Throughout the spring and summer of 1885, Louise and Higham regularly took part in exhibition races on a quarter-mile track at Athletic Park in Washington. This time, she did ride a fifty-one-inch Royal Mail bicycle. Dressed in a wine-coloured tunic with navy blue tights, she went up against Higham

6.2 Lithograph of Louise Armaindo standing beside a Yale high wheel, *Breeder and Sportsman*, 12 April 1884 (Author's collection)

in one-, five-, and twenty-mile races. She was not given a handicap and sometimes she won. Eck and Woodside joined them eventually, but it was clear that Eck no longer played his previous central role in Louise's life. She formed partnerships with others to suit her racing ambitions and the need to make money. It is difficult to assess if she and Eck were still romantically involved, but it is unlikely.

Louise was a star attraction in mid-October at the Fort Smith fair in Arkansas, performing in bicycling exhibitions that included a daily ten-mile race against horses for five hundred dollars a side. Also featured

were Roman Chariot races, Japanese fireworks, and Indian ball play between two Choctaw tribes.[15] Louise disappeared for the remainder of
the fall and into December. A brief report in a Chicago paper explained
why: "Louise Armaindo, whose long distance abilities made her the ter-
ror to members of the opposite sex, has gone to Canada, where she pro-
poses taking a long-needed rest."[16] It also noted that William Woodside,
one competitor who had been beaten by Louise in a six-day race, now
held all the American records from four to fifty miles and the world's
records from six to ten miles. Considered one of the "squarest" riders
ever to race, he was never known to employ underhand methods, or to
become involved in shady schemes.[17] At the end of 1885, Louise still
held the American long-distance record of 843 miles in seventy-two
hours, which she had established two years earlier.[18]

Inevitably, there were an increasing number of racers wishing to challenge Louise for a record since she had already defeated most of the better
long-distance riders in the United States. One such challenger was Fred
M. Shaw, the champion of Dakota, who wanted to race Louise over
twenty-six hours on an indoor track in Minneapolis rink. "As I have ridden within a few miles of the best record on the road," he stated, "I think
I could defeat her in a long race and on an indoor track."[19] At the beginning of 1886, Louise resurfaced in Boston, where she was attempting,
unsuccessfully as it turned out, to arrange a six-day race with Robert A.
Neilson, who brazenly claimed to be the professional champion of both
the United States and Canada.[20] Tom Eck, still Louise's manager, replied
to Shaw that he would contact her and try to arrange the match for $100
a side. The race took place in mid-January with the result that Louise
beat Shaw by completing 182 miles over the twenty-six hours despite
the fact that she was out of shape and had gained fifteen pounds during
her lengthy sojourn in Quebec. Shaw withdrew after completing only
162 miles.[21] There was, as he discovered, considerable difference between
racing on a straight outdoor road compared to a tight indoor track.
Louise had become an expert at the latter, especially on her twenty-one-
pound Royal Mail high-wheel, at the time considered the lightest racing
machine in the country.

Meanwhile, Tom Eck was in the process of creating a permanent
indoor six-day racing facility in Minneapolis. Roller skating was enor-

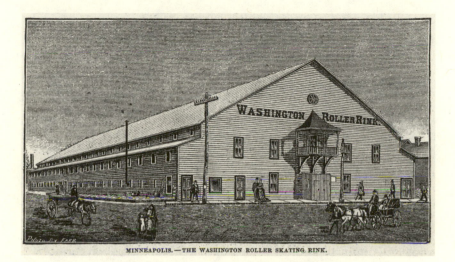

MINNEAPOLIS.—THE WASHINGTON ROLLER SKATING RINK.

6.3 Washington Roller Rink in Minneapolis, 1885, used by Tom Eck as a training and racing facility for professional athletes (Minnesota Historical Society)

mously popular in the early 1880s and entrepreneurs responded to the craze by building indoor rinks. Minneapolis had more than a dozen by 1885, but very few were profitable, with others slated for the auction block. The *St. Paul Daily Globe* commented that declining attendance was a natural reaction to an unnatural craze, but, more importantly, public sentiment regarded these rinks as immoral. The mixing of young men and women at the roller skating rink was viewed as a corrupting influence by the city's religious leaders, who also bemoaned the sparse attendance at weeknight religious services. "The press," said the paper, "has damned them with faint praise and the pulpit has denounced them unequivocally."[22] As interest in skating waned and attendance declined, roller rink owners sought to expand their usage and clientele.

Tom Eck cared not a whit about the so-called depravity of the rink. What he saw in the Washington Roller Rink in Minneapolis was a huge covered structure with a cement floor that was the perfect venue for six-day indoor bicycle races. Even better, it had steam heating and electric lights. Eck took over management of the Washington rink and immediately constructed a banked or raised track, eight laps to the mile. With his usual bravado, he pronounced it to be the fastest indoor track in the world.[23] He now had a base for races, and also for training.

Eck also rented a rooming house a block or two from the rink where athletes could live while they trained under his guidance. When a reporter from the *St. Paul Daily Globe* visited this establishment one day, he found heavyweight boxer Patsy Cardiff stretched out on a couch, bicycle racers Phil Hammel and Albert Schock lounging about, and Louise Armaindo superintending the household affairs. The reporter's description of the scene was quite comical:

> Here these sporting lights live. They are equipped with all the utensils necessary for housekeeping and the little things that go to make up the comforts of home. In fact, the party is about as comfortably situated as anyone need be. Judging from the amount of edibles that were dispatched at the delectable dinner, which was spread at 2:30, one is led to imagine that the grocer's and butcher's bills each week are not inconsiderable. The vigorous exercise they daily undergo is calculated to sharpen appetites until grindstones might be dissipated by their hardy digestive organs.[24]

The reporter also visited the Washington Roller Rink, where boxer Cardiff was undergoing a rigorous course of training in preparation for upcoming bouts with heavyweights George Rooke, Charlie Mitchell, and Billy Wilson. He was impressed with the six-foot, 192-pound Cardiff, who had put on weight and muscle since his last fight.[25] Phil Hammel, an amateur racer from Chicago, took a ten-mile training ride while Albert Schock, a professional also from Chicago, made pace for him. The two followed their workout with a rubdown. Louise's training consisted of swinging dumbbells, riding her bicycle, and rollerskating. She was determined to get in shape and reduce her weight. No doubt there were other athletes taking advantage of the new training facilities and Eck's expertise. The rink marked another step in Eck's long and successful career as a professional trainer of many athletes and teams in a variety of sports.

With a proper training facility and other athletes with whom she could train, Louise stayed put in Minneapolis for at least a few months.

She spent long hours building up her fitness and endurance, and occasionally travelled locally for a challenge race. Eck was still her manager and business agent, although by this point he was also training several other athletes. In Faribault, Minnesota, and billed as the "world champion lady cyclist of Canada," Louise took on local rider John W. Snyder in two one-hundred-mile races. She beat him in the first, but he won the second with the betting such that "much money changed hands."[26] Back at the Washington rink, and just as Eck had predicted, records were being broken quickly and frequently. *Bicycling World* pointed out that the current world's records from thirty-five to fifty miles and from 100 to 1,042 miles had been made at the rink.[27]

William Morgan decided to team up with Louise on a tandem tricycle in an attempt to establish a new twenty-four-hour record. He optimistically predicted that they would "roll up a record for a man and woman on a tricycle that will stand for years," and that even two men would not be able to beat it.[28] They would ride continuously for twenty-four hours taking meals while on the track. Louise boasted that she would never give up until she was so tired she could not move. The event took place in October in Lynn, Massachusetts, just north of Boston, on an outdoor track. They were indeed successful, and decided to stop riding after completing 250 miles with twenty-six minutes to spare. After the race, Morgan said of Louise, "You have no idea of her wonderful capabilities in cycling and there is not a woman in the world who can stand such an ordeal. Her endurance is something phenomenal and even after her long jaunt she did not feel the effects to any extent … There is no woman who can approach her, and but few men." He also admitted that "she is a much better companion in riding than a man. She never frets, grumbles or complains, and instead of needing encouragement she administers it."[29] He promised they would do more tandem tricycle racing next season, especially in warmer weather, and break even more records.

Louise's final race of 1886 was a gruelling six-day contest held in the Washington rink in Minneapolis with Albert Schock and William Morgan. At stake were the championship of America and a prize of $2,500. No one thought she could win, and it was stipulated that she must complete 1,000 miles to get any share of the gate. The race was the go-as-you-please variety, where riders were in the arena at all hours of the day or night, riding for as long as they could, and taking breaks whenever they were needed. Each rider had a private room and a team of two to three trainers or attendants whose responsibility it was to prepare food, draw baths, give rubdowns, lay out clean costumes, repair bicycles, and keep track of what the other riders were doing. What is interesting is that one of Louise's attendants for this race was "Ellen Armaindo," possibly her younger sister Hélène Brisebois, mistakenly called Ellen because that was how her name sounded in English. The press likely did not know Louise's real last name.[30] Hélène was living in Chicago at the time and could easily have travelled to Minneapolis by train.

At the start of the race Louise seemed ill and she retired frequently from the track, which meant that Morgan and Schock gained a substantial lead. These two paid strict attention to each other and for most of the race they were less than a mile apart. Louise perked up considerably later in the race but was never able to get closer than two hundred miles to the two leaders. She often changed her costume, and one time came out in maroon tights, a red jacket, and a short skirt with a white sash that gave her the appearance of having wings. Morgan and Schock closed up behind her and began warbling "White Wings that Never Grow Weary," much to the amusement of the crowd.[31] Another time, Louise fell asleep and took a header over the front wheel, landing in a heap on the outside of the railing, but she revived quickly and started off again. Morgan fell ill on the fifth day with stomach trouble and consequently lost time to Schock, who won the race with a record-breaking 1,405 miles. Morgan was second with 1,165 miles, and Louise completed 1,050 miles. Physicians from a local hospital monitored the riders, noting that each had lost four to five pounds during the race. As for Louise, they found "her condition as good as when she entered the race," which meant that she had recovered well from her initial illness.[32] It was, however, a harbinger of things to come.

Among the professional cyclists of the day, Louise clearly saw herself as one of the "guys." She lived with them, travelled with them, raced with them, fought with them, and on occasion beat them. "Louise was always good to the boys," Tom observed, and "when any one of them was busted, she would willingly divide her last cent with him. And

6.4 William J. Morgan, who often teamed up with Louise Armaindo
to establish long-distance records, 1889 (William W. Cecil collection,
History Colorado)

another good trait of hers was that when she borrowed any money she always returned it."[33] However, as six-day bicycle racing became increasingly popular and younger men entered the field as professionals, it was obvious that Louise could no longer match their strength and endurance. She did not stop racing but instead took up or sought challenges from those she thought she could beat. Early in 1887, for example, she raced Fred Straub in Faribault, Minnesota, over fifty miles but unfortunately was defeated. Louise claimed that Straub won more by trick riding than speed because the narrow track was seventeen laps to the mile.[34] She also took on pedestrian Richard Hale in Minneapolis in a unique race where Louise rode ten miles on a bicycle and Hale walked five miles. Again, she lost by a few laps. Then she agreed to walk two hours a night for six nights in Minneapolis against three men; however, she quit after a short while because of sore feet.[35] An entertainment benefit was held for Louise in the Washington rink in Minneapolis, with the proceeds going to her, a sure sign that she was not earning much money through racing.

It was a total surprise to most, and certainly to Louise, when on 15 July 1887, Tom Eck married Jennie Carlisle of Minnesota, the sister of his manager, Steve Carlisle. Eck was thirty-one years old and his bride was eighteen. The wedding took place in Omaha, Nebraska, at the home of John Prince and his wife.[36] Jennie was secretly married against the wishes of her parents, although Eck claimed that he had advised them by letter about his plans to marry their daughter. They were indignant and the press equally so: "She was but a school girl and very susceptible, and the feeling among her friends is that Eck acted dishonorably in beguiling her from her home."[37] As for Louise's reaction, she arrived in Omaha a couple of days after the wedding and the rumour immediately spread that she was "after Eck's scalp." She denied this, claiming that his marriage caused her "surprise rather than pain."[38]

A few weeks later, there were reports that Louise had married a Mr Burnett, a prominent and wealthy real estate owner in Eau Claire, Wisconsin. There was no truth to the rumour whatsoever. Nevertheless, *Bicycling World*, affiliated with the League of American Wheelmen (LAW), and not at all sympathetic to Louise, took the opportunity to publish a diatribe against her:

It is hoped *for the sake of the sport* she may never again mount a wheel. I think the sooner the female bicycle rider is hooted off the race track, the better for our sport. We should not encourage anything so questionable. Many of us have sisters, and wives and mothers, who would instinctively blush to be seen at a race meeting where ex-trapeze performers and variety queens rode against time and morality in an unbecoming and unwomanly position. The sight of abbreviated ballet skirts and tinsel at a race meeting is one which should meet with nothing but hisses, and even the abbreviations are often omitted. The "whoop-it-up-Eliza-Jane" spirit of old Black Hills dance houses is being gradually supplanted by one of appreciation for square and sportsmenlike races between men of good character.[39]

This tirade was in all likelihood written by Charles Pratt, the editor of *Bicycling World*, and also one of the founders of the LAW. By "men of good character" he meant amateur racers and certainly not professionals. The LAW stipulated that an amateur must never engage in, assist in, or teach any athletic activity for money, or in the case of racing, never compete against a professional for a prize.[40] Therefore, not only was he opposed to women racing, he was also against men's professional racing, which the LAW considered a cheap form of entertainment. In his opinion, women engaged in bicycle racing – no matter how few – made them no better than showgirls.

None of this mattered to Tom Eck, who secured a deal with the bicycle manufacturing company Gormully & Jeffery in Chicago to sponsor a travelling racing team. It covered the team's expenses and rewarded individual members with bonus money for winning races and breaking records. Eck recruited some of the best professional racers in the country, including Stillman Whittaker, John Prince, Wilbur Knapp, L.D. "Birdie" Munger, and Frank Dingley.[41] He also invited Louise to join the group. The team's first indoor six-day event was held in February 1888 in Philadelphia. Arriving in the city two weeks earlier, Louise was again overweight at 155 pounds and admitted that she had done very little riding over the past year. Although she embarked on a rigorous training regime, it was not enough to get her in racing condition and she did not start. The seventy-two-hour, twelve-hours-a-day race was a great success and attracted huge crowds. As an added feature, Louise performed exhibition rides of three or five miles against time; the audience cheered wildly whenever she passed one of the male competitors.

Louise was overly confident that she could surpass some of the existing six-day long-distance records, if only given the chance.[42] Still in Philadelphia, she went up against two male pedestrians in a six-day, four hours per day race whereby she hoped to beat the combined score of the walkers. Initially, there was little interest in the event and at Louise's invitation "ladies" were admitted free. When it became a close race the crowds picked up substantially, as did the betting, but Louise lost by a couple of miles; nonetheless, she had ridden almost 327 miles over the six days.[43] Again, the journal now called *Bicycling World and L.A.W. Bulletin* took a swipe at Louise: "The rumour that the bicyclienne, Louise Armaindo, is again going to nauseate cycling America by her disgraceful performances is not without foundation."[44]

Louise never ceased to surprise. On 21 April 1888, she quietly married Norman Burroughs Stewart in the Union Methodist Episcopal Church in Camden, New Jersey.[45] Very little is known about Stewart other than he was born in Camden on 21 December 1866, the fourth child of Alexander and Emma Stewart.[46] Even less is known about how Louise met him, and indeed why she married him. He was only twenty-one, and although her age was listed as twenty-four on the marriage record, if I am correct about her 1857 birthdate, she was actually thirty. Stewart's occupation was noted as "travling [sic] agent." There were no press reports at the time, and hardly anyone seemed to be aware of the nuptials.

While Louise took on a husband, Elsa von Blumen had shed hers. In early 1887, after four years of a tumultuous marriage, Caroline Kiner (her real name) was granted a divorce from Emery Beardsley.[47] She continued to earn a living through riding exhibitions, mostly in friendly rivalry against "gentlemen bicyclists," and she still refused to countenance any wagering or gambling at these events. Over New Year's in 1886, for example, as part of the entertainment for the benefit of the Rochester Soldiers' and Sailors' Monument Fund, she competed in a fifty-one-hour race against the combined miles of two men, who alternately relieved each other.[48] There is no report as to who won. Sometimes Elsa went up against a male pedestrian by riding two miles for every one he walked over a set distance, and at summer fairs she rode against trotting horses. In an 1888 newspaper interview, she remarked, "I like the business, and although I say that every year will be my last I stick to it. I do a great deal of riding at country fairs, and sometimes the experience is anything but pleasant, for the tracks are usually horrible, and the country people seem to think that I can ride over anything or through mud or uphill without any difference. After my winter's rest my muscles are soft, and it takes a good deal of riding to get me in condition."[49]

Elsa von Blumen made these comments while preparing to race the English rider Jessie Oakes, who wished to test the relative speed and endurance of American versus English riders. Oakes was originally from Boston in Lancashire, where she learned to ride initially for pleasure and then as a professional racer with over thirty races to her credit against both men and trotting horses. Their first challenge race took place in June 1888 in Pittsburgh, and it was a draw. The two racers then went on tour, racing each other frequently, including a performance at the Great Industrial Fair and Agricultural Exposition (now known as the CNE) in Toronto, Ontario.[50] Both riders would soon be challenged by a growing number of females taking up the sport.

Early in the spring of 1888, Tom Eck went to England with four of his best male racers to challenge another American team managed by William Morgan, and to pit them against European racers. He was gone several months, leaving his young wife, and when he returned to the United States in August, he immediately became embroiled in marital difficulties. Alleging adultery, cruelty, and desertion, Jennie Carlisle had filed for divorce after only a year of marriage and was staying with her parents in Minneapolis. Alleging that Jennie was being unduly influenced by her parents, Eck abducted her and denied all charges. "I think enough of my wife not to lose her," he wrote in a letter to the *St. Paul Daily Globe*, "and I concluded to take no chances, so I have taken my wife away where she will be influenced by no one except myself."[51] He maintained that it was Jennie's parents who were behind the divorce, and not his wife. The sordid affair received substantial publicity even in the *New*

6.5 Jessie Oakes, originally from Lancashire, England, 1889 (Collection of Lorne Shields, Toronto, Canada)

York Times, but nothing more was heard of these divorce proceedings.[52] Nine months later, on 18 July 1889 in Minneapolis, Jennie Carlisle gave birth to a daughter, Irene Carlisle Eck.

Meanwhile, Louise was still seeking someone to race. Calling herself "the Champion Female Bicyclist of the World," she sent a challenge to the *Chicago Inter Ocean* indicating she would be pleased "to compete with any man in the world in a race of 142 hours straight-away for $500 a side, or the gate receipts and the championship."[53] If no one accepted the challenge, she would take a fair start and ride in a twelve-hour-a-day race for seventy-two hours. She was willing to wager that she could beat her best record of 843 miles by riding at least 900 miles or even 1,400 in a longer race. Louise also went to Pittsburgh seeking out Elsa von Blumen and Jessie Oakes, but they had already left on their exhibition tour. She boldly claimed that she would race them both together in a six-day race, their combined score to go against hers.[54] Louise was as confident and boastful as ever, but unrealistically so, and she would soon learn that her star was fading.

CHAPTER SEVEN

BEAUTY ON WHEELS, 1888–1890

As 1888 drew to a close, Louise was in Omaha, Nebraska, busily training for a six-day, eight-hour race that would include several of the top male professional racers in the country. It took place in the Omaha Coliseum, now managed by John Prince,[1] where a new, very fast, ten-lap track had been constructed. There was controversy over the number of miles Louise wanted as a head start or handicap. Where the men were willing to give her 100 miles, the equivalent of over ten and a half miles for each eight hours, Louise wanted 150 miles. William Morgan, who had been defeated by Louise before, was adamant: "Miss Armaindo is a well-trained athlete, and to defeat her is no small task; but, of course, being a woman, we are expected to treat her with the usual indulgence of her sex."[2]

Louise started the race with 100 miles to her credit along with Frank Dingley, William Morgan, Wilbur Knapp, C.W. Ashinger, Tom Eck, and "Unknown" who had been entered by Prince to protest against Louise's head start. Now riding a forty-eight-inch light Champion racer, Louise did well for the first four days and then suddenly was taken ill. She suffered from dyspepsia or indigestion, which she tried to brush off, but finally had to give up any serious contention in the race. Knapp won with 711 miles but he only beat an "Unknown" by six laps, who turned out to be Ned Reading, an amateur rider and army sergeant. Louise was out of the money, which was eased somewhat by a benefit held for her a few days later.

During this race Louise was interviewed by a woman reporter from the *Omaha Herald,* and the questions asked were different to those normally posited by men. "Do you think women can become as well qualified in all respects for athletic work as men?"[3] Louise replied that she had given the matter a great deal of thought. She pointed to her heritage that included a strongwoman mother and a father respected for his strength, and to her own background as a strongwoman and trapeze artist. On the subject of women's endurance compared to men she believed that women could stand more pain and complained less about it, and she went on to tell the reporter about her more spectacular racing accidents, pointing out that each time she got right back up on her bicycle and continued. She claimed to have been involved in thirteen six-day races in the past three years, admitting it was too many because she no longer had the same strength.

Her husband, Norman Stewart, whom Louise called Charlie in deference to his Scottish background, came into the room during the interview looking scruffy and younger than his twenty-one years. Louise explained that she loved going out with Charlie. Although he didn't look very slick now, when dressed up he was a handsome fellow, behaved like a gentleman, and boasted about her athletic accomplishments. Louise also let on that she liked to sew and fix up her clothes, which no doubt included her many racing costumes, when she was not training. On the dresser beside her bed were two dumbbells. The reporter summed up her article and Louise with these words:

A thorough Bohemian is Louise. A woman capable of true friendship – fierce friendship even. A woman who would be willing to work herself to death for any one she loved; one who cherishes the memory of her mother with tenderness, and who has made great sacrifices to help her old father in business. Although she might go on remorselessly in any contest till she saw her opponent reduced to a miserable wreck, she would be the first to sympathize in any sort of trouble, and she would be willing to spend money with reckless prodigality upon her friends. One could image her taming a wild beast – or becoming one.[4]

The reporter from the *Omaha Herald* was likely Elia Wilkinson
Peattie, who became a well-known American journalist, short story
writer, novelist, poet, and playwright. She and her husband came to
Omaha in 1888, when Robert Peattie became the managing editor of
the *Herald* with the promise that his wife would also be hired by the
newspaper. Elia's first article appeared in the *Herald* in December 1888,
at which time it was announced that she was now a regular staff corre-
spondent.[5] Louise apparently made a considerable impression on Elia
Peattie, who a few months later published a fictional story about one
"Louise Viellard Sainte-Foix," a thinly disguised representation of
Louise Armaindo and her husband, Charlie. It was published in a magazine called *America: A Journal for Americans*. Peattie used the basic
facts of Louise Armaindo's background to trace her fictional character's
rise to athletic stardom. As a successful six-day bicycle racer, the track
was Louise Viellard's entire life until the day she met Charlie Stuart, who
won her heart. Soon, the two were married. Viellard doted on Charlie,
bought his clothes, jewellery, perfumes, and wine, and also gave him
money. One day she discovered him walking arm and arm with another
young woman, who mysteriously turns up dead (see appendix 2 for the
complete story). Peattie's story authentically captures Louise Armaindo's
life, and it is possible to imagine how Louise may have spoken with her
French accent. The ending, however, was entirely fictional.

For the real-life Louise Armaindo, her competitive life was about to
change dramatically with the entrance of several more women into the
world of high-wheel racing. No longer would she be forced to race
against men, especially those unwilling to grant her a fair handicap.

Pittsburgh, Pennsylvania had seen many a contest among pedestriennes, but it had never witnessed a six-day women's bicycle race. William
B. Troy, a local sports and entertainment promoter, decided that such an
event would make money, but he needed competitors. Somehow he
found nine willing young women, all from Pittsburgh, though most had
never seen a high-wheel bicycle before, let alone ridden one. For five
weeks before the race, he taught them how to ride, worked them until
they were fit, and had them practice racing against each other. The
women put in at least four to six hours of training a day.[6]

By the end of November 1888, all were ready for a six-day, forty-eight-hour race except for Hilda Suallor, who fell off her bicycle, sprained her ankle, and fractured her left arm, but would ride anyway.[7] Twenty years of age, Hilda was said to be of German heritage, though perhaps Swedish. At 135 pounds, and just over five feet four inches tall, she had a square and sturdy build. Jessie Woods, seventeen, was thought to be the most graceful rider of the lot. With wavy golden hair, she was small in stature at just over five feet three inches and weighed 125 pounds. Kitty (sometimes Kittie) Brown, nineteen, was also considered a graceful rider, but one with grit because she had ridden five hours during training without dismounting. Tall and slender at five foot six inches, she weighed 125 pounds. Hattie Lewis, twenty-two, and one of the tallest at five feet seven inches, had fallen repeatedly during training. She hauled herself back up onto her fifty-two-inch wheel and tried again and again until she mastered it. Now she was one of the strongest. May Allen (whose real name was Louisa Bertha McCurry, and nicknamed "Birdie") was sixteen and tipped the scales at 120 pounds. Superbly confident that she would accomplish at least one hundred miles on the first day of the race, she proved to be one of the speediest short-distance racers.

Lulu Hart, twenty-two, looked and acted like an athlete. There was not an ounce of superfluous flesh on her body due to the strenuous training she had engaged in over the previous five weeks. At five foot two and a half inches, she was thought to be a "stayer." Pittsburgh was already familiar with Aggie Harvey, whose real name was Maggie McShane, because she was an accomplished pedestrienne. Though not the most graceful rider, she displayed the same dogged determination to keep going as she did as a race walker. Nineteen-year-old Lottie Stanley, the smallest rider at just over five feet and one inch, liked to sink her head down over the handlebars and work the pedals very quickly in rapid bursts of speed. "She is a dashing rider, has a remarkably cool head and a steady hand," proclaimed the local paper predicting she might win.[8] She was certainly the best short-distance sprinter but it remained to be seen how she would do over a forty-eight-hour race.

Finally, eighteen-year-old Helen Baldwin would enter the contest, probably in better condition than the other competitors because she had

spent the past three years training in a gymnasium under the tutelage of her father, a fitness instructor. She was also the best all-around rider among the group and had proven to be an apt pupil. At five foot five and 125 pounds, she was fearless on the wheel but not reckless. Like the others, who were probably in low-paying and boring jobs if they worked at all, Helen Baldwin admitted that she was tired of working in a store for four dollars a week. She embraced the possibility of a new career, hopefully more profitable and exciting, with a great deal of enthusiasm. Only time would tell if this would turn out to be the case.

Although it was advertised as a race, the women were paid a small salary to be the contestants. Prizes amounting to $500 were also offered with the winner receiving $125, second $100, third $75, fourth $55, and fifth $45. The remaining $100 would be divided equally among the others as long as they finished the race. As with all these sorts of races, side betting was encouraged. Grand Central rink, where the contest took place, was tastefully decorated with flags and lanterns. Seats were arranged so that spectators had a clear view of the track and the contestants at all times. A portion of these seats had been reserved for ladies and

7.1 Helen Baldwin, Jessie Woods, and Lulu Hart, c. 1888 (Baldwin is from the author's collection; Woods is courtesy of John Weiss; and Hart is from the collection of Lorne Shields, Toronto, Canada)

their escorts. The oval track; fifteen laps to a mile, was made of smooth, solid boards and slightly raised at each end of the building. At the north end was an elevated stand with chairs for the scorers, timers, and judges. In the centre was an enclosed area for the press, and also a first-class band to cheer the riders and entertain the crowd. Everything was set for the race to begin.

At 3:00 p.m. on Monday, 27 November 1888, all nine competitors, in colourful costumes with their bicycles decorated with bright ribbons, lined up at the start. They would ride for eight hours or less, and since it was a go-as-you-please format, they could take breaks whenever required. The crowd was small, with only three hundred people observing the start, though another thousand patrons apparently came to watch the race throughout the evening. At the end of the first day, no one had completed one hundred miles in eight hours, but Lottie Stanley and May Allen had come close at 93 miles each. Hilda Suallor, hindered by her broken arm, was way behind at a mere four miles, and the inexperienced Aggie Harvey had ridden only thirty-eight miles. The second day of the race was more interesting, especially as Kitty Brown, May Allen, and

Lottie Stanley became entangled at one point and were all thrown from their mounts; luckily, no one was hurt and they continued soon after. Throughout most of day, May Allen kept right behind Lottie Stanley's wheel, but near the end she dropped back and was passed by Helen Baldwin, who had ridden 184 miles to Stanley's 186.[9]

Some two thousand spectators were supposedly enticed to Grand Central rink on the third day of the race. The organizers later revealed they had exaggerated the attendance numbers throughout the event in order to convince more people to attend, and thus bring in more money. Early in the evening, Allen rode too close to Lulu Hart causing them both to crash. Hart's bicycle was badly damaged and another one had to be provided, but she lost little time. Stanley continued her fast pace completing 268 miles, with Baldwin, Allen, Lewis, and Hart still in the running. The other four – Suallor, Woods, Brown, and Harvey – were simply not in contention. The fourth day allegedly brought out five thousand people, who were entertained by the women and also by a men's five-mile amateur race, where one rider fell breaking not only his saddle but also the handle bars. Somehow, he remounted and finished the race. Among the women, there was little change in position: Stanley maintained her lead at 361 miles by averaging 90 miles a day; Baldwin had completed 343; Allen and Hart were tied at 305 miles; and Lewis had fallen behind with 283 miles. By the end of the fifth day, Stanley still led with Baldwin close behind. On the sixth and final day of the race, Stanley won by completing a total of 520 miles, twelve laps to Baldwin's 500 miles.

The event was not without controversy. Manager William Troy was accused of absconding with the gate receipts, when in fact he had left immediately afterwards for New York to arrange for a women's race to be held in Madison Square Garden. He was also thought to have bet a large sum of money on Helen Baldwin, but when it was clear that she would be beaten by Lottie Stanley he allegedly offered Stanley money to stay off the track on the final day, although she would receive a certificate verifying that she was the real winner of the race. Both these rumours were vehemently denied by Mr A.C. Banker of the Pittsburgh Bicycle School, an associate of Mr Troy, who admitted they had not made money on the event and were having some difficulty paying the bills, though the balance was less than $300. Expenses, he claimed, amounted to $1,236, but he did not say what, exactly, they had made through the gate. He also assured everyone that the racers were paid what they were due, and their hotel bills and other expenses had been covered.[10] Still, the controversy and innuendos about money, gambling, and expenses were worrying and a harbinger of what was to come.

Not long after the controversial race, Elsa von Blumen's manager, Bert Miller, came to Pittsburgh reportedly to convince Lottie Stanley (and also Aggie Harvey) to switch managers. They were both under contract with William Troy for a year, and were unable to ride under any other management during that time. Miller also complained that Birdie McCurry (competing as May Allen) was a minor, and as a result her contract with manager Troy should have been signed by her father. Regardless of the controversy, Troy was intent on keeping Stanley, Harvey, and McCurry under his exclusive management.[11]

On Christmas Day 1888, five women from Pittsburgh competed in an eight-hour (hundred-mile) race at the Palace Rink in Brooklyn, New York. The contestants were Helen Baldwin, Jessie Woods, Lulu Hart, Aggie Harvey, and Lottie Stanley, who were all still under the management of William Troy. Dressed in jersey knickerbocker trousers and small jackets of various colours, the riders were a pretty sight. One report was especially complimentary: "How graceful a graceful woman can be astride the two-wheeled steed, and what endurance a little training can develop in her."[12] After eight hours, none had accomplished one hundred miles. Even so Stanley, "a chunky mite of five feet," was declared the winner having ridden more miles than the others. She received a diamond medal and a purse of five hundred dollars, but more importantly, she was also awarded the title of champion female bicycle rider of America.[13]

William Troy was determined to keep his riders in the public eye. Another six-day event, racing eight hours a day throughout the afternoon and evening, was scheduled in Pittsburgh to begin on New Year's Day. Competing this time were regulars May Allen, Hattie Lewis, and Hilda Suallor, who were joined by professionals Elsa von Blumen and Jessie Oakes. The *Pittsburgh Dispatch* provided daily coverage of the race at the Grand Central Rink, and though mostly positive in tone, the journalism was at times condescending. The reporter assured readers that

7.2 Lithograph of Lottie Stanley, *National Police Gazette*, 27 April 1889
(Library of Congress)

although the bicyclists were charming and pretty, there were more
than good looks to attract their attention: "Five good looking young
ladies, real athletes, if the term applies to the sex." He went further:
"We seldom will listen to anyone who says that a woman can make
anything like a reasonable showing in any contest that demands grit,
stamina and skill."[14] If spectators came to see for themselves, he suggested,
they would be astounded at the terrific race taking place. Since most of
these races produced spills, the crowd was treated on the first day to a
spectacular accident when a man crossed the track and came in contact

with one of the bicycles. This caused three riders to be thrown violently from their wheels, including Elsa von Blumen, who fell against a post at the side of the track, which resulted in a deep gash to her head. She lay senseless until she was picked up and carried into a room where her wound was dressed. She soon reappeared and pluckily began to make up for lost ground. At the end of the first day and to everyone's surprise, one of the local contestants, Hattie Lewis, was in the lead.

As the race went on it attracted an increasing number of female spectators, and by the fourth day at least half of the 3,000 to 4,000 who entered the rink were "ladies." Jessie Oakes, the prettiest and speediest rider, unfortunately became ill later in the race putting her out of contention. Both Suallor and Allen had ridden well, and despite her terrible fall, von Blumen made up considerable distance, but in the end it was Hattie Lewis who won the race by completing 455 miles, only four miles more than Elsa, and earning $150 for her efforts. In his final article, the *Pittsburgh Dispatch* reporter had this to say: "It has been well contested from the beginning, and the fact that a local contestant has won somewhat knocks on the head all notion of hippodrome."[15] In other words, the race was not fixed, and the fact that substantial betting took place during the event was evidence that gamblers considered it a legitimate one.

Armaindo now had to contend with Lottie Stanley, who had appropriated her title as the best female racer in North America, indeed the world. Louise's response was entirely predictable and appropriately indignant: "I'm the champion lady bicyclist of the world. I hold all the medals and have defeated all comers for the title, and am willing to race all the women cyclists of the world one after the other for six days. For over five years no one but Elsa von Blumen has had the nerve to race me and Miss Blumen met with defeat. This Miss Stanley has been presented with my title in New York and Brooklyn because she won a one-hundred-mile race from five ladies who had only just begun to ride, which is no credit to her."[16] To show that she meant business, Louise deposited $100 with John Prince for a match with Stanley, or any other lady bicyclist in the world, for stakes of $500 to $1,000 a side over any distance from 10 to 100 miles, or a six-day race, as long as it took place in Omaha. The information was sent to Stanley by Morgan and Eck via the *New York World* and the *Boston Herald*. A cycling journal advised William Troy, Stanley's manager, "not to permit Miss Lottie to come within telephone distance of Morgan or his party unless she wishes to lose her reputation."[17] A story about Stanley also appeared in the *National Police Gazette*, calling her "the most promising bicyclienne now before the American public."[18]

After the successful races in Pittsburgh and Brooklyn, William Troy convinced William O'Brien, manager of Madison Square Garden in New York, that it was the perfect venue for a six-day women's race. Troy already had his Pittsburgh racers under contract, and von Blumen's and Armaindo's managers agreed to their participation. The race would not only match these two old rivals for the first time since their epic duals in 1882, but it would also allow for a new wave of women racers to challenge for championship laurels. Of course, not everyone agreed and certainly not the editor of *Bicycling World and L.A.W. Bulletin*. He disparaged Madison Square Garden by calling it that "irredeemable old cycling murder mill, otherwise called 'a track,'" with a reputation of "being the most dangerous place possible for wheelman to attempt to race upon."[19] As for women racing, he was equally disapproving: "when it comes to a question of women bestriding an ordinary, and riding around a track for the purpose of being guyed by a curious public, then I want to go on record as voting decidedly in the negative. I had thought that this type of cycling disgrace met its birth and death in the performance of Louise Armaindo, but alas I was mistaken."[20] On a more positive note, a cycling enthusiast wrote to the same magazine with a story about the unusual sight of a cyclist in downtown New York, something that took his breath away. "My surprise was, perhaps, natural, when I discovered that the rider was Miss Helen Baldwin, who was mounted on a fifty-inch Rudge ordinary, and was engaged in doing a forty-mile practice spin in training for the forthcoming ladies' – I beg your pardon! women's – bicycle race at Madison Square Garden."[21]

The six-day, eight-hours-daily race began on 11 February 1889. Twelve riders lined up at the start: Hilda Suallor, Jessie Woods, Kitty Brown, Jessie Oakes, Elsa von Blumen, Lulu Hart, Maggie McShane, Lottie Stanley, Helen Baldwin, Hattie Lewis, Louise Fox, and Louise Armaindo. Most were dressed in tights or knickerbockers along with brightly coloured, tight-fitting jackets and jockey caps, except for von Blumen, who was resplendent in her usual costume of dark red, knee-length skirt and jacket, black stockings, and helmet. They began each day at three o'clock in the afternoon and rode until six in the evening. After a two-hour break, they started again at eight o'clock and continued until one in the morning when they retired to neighbouring hotels. Armaindo was the favourite, and her trainer, William Morgan, was so certain she would win he offered to bet a thousand dollars on her.[22] As for Louise herself, she expected to make at least six hundred miles, dismissing newcomer Lottie Stanley with the comment: "Who is this little monkey, anyhow? I'll send her home sick before long."[23] Louise would regret those words, and luckily Morgan never made the wager.

The race was eagerly covered by the major New York newspapers, which provided readers with detailed, daily reports of how the contestants were faring. The press coverage was generally fair and respectful. One paper commented favourably upon the modest demeanour and ladylike bearing of all the riders, and the absolute respect with which they were treated by the spectators.[24] The first day brought several spills and crashes as the riders got used to the track with its tight, unbanked turns. Louise Fox, the "Jersey Buttercup," who was the least experienced racer, withdrew after riding only six miles. Towards the end of the first day, Louise was in the lead with Stanley not far behind. Just before midnight, Louise fainted and was carried off the track. A doctor reported that she had been ill and as a result had not eaten much over the previous couple of days. She appeared again at the beginning of the second day, but rode only for a little more than an hour. She continued this pattern for the rest of the race, sometimes riding longer, but clearly was out of contention.

Stanley held the lead for the remainder of the race and was never seriously challenged. By the fourth day she had ridden over 400 miles and was nearly twenty miles ahead of the rest. Von Blumen, Oakes, and Baldwin were working hard and keeping up, but the others were showing fatigue. Jessie Oakes unfortunately suffered several painful accidents but she hung in the race, much to the appreciation of the crowd. Spectators increased substantially throughout the week and on the last day there were nearly 6,000 in attendance. Stanley rode just over 624 miles to win the race, whereas Armaindo was a disappointing tenth.[25] All were in excellent condition after the race except for Elsa, who was sore from a serious crash, and Louise, who was confined to bed and under the care of a physician. She complained of headaches and dizziness, and thought her ailment was a bilious attack, but optimistically predicted she would soon be back in training for her next race.[26]

The aftermath of the race was a messy wrangling over money, and it also became clear that the public had been duped because the racers were in fact paid employees. Troy and O'Brien agreed to split the gate receipts with 60 per cent going to O'Brien, who would pay expenses connected to the race, and 40 per cent to Troy. It was reported that each rider would receive a portion of Troy's take depending on where they placed in the race. In the end, the total gate receipts amounted to $10,212 of which 40 per cent was $4,084.80. The winner, Stanley, was to receive 40 per cent of this amount, which was $1,633.92; von Blumen, the runner up, was entitled to 20 per cent or $816.96; third place finisher Oakes to 15 per cent or $612.72; and the others would receive 10, 8, 5, and 2 per cent, respectively.[27] O'Brien, and not Troy, apparently gave Armaindo $300 to defray expenses, and $50 to each of Woods, McShane, and Brown so they would not be left without anything for their efforts.

However, since most of the racers were under contract to Troy and paid a weekly wage, they did not receive anywhere near these amounts of money. It all came to a head when several of Troy's riders, including Stanley, complained to O'Brien that Troy would not pay them their winnings. For his part, Troy argued that his racers were under contract for which he paid them a wage, and that he trained them, paid their board and transportation, and supplied their machines.[28] Bert Miller, Elsa von Blumen's long-time manager, was at odds with Troy throughout the entire race, and at one point they indulged in angry fisticuffs. In the end, it is not clear what the racers were paid. One report said that Stanley received $250 as the winner and the others $65 each.[29] Consequently, the race was branded a "hippodrome" because the racers were paid regardless of where they finished in the race. This left a bad impression with spectators, and did not bode well for public interest in future races. As for the women Troy had under contract, they were so fed up they left

7.3 Fanciful depiction of Lottie Stanley winning a six-day race in Madison Square Garden, New York, *National Police Gazette*, 2 March 1889 (Library of Congress)

him immediately and signed on with Tom Eck and William Morgan. Elsa von Blumen retired, and never competed again.[30]

The troupe was advertised as "Beauty on Wheels." From the end of February until mid-June 1889, they travelled by train to a half-dozen cities from New York and Philadelphia in the east, Denver in the west, and Chicago, Kansas City, and Omaha (three times) in between. With such huge distances to cover, they were constantly on the move except for the time spent in one location for a six-day race. The group consisted of Jessie Woods, Hattie Lewis, Helen Baldwin, Kitty O'Brien, Hilda Suallor, Jessie Oakes, and Louise Armaindo. During their first contest in Philadelphia, Suallor again broke her arm, which caused her to drop out. At the next stop in Omaha, twenty-one-year-old Lillie Williams was added to the troupe. She was a protégé of Patrick Fallon, a well-known sporting promoter in Omaha, but had only been riding for four months. A printing compositor by trade, she was also married (Mrs Sutton), but apparently unhappily so.[31] She surprised everyone by winning the first Omaha race, and subsequently was invited to join Eck's group for the rest of the tour. Louise was simply not fit enough to race eight hours a day for six days, and when she did appear on the track, she looked worn and disheartened. Her contribution to the entertainment was mostly through exhibition races such as five miles against time.

Also made public were serious difficulties between Louise and her husband of less than a year. There had been reports of Norman Stewart's refusal to seek employment, and that Louise was supporting the two of them through her meagre earnings. She had gone through most of her savings and was forced to sell some of her jewellery and medals to keep them going. Stewart was gaining the reputation of a hoodoo, someone who brings bad luck and ill fortune to those around them. What happened in Omaha, while Louise was still recovering from her illness, finally brought their differences to the public's attention. As reported in the *Omaha Herald*, "Norman dropped in and began worrying her and concluded by striking her as she lay in the bed. Forbearance has ceased to be regarded by the little Frenchwoman as a virtue, and after a season of abuse she rose from her bed, and seizing the stripling husband by the scruff of the neck, she slammed him against the wall, and across the bed and over the trunk, and down the stairway to the ground floor."[32] The landlady evicted them both from the rooming house. Louise's friends, likely Eck and Morgan, announced their intention of procuring a warrant for Stewart's arrest for assault and battery. The general consensus was that this disastrous marriage had been responsible for Louise's racing decline during the past year.[33]

Although press reports about these races were generally positive in tone, there was also some negative editorial criticism. Admitting that the event had been exceptional sport, as proven by substantive box office receipts, the *Omaha Herald* was concerned that bicycle racing might become popular among women. One concern was that once a young woman became a racer, the chances of returning to a quiet home life were slim: "The dull round of duties which a daughter or a wife must perform is greeted with no plaudits, and when once the taste for applause is acquired it is as hard to break as the whisky habit." Another worry was that women racers would ruin their health and be permanently injured, citing Louise as an example: "Louise Armaindo has stood it for years, but she comes from a family distinguished for its strength, and even she is broken down – 'gone to stable,' as her friends in the ring put it."[34] Fed up with the constant criticism of women racers in *Bicycling World and L.A.W. Bulletin*, William Morgan, who would soon marry Jessie Oakes, wrote, "I notice you are severe on the lady bicyclists, but please remember, Mr. Editor, that they are making their living at cycling, and as they are well behaved and intent on earning an honest living, I think their course is commendable. I do not think they will injure the sports or themselves so long as their appearance and conduct on and off the track is the same as it was at Omaha and Kansas City."[35]

Morgan's prediction was about to be tested. Before the six-day race in Battery D in Chicago, Louise told a reporter that she felt stronger and in every way healthier than before. "Bicycling," she added, "is the best exercise for ladies, as it does not cause that tired feeling walking, running, roller-skating, boat-rowing makes one feel after such exercise, and the vibration of the body is not half as much."[36] However, on the first day of the six-day race, Louise could not keep up and she accomplished only twenty-six miles in three hours (compared to forty-two miles by Woods, the leader). On the second day, Louise was annoyed about a new bicycle that Helen Baldwin was using but eventually had agreed to start when someone in the crowd yelled, "Aw, you're no good." Louise was so upset she dismounted, burst into tears, and flew off the track in a huff. To make matters worse, Louise's husband arrived from Omaha at Battery D, made a nuisance of himself, and was ejected by Eck and Morgan. After this, Louise absolutely refused to return to the track.[37]

Following another race in Omaha, next up was Madison Square Garden in New York with Armaindo, Baldwin, Woods, Brown, Lewis, Oakes, who were also joined by Lottie Stanley and Maggie McShane.

Stanley had not raced since the last women's race in the Garden in February, and McShane (under her other name Aggie Harvey) had been racing earlier in May in Wheeling, West Virginia, with Lulu Hart and Lulu Gordon.[38] Louise, supposedly now in "splendid shape," was described by one paper as a "short, plump, little creature, with imposing masses of muscle."[39] Where Stanley was sadly out of form, and also ill at the beginning of the race, Louise was prepared for the daily eight hours, and in the end she came fourth, having ridden 598 miles. The winner, Jessie Oakes, completed almost 670 miles. The final race for the troupe, six days but only two hours daily, was held in Athletic Park, Denver, where Louise came third. At the end of the race, Jessie Oakes and William Morgan were quietly married, followed by a cozy supper with all members of the team present.[40]

The group then split up, with Oakes, Brown, and Baldwin managed by Morgan, whereas Eck took on Woods, Lewis, Stanley, Williams, and of course Armaindo. Morgan and his racers went to the West Coast, and from there they hoped to travel to Australia. Eck's troupe, still called "Beauty on Wheels," planned to invade the eastern United States, and then go to Europe for an extended to tour.[41]

After travelling across the country, William Morgan and his wife, Jessie Oakes, along with Helen Baldwin and Wilbur Knapp, arrived in San Jose, California. Also accompanying them was Kitty O'Brien from Ireland, who in reality was Kitty Brown from Pittsburgh. Whether she simply changed her name or was married is unclear, but from then on she was known as Kitty or Kittie O'Brien. In San Francisco, they took part in a seventy-two-hour race held over seven days in the Mechanics' Institute Pavilion. Riders were on their bicycles from two to five in the afternoon, and then from seven until midnight. Also in the race were four other males, including one who had ridden his bicycle from New York to San Francisco and another who was a pedestrian but had little experience racing a high wheel. The women riders were granted a one-hundred-mile head start, and given their competitive experience, commentators thought the men, even Morgan and Knapp, would have difficulty making this up and overtaking the women. The winner would collect $1,000, second $750, third $500, fourth $250, and so on.[42]

On the first afternoon of the race, and to promote the event, organizers let thousands of school children into the pavilion for free. Unable to contain their excitement, some children crawled under the railing and onto the track, causing at least one rider to crash in order to avoid them. Luckily, no youngsters were hurt. The two inexperienced men quit the race after the first day, with the women leading and Baldwin in front of everyone. Spectator attendance improved as the race continued, and despite taking a header on the last day and being run over by Oakes, Helen Baldwin won the race having ridden 884 miles; Knapp came second and Morgan third; Oakes and O'Brien pulled up the rear.[43] With sixty-nine miles between Baldwin and Knapp, and eighty-two between Morgan and Baldwin, it demonstrated that two of the top male riders could not come close to making up a one-hundred-mile head start given to probably the best female racer in America. From San Francisco, the group travelled north giving exhibitions along the way, and spent some time in Portland, Oregon. They did not travel to Australia as planned.

On 28 August 1889, a small group of women bicycle racers boarded the White Star steamer *Germanic* in New York and set sail for Liverpool, England. Among the group were Louise Armaindo, May Allen, Lottie Stanley, Jessie Woods, and Lillie Williams, accompanied by Tom Eck, their manager, and Mr J.N. Gannon, their advance agent. Once in England the plan was to train for a few weeks, then race in several towns and cities before heading to the Paris World's Fair to ride in a series of events against the cowboy horsemen of Buffalo Bill's Wild West show. Brief but arduous training took place at the Recreation Ground in Long Eaton, Derbyshire. By 21 September they were ready for an initial appearance in Leicester at the Belgrave Road Cycle and Cricket Ground, which had an outdoor four-lap cycle track of one mile. Louise did not appear because she was yet again ill – inadvertently poisoned through taking the "wrong" medicine. It is impossible to know what this meant, but she could have become ill through the use of a stimulant such as caffeine, cocaine, or even strychnine.[44] The other four raced each other at various distances and accordingly "gave pretty exhibitions of spirited wheel racing and came in for loud plaudits."[45] Although the weather was fine, a strong wind made the going exceedingly difficult; nevertheless about a thousand spectators paid admission to see the women ride. Since racing the high wheel among women was virtually unknown in England, their appearances brought forth the curious.

Next they appeared at a charming little cycling enclosure in Victoria Gardens, Northampton, still in the East Midlands. The eighteen-foot-wide track was seven laps to the mile and banked at the corners. Louise, advertised as the "Champion of the World," was now back riding, and although she was beaten by Stanley in a five-mile race, she rode well.[46] Then it was back to Long Eaton, where in the cold and wet Louise beat Stanley in a ten-mile race by preventing her from getting past at the finish. Stanley entered a formal protest of "foul," further evidence that she and Louise were still not getting along.[47] There was also a rumour that His Royal Highness the Prince of Wales was particularly taken with Louise, and had shown his admiration with several beautiful floral pieces.[48] Derby was their next venue, where they were forced to race in tall, wet grass; needless to say their times were not up to speed.

From the Midlands they travelled north to coastal Sunderland just south of Newcastle upon Tyne. At the skating rink they competed in an eighteen-hour six-day race on an excellent track of sixteen laps to the mile, with £60 offered in prizes and £10 to the rider who could beat Lillie Williams's world record of 261½ miles. A large crowd of spectators gathered for the start. All went well for the first half hour until Williams lost control of her machine and came down heavily. Armaindo and Allen were close behind; consequently, they collided with Williams and fell from their bicycles. Williams wasn't hurt, though her machine was so badly damaged she could not continue. Louise received a nasty cut on her forehead and was bruised about the arms, but she remounted; whereas Allen sprained her wrist and was sufficiently shaken to retire for the night. The second day was also marred by an accident, and this time Louise was forced to withdraw, but Allen returned. The track was altered to make it safer, and there were no more crashes. After eighteen hours, Stanley won with 269¾ miles not only beating the record, but also establishing an English eighteen-hour record. Woods came second with 263 miles, which also beat the record.[49] The group then travelled to a small mining town in East Northumberland, and were hosted by the New Delaval Amateur Bicycle Club, which had a newly built

7.4 May Allen in her high-wheel racing costume of bloomers and tights, 1889 (Collection of Lorne Shields, Toronto, Canada)

enclosed track. The women raced against several male club members, who were given a head start, but the women won anyway. They also raced amongst themselves.[50]

It is not clear what the women were doing in England between mid-November and the end of December. They did not go to Paris as planned because Buffalo Bill's Wild West show at the World's Fair was finished by the end of October. No reports were found until the women's appearance in a six-day, four-hour-daily race in Sheffield's Artillery Drill Hall beginning on Christmas Eve. All five started the race before a sparse crowd, which picked up as the race progressed. "Spectators saw a tastily dressed lot of athletes," reported the *Sheffield & Rotherham Independent*, "who rode with speed and skill worthy of the best male bicycle riders."[51]

Tom Eck had returned to the United States by the end of December, having left his wife and new baby in Minneapolis for several months. There was a report that he was hired as a trainer at a gymnasium run by the Minneapolis Athletic Association, and perhaps he planned to stay put for a while. What happened to the group in Europe after Eck returned home is unclear, though it is possible that some went to France. Lillie Williams, for example, claimed later that she rode against three French women in Paris in February 1890 by competing in a one-hundred-mile race on a twelve-lap asphalt track, which she won by a mile.[52] Louise also appears to have been in France, perhaps accompanying Williams because she spoke French, but no reports were found.[53]

May Allen found love when she met a young British sprinter named Harry Jeffs. He shared her passion for sport, and more importantly, earning a living through competing. They were secretly married in 1890 and Jeffs accompanied May back to the United States. He became her trainer and manager, and their partnership was rarely publicly acknowledged.

By June most of the group had returned to the States with only Lottie Stanley remaining in Europe. She had ventured off by herself and continued to race in England. Billed as the "Champion Lady Cyclist of the World," she rode a fifty-inch wheel, dressed in male attire, and competed against professional male racers. Between May and October 1890, there are reports of her racing in Wallsend in the northeast; in Woverhampton, Aston, and Coventry of the West Midlands; then back north to West

Hartlepool, Durham. Stanley remained in Europe possibly until the end of 1892, although it is not clear where she was or what she was doing.

As soon as Louise arrived back in New York in March 1890, she dropped into the offices of the *National Police Gazette* and had them issue the following challenge on her behalf: "I am ready to ride from 10 to 1,000 miles on a bicycle against any lady rider in America for the 'Police Gazette' championship medal and $500 or $1,000 a side and the championship of the world."[54] She made it clear that she meant business, and every lady rider should understand that she was still the female bicycle champion of the world. Presumably this was a not so subtle dig at her arch rival, Lottie Stanley. Louise reportedly returned to the track at Battery D in Chicago in June and again in July by racing her high wheel against the combined score of two male pedestrians over six days. However, there was little interest in the contest, and no report as to the outcome of the races appeared in any Chicago paper.[55]

Meanwhile, a twenty-four-hour "championship of America" race took place at the Wyatt Park Amphitheatre in St Joseph, Missouri, without Louise. Riding three hours a night over eight days, Helen Baldwin, Hattie Lewis, Lillie Williams, and Frankie Nelson (who previously raced as Lulu Gordon) competed for a $400 purse and a gold medal. Kitty O'Brien had also intended to enter the race, but she was still recovering from injuries suffered when she took a header while training. The race was a novel sight in St Joseph, prompting the local paper to cover it extensively. Advertising assured spectators that "the race was for blood, not exhibition"; in other words, it was not a hippodrome. St Joseph residents responded favourably with five thousand showing up on the final night. Williams, the betting favourite, won the race covering 340 miles and four laps with Baldwin, Lewis, and Nelson very close behind.[56]

The era of the iconic high-wheel bicycle was coming to an end. Most everyone agreed it was not safe due to the mounting number of injuries resulting from a high fall over the handlebars. Tricycles, most with chain drives, were popular, especially among well-to-do couples and women. Bicycle manufacturers also began to crowd the market with two-wheel alternatives called "safeties." Although initially expensive, the sleeker, low-mount safety bicycle soon replaced the clumsy tricycle, especially among society women, and a new era was born.

CHAPTER EIGHT

SAFETIES, BACKLASH, AND DISASTER, 1890–1896

In the summer of 1890, a Chicago newspaper article about "Ladies Who Ride Wheels" claimed there were at least five hundred women cyclists in the city, whereas three years before there was not a single one.[1] Much the same pattern occurred all over North America, especially in major centres. As long as the only available bicycle, aside from a tricycle, was the high-wheel machine, women were not attracted to cycling. Everything changed with the introduction of the two-wheeled "safety" bicycle, so named because it was safer to ride than the high wheel or ordinary.

The most important development in the safety bicycle was to apply drive to one wheel (the back) while steering with the other (the front), rather than trying to drive and steer the same wheel (the front) as in the high wheel.[2] Safeties had roughly two equal-sized wheels, usually about twenty-seven inches in diameter. While seated, the rider's feet were just a few inches from the ground. In the woman's version, the seat was arranged so there was no bar or rod in front of it except at the level of the feet. Therefore, the rider did not sit astride, one of the major difficulties with the high wheel for women in long skirts. This drop-frame version of the safety made it possible to step through the frame between the wheels, therefore allowing for an easy and comfortable mount. The rear wheel was covered with strings, netting, or some other construction to prevent a women's skirt from becoming caught or entangled in the chain or spokes. It was easy to learn to ride the safety, since three half-hour lessons were all that was necessary. Although various versions of the safety were in development from the mid-1880s, it wasn't until pneumatic tires were introduced in 1890 that it became truly popular.[3]

Early safety bicycles, such as the Rover, were more expensive, heavier, and rougher to ride than a racing high-wheel, which meant that racers were at first not keen on switching. Two Wisconsin racers went head-to-head in 1887 to determine which was faster, the safety or the high wheel. Racing over twenty-one miles, the rider mounted on a massive fifty-four-inch ordinary beat the fellow on a safety "bicyclette" by nearly six minutes.[4] However, even observers of the race could see that the days of the high wheel were numbered. Once pneumatic tires brought increased speed to the safety design, and a strong diamond-shaped frame made for a smoother ride, high wheels became relics in the world of bicycle racing.

It is difficult to pinpoint exactly when women racers in the United States ditched their high wheels and switched to safeties. They did not seem to change machines as early as male professional racers. By 1888, for example, at an international men's event in Buffalo, races were held separately for the high wheel and the Rover safety.[5] Certainly by 1890, with pneumatic-tire safeties gaining in popularity alongside a growing proliferation of racing tracks and velodromes, most male amateur and professional racers were making the switch.[6] It was several more years before safeties were the choice of American women professional racers. Women rode safeties for certain in races held in Saint Paul, Minnesota, and in Rochester, New York, in July 1895, but it is likely that safety races for women took place before this date. For example, an amateur half-mile race for women billed as the "first ladies' bicycle race in America" took place in September 1894 in St Louis, Missouri. There were only four contestants and they were all riding safeties.[7] Sometimes, however, it was simply not clear from press reports what type of bicycles they were riding.

Why were women professional racers more reluctant to switch to the safety? After thousands of middle- and upper-class women took up cycling for recreation and pleasure, there was no longer a clear distinction between racers and everyday riders. However, scorching – leaning low over the handlebars and riding fast – was considered unsightly and inappropriate for the everyday woman rider. Commentators were careful to make a distinction between racing and recreational riding. Maria Ward, who wrote a popular handbook on bicycling for ladies, was not opposed to women training and riding fast. She offered suggestions as to how to do it properly, especially on a track, but she cautioned that "scorching and racing, however, are not properly part of the subject of bicycling, but are a sport, and should be separately considered." In her view, sprinting was comparatively harmless, but scorching was a form of "bicycle intoxication" not to be commended, and reckless scorching was to be condemned at all times.[8]

High-wheel races had proven to be an exciting mixture of cutthroat competition replete with the inevitable spills, collisions, and drama. Lottie Stanley, one of the stalwarts of the high wheel, who continued her racing career on a safety, made an interesting observation at a race in Omaha, Nebraska. Formerly a hotbed of women's high-wheel racing, Omaha had not witnessed a race for several years, but in 1895 a six-day event (all on safeties) was scheduled. Local bicycle clubs objected to the race claiming it would be detrimental to women's cycling. As Stanley observed,

> So they talk about not letting us ride do they? Well, I'd like to know why. When I was here six years ago, they didn't talk of stopping the races, and things were entirely different then from what they are now. Then there were no women riding bicycles, now there are thousands. Then there was danger in riding, either to a man or a woman, for a fall from a wheel five feet up in the air meant something, now it is next to impossible to get a fall. Then people were unused to seeing women in the semblance of the apparel of men, now hundreds of women on the street wear bloomers, and their conduct is not called into question.[9]

On safeties, women racers were more threatening to middle-class wheelwomen, who were working to justify and promote their new cycling practice. Far from supporting women's professional cycling, these same women were concerned that working-class racers would derail the acceptance of women's cycling, because men might assume the racers' dress and riding style were the norm for all wheelwomen.[10]

8.1 Lottie Stanley with a safety racer, *Minneapolis Tribune*, 18 August 1895 (Minnesota Historical Society)

Women's high-wheel races were still featured in the 1891 racing season. The first one was held in April at the Washington rink in Minneapolis, which had seen many a previous contest. It was an eighteen-hour race (six days, three hours a night) managed by Tom Eck that attracted Louise Armaindo, experienced racers May Allen, Helen Baldwin, and Aggie Harvey, as well as rising stars Lillie Williams and Frankie Nelson. Williams was the odds-on favourite because she held the eighteen-hour record of 262 miles. The *St. Paul Daily Globe* assured readers that the race, billed as the "greatest event in the history of Northwestern cycling," was not a hippodrome: "And they are riding for blood. Women are not fakers. They don't put up jobs to make a bluff and divide the receipts, no matter who wins. The inherent jealousy of the sex prevents anything of that sort."[11] Four thousand curious people – fully half were "ladies" – showed up at the start to watch the six racers clad in coloured tights and blouses, while Louise added a red sash and cap to her dark blue costume in recognition of her French Canadian heritage.

Before the race began, there was heated public debate over the McHale Anti-Tights Bill before the Minnesota state legislature. The bill, sponsored by Senator McHale, was directed primarily at actresses performing in operas, plays, and comedies who wore tights on stage. McHale wanted them to cover up with skirts or bloomers. Although the bill was a laughing stock among the media and general public, the Minnesota senate took it seriously enough to approve it. Theatre productions ridiculed the proposal by outfitting their actresses in bloomers for several performances. If the bill became legal, the bicycle racers' costumes would also be at risk, prompting Tom Eck, with his usual bluntness, to state that the race would be held even if the contestants had to wear trousers and overcoats.[12] Luckily, the bill died before coming to the legislature.

As for the race, it was close until the second night when Williams took a spectacular header while rounding a corner. She was obviously hurt but insisted on getting back up on her high wheel. She rode in pain for a few laps but finally quit and was taken to her dressing room where a doctor diagnosed a broken collarbone and shoulder. With Williams out of the race, Louise and Nelson took the lead averaging fifteen miles an hour by trying to outspurt each other. Baldwin was not in the best condition and could not keep up, though Allen and Harvey were still in contention. By the last night, the crowd had swelled to over seven thousand to watch Nelson win the race and break the record with 264 miles. Louise dropped back to fourth at 224 miles behind Harvey and Allen because she lost time one evening when she was sick. At thirty-three, she was more than a decade older than her fellow competitors, though still capable of keeping up with them.[13] Throughout the remainder of the 1891 season, there were reports of more races in

Minneapolis and Saint Paul, Minnesota, and also in Fargo and Grand Forks, North Dakota. The Armaindo-Nelson-Baldwin-Harvey-Allen-Williams troupe travelled about competing in mostly six-day, two-hour nightly races. Frankie Nelson was the usual winner, though Louise was pushing her and often came second.

By 1892 it was becoming increasingly more difficult to find backers and venues for these races. Some racers, including Louise, resorted to competing in pedestrian or walking races. One such race took place in the Cyclorama Building in Minneapolis in April 1892. It was a seventy-two-hour go-as-you-please race. Among the eight competitors were long-time pedestrienne Sarah Tobias and the Canadian short-distance champion Louisa Ruston, in addition to Aggie Harvey and Louise, both of whom began their bicycling careers as walkers. Although Harvey had recently competed in a few pedestrian matches, Louise had not been on the sawdust track for many years. She simply could not keep up and dropped out after the third day. Harvey was the winner by completing just over 256 miles, clearly proving she was a force as both a pedestrienne and a cyclist. Another walking race took place in Saint Paul in May with Louise advertised as competing, but she did not show up. Throughout the summer there were reports of her being secured by a local fair to race horses, but whether she did this is not known. A telling announcement concerning Louise appeared in September 1892: "To-day the ex-queen of the cinder path races back and forth through the length of a Minneapolis restaurant in the humble guise of a waiter 'girl.' ... How sad is the sight of fallen and forgotten royalty."[14] Would she race again?

Early in February 1893, Helen Baldwin wrote a letter to the editor of the *Chicago Herald* suggesting that a women's bicycle race be held in May to determine once and for all who had the right to claim the American championship.[15] Baldwin suggested an eighteen-hour race because she, Armaindo, Williams, Woods, Nelson, and Oakes had all won races at that distance. In fact, as Baldwin pointed out, she had won the forty-eight-hour championship, several eighteen-hour races, and her share of shorter races. She wished to do her racing early in the season because she planned to tour the United States during the summer and fall giving exhibitions of riding and fancy rifle shooting.

The race, expanded to forty-eight hours, took place in a Chicago armoury in mid-May, not long after the World's Columbian Exposition opened. Perhaps the organizers thought it would be an added attraction for visitors to the international fair. It is unclear whether the women were riding safety bicycles. Louise, for example, rode a "geared ordinary," which was basically a high wheel with a small, geared driver instead of a large, direct driver. It was also lighter and lower to the ground.[16] The prizes offered were a $1,000 purse and a valuable trophy representing the championship of America. In the race were Armaindo, Baldwin, Williams, Harvey, and Stanley, as well as two local amateurs who competed for a special prize. Whatever the organizers expected, they certainly miscalculated because attendance was poor, there was little press coverage, and the event lost money. As for the results, Baldwin won by covering 471 miles; Williams was a close second; and Louise came third but was 55 miles behind Baldwin.[17] This, as it turned out, was Louise Armaindo's last recorded bicycle race.

Louise remained in Chicago for much of the world's fair, which lasted until the end of October 1893.[18] She possibly took part in a parade organized by the League of American Wheelman on a summer night in August. Nearly seven hundred cyclists, including more than one hundred women, participated in a lighted procession throughout the fairgrounds. Riders decorated their bicycles, and every wheel carried Chinese lanterns attached to the handlebars or on a framework above the bicycle.[19] Louise was not heard from again until the following February when the *Chicago Inter Ocean* reported that she was looking for a male partner to ride a bicycle built for two against racehorses "or anything else that can set a warm pace."[20]

Louise disappeared for the remainder of 1894 until she showed up again in Montreal in mid-December seeking permission from the military to use the Montreal Drill Shed, an enormous building located at the corner of Craig and Hotel de Ville streets, for an amateur long-distance race to last six days. The application was submitted on behalf of Louise, the "Long Distance Lady Champion Bicyclist of the World," by the *Montreal Star*'s sporting editor Peter Spanjaardt. The request was refused because the shed was undergoing renovations and the military did not know

8.2 "Beauty" Helen Baldwin on a safety racer, c. 1895
(Alice Olson Roepke Collection)

when it would be finished. Regardless, they could not give up its use for a whole week.[21]

In January 1895 Louise again announced her intention to break the one-thousand-mile women's record, but there was no indication she was able to organize such an event.[22] She seemed to be wandering all over the state of New York looking for somewhere and someone to race. In April there was a report in a Brooklyn newspaper that she wanted to race any professional man or woman at fifty or one hundred miles for $250 a side.[23] She even tried to sneak into a strictly amateur women's race in Rochester in June where the first prize was a diamond ring, but her real identity was discovered well beforehand.[24] This race and several others were organized by Billy Madden, a former lightweight boxer turned manager and promoter, who believed there was money to be made in reviving women's cycle racing. Presumably if Louise planned to race, it was on a safety bicycle. In July she was still in Rochester claiming that her reputation was based on being able to put more miles behind her in a long-distance contest than any other living rider, male or female. She was willing to meet any ten women in the world in a six-day race, riding four hours each night, a fresh woman being started against her every hour. She would also race any man in the world for 144 hours.[25] These were not entirely outrageous challenges, but again nothing came of them.

As more professional racers switched to safeties and inexperienced amateur riders were allowed to enter races, the backlash against women's cycle racing became more intense. Races held in Louisville, Kentucky, and St Louis, Missouri, reported women fainting and falling on the track, which drew the ire of a local newspaper: "Since the days of the unsavory professional combination of women high-wheel riders, ladies have happily cut a very small figure in cycle racing, and it is sincerely to be hoped the spectacle of women contesting racing honors will not receive a revival."[26] Ladies, advised the newspaper, belong in the grandstand. The influential *Referee and Cycling Trade Journal* published a diatribe against women racers, arguing that "when members of the fair sex attempt to ape the lords of creation by competing in cycle races of their own, they take a step which ... can benefit neither themselves nor the sport to which they engage."[27] Women's cycle racing, added the writer, should not be encouraged in any way; rather it should be strongly discouraged. The *Pneumatic* magazine, devoted to cycling literature and trade news, suggested that women track racers would suffer the same fate as female baseball teams – "all of whom have been looked upon as degrading in the eyes of the public."[28]

The League of American Wheelmen had never approved of women racers and mostly ignored them during the high-wheel era. When women on safeties appeared on the track, it prompted LAW secretary Abbot Bassett to declare, "It has come at last. Heaven save the mark. Women on the race track. We are glad to note that the innovation was not a success and the reception of the women was not enthusiastic. In riding the wheel, as in everything else, our fair sisters should not forget to be womanly. We look to them to elevate the sport, not drag it down."[29] LAW membership, which increased steadily as more bicyclists took to safeties, was predominantly affluent males, who sought to maintain the status quo especially where women were concerned. By 1895 the LAW included the following clause in their bylaws: "No race meeting shall receive official sanction if it ... has upon its schedule any event which is open to women competitors."[30] The American League of Racing Cyclists, formed in the summer of 1894 to protect racing *men's* interests, was comprised of male racers, managers, and trainers, and did not include women in their membership.[31] Whether any woman racer tried to become a member is not known.

Despite increasing condemnation and little organizational backing, women continued to look for opportunities to race. What was apparent was that the public wanted something new and different. The men's professional races still followed the style of the high-wheel era, which were gruelling six-day, twelve-hours-per-day endurance contests. Spectators began to tire of the race monotony with the excitement mounting only in the last few hours. In Minneapolis, Minnesota, a former pedestrian competitor, now a manager and promoter by the name of H.O. Messier (his first name was Henri) decided to try something different, almost at the same time as Billy Madden's uninspiring races in Rochester.

Although it took place over six days, Messier shortened the contest to just three hours a day, which made for an exciting race each evening. He also signed up several former high-wheel racers, all successful and

well-known: May Allen, Helen Baldwin, Frankie Nelson, and Lottie
Stanley. Allen, now billed as from Liverpool, was trained by her English
husband and manager Harry Jeffs. She was returning to the track after
almost four years following the birth of their child in 1892. Baldwin,
Nelson, and Stanley were very experienced and had made a smooth tran-
sition to safety racers. Also in the contest was Jessie Oakley, a nineteen-
year-old, all-around athlete who had taken part in many shorter races,
though this was her first eighteen-hour contest.[32] The race took place at
Saint Paul's new Aurora baseball park, where Messier built a small,
saucer-shaped wooden track on the grounds. A grandstand and bleachers
provided an excellent view of the lighted track. Ladies were admitted
free of charge. Helen Baldwin, who was sponsored by the Monarch Bicycle Company, had been training for a month in Chicago under respected trainer Edward W. Moulton. Clearly she was out to win, and
that is exactly what she accomplished. With 277 miles and eight laps,
she beat Nelson by only a lap, setting a new American record.[33] The
event was a roaring success with Messier purportedly selling twenty
thousand tickets over the week.

Messier also managed a similar eighteen-hour race in August at Athletic Park, Minneapolis, with Baldwin, Nelson, Allen, and Stanley competing alongside several amateur riders. Among them was Mate
Christopher, a Minneapolis sales clerk, who had been riding for only
four months. Allen and Baldwin were involved in a crash on the second
night causing Allen to drop out, but Baldwin persevered. To everyone's
surprise, Christopher proved to be a superb racer and she missed winning
the race by less than a lap. Nelson crossed the tape first with 293.4 miles,
yet another record.[34] Subsequently, Nelson and Christopher signed a contract to race each other over twenty-five miles to see who was better.
Over 6,000 people came to Athletic Park to witness the event, won by
Christopher in the respectable time of one hour, twenty-five minutes, and
fifteen seconds.[35] Time and time again, Nelson tried to pass her competitor but Christopher set the pace and would not let her through.[36] These
types of races, where speed was privileged over endurance, were clearly
a success and they brought in thousands of spectators. It did not mean,
however, they were not without controversy.

In mid-September, at the Nebraska State Fair in Omaha, the racers were at it again, despite considerable opposition. One of the highlights of the fair was the celebration of the Feast of Mondamin by the Order of the Knights of Ak Sar Ben (Nebraska spelled backwards), an organization of leading business and society men. They objected to young women dressed in suggestive attire while racing their bicycles, whereas local bicycle clubs claimed the race hurt cycling. Lottie Stanley was incensed: "What is the matter with Omaha? Are they getting to be churchgoers to such an extent? Why didn't they stop the women acrobats at the circus that was here Monday from showing unless they would consent to turn their flip flops and double somersaults in long flowing trains and gowns of the latest patterns?"[37] Another contestant, Jessie Oakley, intimated that her racing costume was less suggestive than some of the bloomer outfits she had seen women bicyclists wearing on the streets. She had a point.

The racing costumes worn by some of the women described in this chapter (see Figures 8.1 to 8.4), when compared to those of the women high-wheel racers of earlier chapters, especially where there are comparative photos or lithographs, are more prudent and discreet. Gone are the short skirts or tunics, form-fitting tights, and lacy tops with a modest amount of exposed skin. High-wheel racer Elsa von Blumen, with her attention to decorum and modesty, was an exception (see especially Figures 3.2 and 5.3) in that she was always fully covered in spats, breeches, blouse, jacket, and helmet. Louise Armaindo, on the other hand, usually wore a very short, long-sleeved dress with tights to show off her shapely body (see Figures 5.2 and 6.2). Among the early safety racers, these outfits were replaced by bulky bloomers or breeches, leg coverings, fluffy blouses, or long-sleeved jackets all designed to hide women's shapeliness and to expose as little bare skin as possible. It wasn't until at least 1897 (see Figure E.1 in the epilogue) that women racers dressed in slimming wool tops and shorts with tights covering their legs.

The six-day, eighteen-hour Omaha race went ahead but it was cancelled on the evening of the festival celebrations. Competing in the race were some of the regulars – Nelson, Allen, Stanley, Oakley, and Williams – but also two untested Minnesota riders, Bessie Moore and Caddie

Stevens. Early on, Williams had a bad fall and was forced to quit; Moore could not keep up and also dropped out. Nelson won the race with 275 miles, well below her record, and Allen was a close second.[38]

On 26 December 1895 a curious report appeared in the *Bearings*, a Chicago-based publication of the Cycling Authority of America. It said that Louise Armaindo was in Buffalo "trying to negotiate an engagement to disport herself in a show window."[39] The item also suggested that she had not "caught on" and was missing a chance to win fame and money in the big garden. The article was referring to a women's six-day race held in January 1896 in New York's Madison Square Garden, which was not a success, financially or otherwise. It was yet another of Billy Madden's attempts to interest spectators in a six-day event that was more about endurance than speed. Billed as a "ladies' six-day international," the event was also more spectacle than legitimate contest primarily because most of the twenty-four racers were young and inexperienced. The only seasoned professionals among them were Nelson, Baldwin, and Allen. The racers were divided into two squads with each squad riding two hours, resting for two, and then riding two more hours each night. The track was crowded, and the less experienced riders slowed down the professionals even more, making for an uninteresting and unexciting event. As a result there was little public interest. Both Nelson and Baldwin accomplished 418 miles and six laps, with Nelson just ahead of Baldwin at the finish.[40]

An interesting revelation is that both Nelson and Allen took the patent medicine bovinine, a mixture of beef blood, glycerine, and sodium chloride, throughout the race in Madison Square Garden. Both racers were monitored during the contest by a physician using urinalysis, and the results subsequently published in a medical journal.[41] Later, Nelson claimed, "I was greatly handicapped at the beginning by being out of condition and really not fit physically to endure the fatigue of the contest. As soon, however, as I began to take bovinine, which I did by the advice of my physician as well as of Albert Schock, and other prominent professional wheelmen, I soon regained my strength and vigor, and suffered no inconvenience from the violent exertions I was obliged to put forth to keep my position at the fore-front of the races."[42] Nelson publically endorsed the use of bovinine in athletic competition.

8.3 Former high-wheel racer Lillie Williams, c. 1895
(Alice Olson Roepke Collection)

Although this may have been the first time there was any explicit mention of medical intervention in a women's race, it was fairly common in professional cycle racing. Both pedestrians and cyclists, especially those competing in six-day races, used stimulants such as coca leaves (caffeine and cocaine), kola nuts (caffeine), and strychnine (in low doses) to stay alert and functioning during a long race. Scientists in America and Europe conducted experiments on potential stimulants and reported their findings in medical journals.[43] Whether trainers and athletes were aware of these scientific reports is another matter, and they likely experimented on their own. The practice of taking drugs in sport was common enough that it prompted the *New York Times* to publish this editorial rebuke in 1895:

> We feel sure that all true athletes would disdain any such injurious and adventitious aids, but there is a vast number of persons who take such things thoughtlessly and injury is done thereby. The announcements which are made in advertisements of various stimulants, in which it is claimed that they save the strength and promote the endurance of bicyclers and athletes generally are very much to be deprecated. There are no drugs, which will help one to win a game that could not be won without them, and the general effect of drug taking, and especially of the use of drugs belonging to the caffeine and cocaine class, is distinctly bad. We believe that the medical profession ought seriously to warn those with whom they come in contact professionally against the use of such things.[44]

The year 1896 was an exciting one for women bicycle racers. Though there were setbacks, a new crop of racers alongside the older, more experienced women appeared in a variety of races throughout the United States and Canada. Among the newcomers were Dottie Farnsworth, Lizzie Glaw, Ida Peterson, Frankie Mack, and Tillie Anderson. The LAW prohibition against holding sanctioned races for women did not seem to matter, since venue managers saw the potential to make money by organizing women's professional races. There was, however, an unfortunate episode in San Francisco when a women's six-day race, scheduled to take place after a men's contest, was started and then cancelled because of wheelmen's opposition and public disinterest. Bicycle dealers, who had exhibited during the men's event, removed their wares before the women's race began.[45]

It is difficult to assess whether this was a protest against women racers, or the recognition that marketing bicycles to ladies via women's racing was a risky business. The relationship at this time between women racers and bicycle manufacturers was not as symbiotic in the United States as it was in Britain and Europe.[46] Unlike male racers, initially little association was made between female racers, bicycles, or cycling equipment even though manufacturers hoped to sell more safeties to women. It was predicted that 1.25 million bicycles would be manufactured in the United States in 1896 and fully half of these designed for women. Whether they actually sold them was another matter.[47] The LAW, still vehemently opposed to women's races, was slowly attracting female recreational riders – out of a total of 41,000 members, 1,500 were women. The organization's mission remained the same: promote bicycling in general; advocate for better roads; and oversee the sport of bicycle racing.

At the international level, women's cycle racing was occurring more frequently and gaining the attention of the sporting press.[48] One notable event took place in England in November 1895 at London's Royal Aquarium, a huge, glass-covered hall used for popular amusements and exhibitions, including performing animals, flying gymnasts, acrobats, wire-walkers, strongmen and women, jugglers, and much else, all happening at the same time. For the bicycle race, a wooden track, banked at the ends and measuring a tenth of a mile, was laid out in the main hall of the building. Twenty entries were received from mostly British, French, and Belgian racers, and to accommodate them on the track, they were divided into two lots of ten riders each for a six-day race. Included among them was the French champion Lisette Marton, whose real name was Amélie Christinet (née Le Gall). She rode for the highly successful Gladiator/Simpson team, and was trained by the Englishman James "Choppy" Warburton. Most London papers, including the *Times*, reported on the race and were mostly complimentary: "Thus far it is a wonderful exhibition of fast and graceful riding, and the *costumes* are of a character to which no exception could be taken."[49] Crowds flocked to the novel contest, which proved to be exciting entertainment, made

more so by a number of spectacular crashes. Luckily, no one was seriously hurt, and after six days and 371 miles, the surprising winner
was Monica Harwood of England, who apparently had been cycling for
just a few months. She was also club captain of the Chelsea Rationalists,
a progressive women's cycling club whose members were passionate
about dress reform.[50] Women's races continued at the Royal Aquarium
as part of its featured entertainment for the next month.[51]

Given the increasing interest in women's cycle racing both in Europe
and North America, sports promoter Billy Madden decided to take several American riders to England to compete in women's international
races being held in London. One report indicated that several racers
would go abroad, including Mate Christopher, Helen Baldwin, May
Allen, and Dottie Farnsworth, but in the end only Frankie Nelson, the
winner of the six-day race in Madison Square Garden earlier in January,
made the trip.

There was considerable excitement in the British sporting press when
Nelson arrived in London, and she immediately went into training at the
outdoor Putney Velodrome. The six-day, four-hours-a-day race for the
championship of the world and £250 in prize money began on 20 April
1896 in the Royal Aquarium, with fourteen competitors divided into
two divisions. Competing in the first section were Monica Harwood of
England and Hélène Dutrieu of France. Nelson was in the second division, where she was up against the celebrated Scottish professional
Clara Grace and the French star Lisette Marton, often known simply as
"Lisette." There was great interest in the race, especially among women,
who may also have been attracted to the Collie and Old English Sheep
Dog Show going on at the same time.[52] On the first day, Harwood ran
away from her opponents in the first division. The second-division riders
were more level with Grace and Marton, sharing the lead. The aquarium
track was narrow, and though most of the racers were familiar with its
eccentricities, Nelson and Marton collided near the end of the first day
and both were severely shaken. Again on the third day, there was a serious crash that sent Miss Field to the hospital. Several riders, including
Nelson, strongly protested, but to no avail. After completing just over
137 miles, Nelson refused to continue in the race.[53] In the end, the new

8.4 Frankie Nelson in her smart, sailor suit racing costume, c. 1895
(Alice Olson Roepke Collection)

world champion was Lisette Marton with 437 miles, seven laps, and
Monica Harwood was second at 429 miles, three laps.[54] Nelson was
scheduled to race in another six-day event at the Royal Aquarium and
also at the Vélodrome D'hiver in Paris, but whether she did or not is unknown. The American cycling press totally ignored Nelson's misadven-
tures in Europe except for a comment by Albert Schock, who witnessed
the race in London, and suggested that she could not hold her own
against the well-trained European racers.[55]

Back in the United States, and especially in the east, larger cities were
willing to promote women's racing despite the criticism and the LAW
ban. A cycling trade show in Minneapolis included a ladies' six-day (two
hours a night) race because women were much more graceful in their
riding than men, and "not the least of the attraction being their pretty
faces and physiques."[56] With seven hundred dollars in prize money at
stake, the race attracted some of top riders: Baldwin, Allen, Farnsworth,
and Peterson alongside a couple of local women, Zella Villarde and Min-
nie Hokenson. The pace was too fast for Villarde, who dropped out on
the first day after completing only fourteen laps. Dottie Farnsworth won
the exciting race by beating Helen Baldwin by a mere foot at the finish.[57]
A week later, in a match-up with Farnsworth and on the same track,
Baldwin set a new twenty-five mile record of one hour, sixteen minutes,
and thirty seconds.[58] She accomplished this on her royal blue Napoleon
bicycle, which Saint Paul's A.D. Smith cycle house noted in a newspaper
advertisement the next day.

One of the first women's six-day safety races held in Canada took
place at Fort Garry Park in Winnipeg, Manitoba. Two thousand people
witnessed the opening night in early June 1896 with Baldwin, Allen,
Farnsworth, Peterson, and Hokenson lined up at the start.[59] Baldwin
was ill when she arrived in Winnipeg, and though she rode hard on the
first night, she reluctantly retired from the race. On the second night,
Allen's front wheel touched Peterson's back wheel, which caused Allen
to fall down hard onto the board track and strike her head (no helmets
were worn in those days). She got right back up, and continued riding at
a furious pace, spurred on by enthusiastic spectators. On the final night
the grandstand was packed from top to bottom with spectators, mostly
women, with boys and men crowded around the track. Farnsworth,

Peterson, and Allen crossed the finish line in that order with Hokenson a distant fourth. May Allen, certainly the crowd favourite, was treated to a magnificent ovation, and people rushed onto the track to get a better glimpse of the racers. The group returned to Winnipeg in late August for another six-day event.

Joining them was Swedish-born Tillie Anderson, a twenty-one-year-old immigrant living with her family in the Chicago neighbourhood of Swedetown. She worked at a laundry during the day and supplemented her income as a seamstress at night. She saved enough money to buy her first bicycle and immediately began riding outdoor centuries (one-hundred-mile circuits) revelling in the new freedom and speed. Coached and trained by her fiancé Philip Sjöberg, she soon learned to ride on a steeply banked, wooden track. In January 1896 she entered her first six-day (twelve-hour) race, which was held in Chicago's Second Regiment Armory. Up against far more experienced riders, surprisingly Tillie won that race and was on her way to becoming the new star of women's cycle racing. It wasn't long before she was called the "second Louise Armaindo."[60]

Women's cycle racing was taken seriously, especially by those who followed it closely. They knew the star riders, and when an opportunity arose to see their favourites, they turned out in large numbers. Such was the case early in July at the Twin City Cycle Track in Minneapolis, when professionals Farnsworth, Anderson, and Peterson were matched against three local amateurs – Lillian Harp, Emma Caska, and Amy Kalgren. Over five days, it was back and forth between Farnsworth and Anderson, since Peterson was slightly injured and the three amateurs lagged behind. Some two thousand to three thousand spectators were enjoying the action, and side betting was extensive. All went well until the last day, when track management inexplicably raised the admission price, and just before the start announced that Farnsworth would not race because she was ill. Fully five thousand people were seated in the grandstand and lined the bleachers, most expressing their disapproval by yelling "fake." As some began to leave, more rushed onto the track and surrounded the frightened riders, who had to be escorted out. A full-scale riot ensued with the police helpless to prevent considerable damage to the facility.[61] The race was never finished.

This small but growing group of women racers ignored Louise Armaindo and her challenges, and she in turn snubbed them. Why she did so is not easily understood, but perhaps she simply could not (or would not) make the switch from her trusty high wheel to a safety. She was also more comfortable racing over a longer distance rather than shorter distances. Possibly she was afraid of losing to much younger, though in some cases less-experienced competitors. By my reckoning, Louise was thirty-eight years old in October 1895. Most important of all, she no longer appeared to have a manager, agent, trainer, or sponsor working with her. Tom Eck was supposedly living in Minneapolis with his wife, Jennie, and six-year-old daughter, Irene, but instead he was travelling all over the country with his newest racing protégé John S. Johnson.

What was Louise Armaindo doing in Buffalo in 1896? Aside from "disporting" herself in a show window, we simply don't know why she was there. The city had a well-earned reputation as a cycling hub. When George Thayer rode his high wheel across the United States in 1886, he visited Buffalo and discovered miles and miles of smooth asphalt and fine park roads around the city.[62] Recreational cycling steadily increased with the arrival of the safety bicycle, which led to the opening of more riding academies, some with special accommodation for ladies. The Buffalo Bicycle Riding Academy, for example, which opened in 1895 on Main Street, offered separate hours reserved for private instruction to women. A female attendant was constantly available to provide ideas regarding the latest riding costumes.[63] Possibly Louise was employed at this establishment. In the spring of 1896 the newly built Buffalo Athletic Field opened with those responsible boasting of the "finest racing track in the United States" and one certainly suitable for bicycle racing. The track was oval and constructed of cement; it was banked high on the outside so that the wheel of the racer was always on a perfect level. It was also very fast.[64] Perhaps Louise hoped to train on this track for a challenge match if she could find someone to race against.

Whatever Louise was doing in Buffalo, she was still there ten months later and residing at the Carlino Hotel, an old four-storey building on Main Street near the harbour, with a reputation as an Italian restaurant and inn. Louise paid a weekly rent to the hotel, and had occupied the same room for the past six months. In the early hours of 2 November

1896, fire broke out on the second floor and soon engulfed the upper two storeys where the twenty or so residents were sleeping. Most were roused and able to flee via the outside fire escapes, although some suffered burns and smoke inhalation. One woman died the next day of her injuries. Wishing to deter unwanted intruders into her room, Louise had nailed shut the window leading to the fire escape and was forced to jump out the other window. She landed on the roof of a shed, suffered a fractured hip and internal injury, and was taken by ambulance to the Fitch Accident Hospital, which was associated with the Buffalo General Hospital.[65] She remained there for five months.

A month after the fire Louise initiated legal action against the owner of the hotel, Robert Ferguson, for failure to provide a "rope or other better appliance" in her room. The case was not heard for a year when it was revealed that Louise, the "alleged world's champion all-round female bicycle rider," was suing the hotel owner for $5,000 (about $140,000 today) for personal injuries. She testified that she was now a "cripple" and unable to make a living as was the case before the accident. She also claimed that she was twenty-seven years old, when indeed she was considerably older, and probably closer to forty.[66] The jury that heard the case awarded her $1,500 in a verdict against Ferguson, but this was not the end of the matter.

Ferguson appealed on the basis that Louise had occupied the same room for six months and never complained about the lack of a rope. There was also the matter of her nailing shut the window with access to the fire escape. To complicate matters, a man (never identified) was also in her room the night of the fire and somehow he managed to open the nailed-shut window and escape down the fire escape. A new trial was ordered and this time the judge agreed with Ferguson. He set aside the original verdict and ruled that Louise was not entitled to recover any costs.[67]

Never again did Louise Armaindo race a bicycle. She had embarked on a professional athletic career when she was fourteen, probably around 1871, and earned her living as a strongwoman, then as a trapeze artist, and more lucratively as a pedestrienne. She learned how to ride a high wheel and raced professionally from 1881 until 1893. Constantly on the move, she travelled primarily throughout the United States, rarely returning to Canada, and then only to Montreal or Toronto. She ventured as far west as San Francisco, and as far south as Galveston, Texas, and New Orleans, Louisiana. Mostly, however, she raced in towns and cities in states south of the Great Lakes – Minnesota, Iowa, Missouri, Wisconsin, Illinois, Indiana, Ohio – and along the eastern seaboard in Massachusetts, New York, Philadelphia, Maryland, Virginia, and the District of Columbia. If she had a base, it was in either Chicago or Minneapolis. In 1889 she crossed the Atlantic to England, and later France, where she spent several months before returning to America.

Louise constantly broke cycling speed and endurance records, although for much of her career she only raced men (and sometimes horses). These records are quite meaningless now because often she was given a handicap or head start. However, there is one record for which she was most proud. In 1883, in Chicago's Battery D Armory, Louise, along with William Woodside and William Morgan, took part in a six-day, twelve-hours-per-day endurance race. Louise won fair and square by cycling 843 miles, and winning the so-called United States championship. It was an amazing feat and the record stood for several years. By the time more women high-wheel racers came onto the racing circuit, Louise was considerably older and past her prime. She was still capable of pushing them hard, but she was no longer a winner. No one deserves a place in history as *la mère du cyclisme féminin*, the mother of women's cycling, more than this French Canadian from Quebec.

EPILOGUE

By 1897 the women's cycle racing circuit in the United States was dominated by the "Big Five" – namely, Tillie Anderson, Dottie Farnsworth, Helen Baldwin, May Allen, and Lizzie Glaw. Baldwin and Allen were the only two racers remaining from the high-wheel era. Allen returned to the sport in 1895 after a three-year hiatus following the birth of her daughter. According to Roger Gilles in *Women on the Move*, a book about women's professional bicycle racing in the United States from 1895 to 1902, or more succinctly the safety era, May Allen was often described as plucky and lovely, but always the "English Girl." It became part of her persona, cultivated by her husband/trainer/manager Harry Jeffs, an Englishman from Liverpool, even though she was born and grew up in Pittsburgh.[1]

Helen Baldwin, known from her early days on the high wheel as the "Queen of the Wheel" due to her racing talent and good looks, retired from the track following a race in Cleveland in August 1897. She was twenty-six and had been racing steadily for nine years. Tillie Anderson was the determined "big, strong, tow-headed Swede," and recognized as the one to beat. Dottie Farnsworth, with "pretty eyes, dark curly hair, and dramatic costumes and jewelry," was a fan favourite. Always a strong contender, she was impetuous and often sulked or pouted over some perceived slight. Lizzie Glaw, from a German family, was the quiet, reticent one though also "heady, strategic, and powerful."[2]

The women's six-day races proved to be as popular as the men's, but were often more exciting and a considerably better attraction. The men mostly stuck to their plodding, endurance, "go-as-you-please" events running for 142 hours from early Monday morning to Saturday night. A round-the-clock schedule required hundreds of race officials. Most racers dropped out before the finish, and those that remained depended on stimulants to keep them going. A lack of spectator interest contributed to the demise of these six-day marathons, but so did negative media commentary, state legislation banning them, and the LAW's refusal to sanction them. The last go-as-you-please men's race was held in Madison Square Garden in 1898.

An entirely different format contributed to the success of the women's six-day races. The contestants were often divided into two squads: the Big Five and other professionals would compete in one, and the less experienced, local amateurs would make up the other. The amateurs raced for two hours in the afternoon, and the professionals for two hours in the evening since they were better able to draw a crowd. The racers also had to complete a certain number of miles to qualify for a prize – more miles for the professionals and less for the amateurs. The LAW refused to sanction women's races, but since men and women did not compete together or at the same venue, it was of little consequence, except that the women could not test their skill against men. The intense rivalry among the women racers was enough to attract an increasingly loyal fan base.

Although Tom Eck was no longer training women racers, he still followed the sport. In March 1897 he watched the Big Five training for an upcoming six-day race at Tattersall's, an exhibition hall in downtown Chicago, and was duly impressed. At the race itself, he was timing on the sidelines when his stopwatch registered 2.24 minutes after Lizzie Glaw's 206th mile. This was the equivalent of twenty-five miles per hour, the fastest mile Eck had ever witnessed by women in competition. Glaw eventually won the race, and at the same time broke the women's twelve-hour, six-day race record by three-quarters of a mile.

If anyone deserves to have a book written about him, it is Tom Eck. He became one of the best known and most sought after athletic trainers in the United States, but less so in Canada because he rarely returned to

E.1 The "Big Five" (L–R): Lizzie Glaw, Helen Baldwin, May Allen, Tillie Anderson, and Dottie Farnsworth at a six-day race in Columbus, Ohio, 22–29 February 1897 (Alice Olson Roepke Collection)

his home country. He also had a substantial reputation in Europe, where he often travelled with his racing protégés or was seeking talented racers to bring back to America. Although known primarily for his work with cyclists, Eck also trained speed skaters, boxers, marathon runners, and track stars. In 1908, for example, he worked with the famous Canadian marathoner Tom Longboat. He was clever, capable, and had all the tricks of his trade at his fingertips. He knew everyone in the athletic world, and they knew him, if only by reputation.

Eck wrote a booklet, called *Points on Training for Wheelmen*, for the E.C. Stearns bicycle company, where he laid out his instructions to young riders interested in racing. He made suggestions as to the proper diet, type of bicycle, what to wear, how to develop speed, and care after exercising.[3] What he knew about the science of training had been gained over many years through practical experience, and he expected complete and unquestioned compliance from his riders, in both training and racing. When the Arnold, Schwinn & Co. signed up John S. Johnson, a rising star from Minneapolis, they also hired Eck to train Johnson and their other racers. In a book about Schwinn bicycles, the authors describe Eck: "He was a silver-haired, intense man, whose commitment to winning gained him more victories than it did friends. Indeed, there probably was room for gentlemen in the world of pro racing at this time; Tom Eck was not usually counted among them. Yet Eck understood better than most that respect in racing came not from good fellowship, but from winning races and setting records. As a result, his determination to succeed was obvious to all who knew him."[4]

Eck's marriage to Jennie Carlisle (or Carlyle), who was fifteen years younger than Tom, was troubled from the beginning. She filed for divorce in 1888 after only a year of marriage, but Tom was able to convince her to stay with him, and their daughter Irene was born in July 1889. After this, Tom seemed to settle down in Minneapolis, where he and his family lived for twelve years, though always with Jennie's parents and family.[5] He was constantly travelling around the American racing circuit, rushing from one meet to another with his protégés, or travelling in Europe sometimes for months. Occasionally, he took Jennie with him, but not often. She once sent a telegram to a Chicago newspaper, which read, "Do you know where my husband, Tom W. Eck, manager of bicyclists is? He has been missing for nearly two weeks."[6] Reporters were immediately dispatched to find him, but it was a week before the mystery was solved. Tom had secretly sailed abroad to sign up racers in London, Paris, and Brussels, and then bring them back to compete on the eastern US and Canadian cycle racing circuit. "I came here," admitted Tom in Paris, "so no one would get ahead of me in developing my business ideas … I did not tell even my wife."[7] There are also indications that Tom, despite his many business interests, was probably not a good provider for his family. By 1900 he claimed to have earned over two hundred thousand dollars (almost six million dollars today) in his time, but unfortunately had none of it left. Judiciously invested, the money could have made him a millionaire.[8] Jennie finally had enough and again she sued for divorce, this time on the grounds of desertion. In October 1901 she claimed that on 29 July 1900, Tom had deserted her at Sault Ste Marie, Ontario, and had not lived with her since then.[9]

E.2 Tom Eck with Canadian marathon runner Tom Longboat in New York, December 1908 (Library of Congress)

It is not known what happened to Jennie Carlisle Eck, although in 1910 she and Irene were still living with her parents (now in their seventies) in Minneapolis and Jennie was working as an insurance agent. Her daughter, Irene, then twenty-two, was married on 16 October 1911 to Roy H. Withian. Both Jennie's parents were still alive in 1920, but she was no longer living with them, although her daughter, son-in-law, and their two children resided in Minneapolis.

Over the years Eck trained and managed many male athletes in a variety of sports, but he also took an interest in a number of female athletes. Mostly he treated them with care and respect, and trained them in the same way he would male athletes. He was often called "Beauty Eck" in the newspapers, a reference to his handsome appearance and attraction to younger women, but there were no reports of sexual scandal. If there were, perhaps they were simply not reported. He and Louise Armaindo were thought to be husband and wife because in those days it was the only way they could travel together without inviting gossip. Louise was much more "one of the guys" than she was ever Tom's "wife," and more importantly, they were never married. For much of Louise's career, he was her manager, trainer, and likely confidant. No doubt she was as stubborn and determined as he was, but they were a good team.

Nonetheless, there was an aspect to Eck's appreciation for female athletic talent that was unsettling. He soon learned that he could make money through them. This was certainly true with Louise, and their partnership might not have lasted for so long if this were not the case. When he took several female racers to England in the fall of 1889, he probably didn't make any money, but his purpose was to demonstrate that female athletes could draw crowds and be admired for their athletic prowess. Similarly, as the originator of six-day bicycle races, Eck understood that having women compete was a novelty, especially in the days of the high wheel.

Lottie Brandon, a nineteen-year-old Canadian based in Brooklyn, joined Eck's Motor Cycle Whirl in 1902, as the only female racer. Motor-paced racing involved motorized and safety bicycles together on a small, specially built track, whereby the pace motor created a draft for the tailgating cyclist, who could reach speeds of forty to fifty miles per hour. Brandon, one of the best track and road racers in the country, held every woman's record from a quarter mile to a hundred miles. Billed as the most fearless cyclist in the world, Eck took her out onto the vaudeville circuit where she performed a tricky and popular bicycle stunt, the loop-the-loop speciality.[10] Her daring stunts along with a trim, well-knit figure and attractive appearance made her a star in both North America and Europe.

Early in 1911 Eck came up with yet another scheme involving attractive young women on bicycles. "Tom Eck's Racing Bicycle Girls" appeared in theatres and auditoriums all over the country. They were mounted on home trainers (stationary bicycles) equipped with a large dial to show the distance travelled. Challenges were issued to any fast riders – almost always male – to compete against the girls. In a five-mile race, for example, local racers rode one mile each, while Eck's racer rode the entire five miles without stopping. If they beat the girls, they could win twenty-five dollars.

Among Eck's racing girls was Jessie Stalter, billed as the "champion of the world."[11] Where Tom and Jessie met is not clear, but unbeknownst to most everyone, they were a married couple. The 1910 United States federal census shows that Thomas Eck (age fifty-four) and Jessie L. Eck (age nineteen) were living in Acquackanonk, Passaic, New Jersey, with Jessie's mother, Estella Stalter, along with Jessie's younger brothers Edward and Louis.[12] The census data indicate they had been married for two years.[13] Eck's praise of Jessie was effusive: "I never had a fighter who would train so faithfully as little Jessie Stalter for her cycle races. She is without a doubt the greatest piece of human machinery ever seen on a wheel, and that is saying something for me."[14]

In 1915 Tom and Jessie moved to Chicago because he was appointed trainer and assistant to Coach Amos Alonzo Stagg at the University of Chicago with the primary responsibility for developing track runners. Eck lived in Chicago for the remainder of his life, and his kindly personality, cheerful humour, and inexhaustible supply of stories made him one of the best-known campus characters.[15] After a series of strokes, he died at seventy on 6 June 1926, and was buried in Chicago's Oak Woods Cemetery. One obituary said that he was survived by his wife and two daughters, but there is no evidence that he had children with Jessie Stalter. Just like his first wife, what happened to Jessie after Eck's death is not known.

What became of Louise Armaindo? Otherwise known as Louise Brisebois, she left this world much the same way she came into it – mysteriously. She was last sighted as a patient in the Buffalo General Hospital when the United States federal census was taken on 1 June 1900.[16] Her ongoing hospitalization was probably related to the serious injuries she suffered in the hotel fire in November 1896. There is also some interesting and confusing information on the census form. Her birthdate, for example, was stated as October 1869, which would make her thirty years old, much younger than was actually the case, but consistent with arguments she presented in the legal case related to the fire that her racing career, and therefore future earnings, had been severely curtailed. If, as I have argued, she was born in October 1857, she would be forty-two years old. She also indicated that she had been married for eight years;

if indeed she was still married to Norman Stewart, it would have been for a little more than twelve years. More importantly, she considered herself married, not single.[17] Finally, she stated the year she immigrated to the United States as 1882, when she was definitely in Chicago by the spring of 1879, and possibly a couple of years earlier. Perhaps she simply didn't remember back that far. One item on the census form that seems entirely accurate is that she had no children.

In a summer 1903 issue of New York's *Police Gazette*, someone wrote in asking if the editors could supply an address for Madame Louise Armaindo, the ex-champion lady bicyclist. The *Gazette*'s response was that they had not heard from her for many years.[18] No one seemed to be aware that Louise had passed away in Montreal on 2 September 1900, possibly due to her lingering injuries. However, it remains a mystery as to how she got from Buffalo, where she was last seen in June, to Montreal if she was incapacitated. On the burial certificate, she is listed as Louise Brisebois *épouse de* (spouse of) Norman Stuart, but her husband Norman Stewart (his name misspelled on the certificate) was nowhere near Montreal in early September 1900.[19] Her age was stated as forty-two, which aligns with the argument presented in the first chapter that she was born on 12 October 1857.

The burial record clearly indicates that Louise was laid to rest in the only cemetery associated with the Notre-Dame Basilica in Montreal at the time, that being Notre-Dame-des-Neiges. However, no amount of searching has located her gravesite, and it is quite possible there never was one. A study of gravestones missing from the cemetery showed that the persons least likely to have been commemorated in the late nineteenth century were young, female, of lower status, Catholic, and French Canadian.[20] These criteria certainly fit Louise. If she was buried in another cemetery in the Montreal area, and the information not corrected in the church register, it would be nearly impossible to locate her grave. Finally, who might have been at her burial? Aside from her husband Norman, who was definitely not there, then possibly her sister Hélène or a brother, or perhaps even her elderly father, who was still alive at this time. We shall likely never know.[21]

LOUISE ARMAINDO: PERTAINING TO HER BACKGROUND

More detailed information is provided here to support the claim, argued in chapter 1, that Louise Armaindo was in reality Marie Louise Brisebois, born in 1857 to Charles Brisebois and Hélène Brunet in Ste-Anne-de-Bellevue, Quebec, Canada.[1] At the same time, others with a similar name were explored, but explanations why they have been eliminated from consideration are also offered here. Regardless, they are all descended from René Dubois dit Brisebois, a French habitant who settled in Quebec around 1658. Among the seven or eight generations following Dubois, there are many descendants named Louise Brisebois and all of them are related mostly as sixth cousins once or twice removed. Almost all can be dismissed because they died too young or were married in Quebec. We know that the Louise Brisebois who became Louise Armaindo married Norman Stewart (using the name Louisa Brisbois) in the United States in 1888 and that she died in 1900 at age forty-two in Montreal. Therefore, our interest is in those born around 1860 – the only published date of Armaindo's birth – with the name Louise or Louisa Brisebois.[2] Some were not considered at all because they were born five years before or after 1860, or in a location too far away from Ste-Anne-de-Bellevue.

Let's begin with a Louisa Brisebois, who was born illegitimate on 3 December 1859 in Ste-Geneviève, Pierrefonds, located east of Ste-Anne-de Bellevue on Montreal Island. She was baptized the next day with god-parents Augustin Brisebois and Marie Josephte Boileau.[3] Possibly, this Louisa was the daughter of Melodie Brisebois, born in 1842 to the same

Augustin Brisebois. According to the 1861 Canada Census, Louisa Brise-
bois was living with Augustin, his second wife, Esther, and their daughter
Melodie. Also in 1861, Melodie married her cousin François Xavier
Brisebois, and by 1871, Louisa, now eleven, was living with them in Pier-
refonds. However, she died two years later and was buried in the Ste-
Genevieve cemetery in Pierrefonds.[4]

Another option is Louise Adeline Brisebois, born in 1858 to Eustache
Brisebois and Philomène Pilon in the Ste-Michel parish in Vaudreuil-
Soulanges.[5] However, like so many of the others, she died far too young
on 22 October 1879 in Montreal. She was twenty-one years old.[6]

Gilles Janson, a Quebec sport historian, maintains that Louise Armaindo was born on 18 August 1863 in Saint-Clet, also in the county
of Vaudreuil-Soulanges.[7] Saint-Clet is located about thirty kilometres
west of Ste-Anne-de-Bellevue. According to Janson, her birth name
was Aglaé Brisebois, and she was the daughter of Moïse Brisebois and
Adeline Charlebois.[8] Moïse Brisebois just happens to be the brother of
Melodie Brisebois discussed above. The full name of Aglaé's mother's
was Marie Aglaé Adeline Charlebois, and although this Louise was
given her mother's name at birth, she appears as Eloise or Louise in census documents. In 1871 the family – Moïse and Adeline with children
Samuel, Léon, Godfrey, Emilie, Henry, Eloise, Adile, and Joseph – were
living in Saint-Clet.[9] Eloise or Louise was seven years old. By 1881 seventeen-year-old Louise was still living at home in Saint-Clet with her
siblings and now widowed mother.[10] The widow Brisebois appeared
in the 1882–83 *Montreal City Directory* as Mrs A. Brisebois, widow of
Moïse. Unfortunately, her daughter Louise died just shy of her twenty-
second birthday and was buried on 21 June 1885 in all likelihood in
the Notre-Dame-des-Neiges Cemetery located in the parish of Notre
Dame in Montreal.[11] Therefore, this particular Louise cannot possibly
be Louise Armaindo.

I come back to my original contention that Louise Brisbois/Armaindo,
born in 1857 in Ste-Anne-de-Bellevue, was the first child of Charles and
Hélène Brisebois. Charles, born in 1830, was a fourth-generation descendant of Jean-Baptiste, a son of René Dubois dit Brisebois. Louise's
younger sister Hélène was born in 1859, and a brother Joseph in 1864,
but he lived for only two years. More tragically, their mother died in

1867. Charles was soon married again to Julia Brennan with whom he had four sons, half-brothers to Louise and Hélène.[12] If we start with this information, has it been possible to trace any of Louise's descendants? Let's begin with her sister Hélène. Their father, Charles, was primarily a farmer, but also somewhat of an entrepreneur in that he conducted his own business affairs and, as it turns out, those of his daughters. For example, Hélène became involved in the real estate business. In 1881, at age twenty-two, she was still living in the family home in Ste-Anne-de-Bellevue but, by January 1882, had moved to Chicago and was using her father as a proxy to buy and sell property back home. Although Chicago was never Louise Armaindo's permanent home, she had used it as a base in late 1881 in order to learn how to ride the high wheel. From then on she travelled extensively wherever racing engagements took her, and she never established a permanent base. Hélène continued to reside in Chicago, and may have married a man by the name of James Harrisson, but unfortunately she cannot be traced beyond 1892. What is also worrying is that there is no evidence that Louise ever mentioned a sister.[13] She did, however, mention a brother and, as time went on, her elderly father.[14]

As discussed in chapter 7, Louise Armaindo – Mrs Norman Stewart – did not have an easy married life. Less than a year after the marriage, with growing concerns that Norman did not appear to work for a living, there was a report that Louise had lost all the money she had accumulated before marriage. Apparently, she had the foresight to purchase a couple of houses in Montreal held by her father in safekeeping.[15] Notary records in Quebec between 1888 and 1900 show evidence of transactions among Charles Brisebois (Louise's father) and a couple of her half-brothers, but there is no evidence directly linking any property in Montreal to Louise herself. Indeed, the properties held for Louise may have been in Ste-Anne-de-Bellevue. News reports about Louise often mentioned that she came from Montreal, even just Quebec or Canada, and rarely the small village of Ste-Anne-de-Bellevue.

What do we know about Louise's half-brothers? Charles, the oldest, became an employee of the Grand Trunk Railway, and eventually moved from Ste-Anne-de-Bellevue. He and his wife, Albina Portelance, buried two infant sons, but eventually their family was comprised of two sons and two daughters. By 1911 the family was living in Alfred, Ontario, al-though it has been impossible to trace them further.[16] Nothing much is known about William Brisebois, other than in 1901, at age thirty, he was still living with his parents in Ste-Anne-de-Bellevue.[17] He cannot be found in either the 1911 or 1921 census. In 1899 Samuel Brisebois, age twenty-eight, married Adele Lavigne, a much older woman from Ste-Anne-de-Bellevue and a widow with three children. He disappeared after the 1901 census.[18] Finally, Ferdinand Brisebois, born in 1875, married Exerine Lauzon in 1899, and eventually had six children. By 1921 Ferdinand had died and Exerine had married Charles Lalonde and the family be-came a blended one.[19] Each of Ferdinand and Exerine's children has passed away, and although many of their descendants are still alive, no attempt has been made to contact them simply because in all likelihood they know nothing about a long-lost cousin, far removed, named Louise Brisebois/Armaindo.

As pointed out in chapter 1, what has been presented about Louise's origins is speculative. However, based on the bits and pieces we know about Louise's background, and eliminating from consideration many others called Louise Brisebois, it is possible that the family outlined here is the correct one. Nonetheless, we will never know for certain until a relative or descendant comes forward with irrefutable evidence of Louise Armaindo's true origins.

"Louise Viellard Sainte-Foix": A Story by Elia W. Peattie

Elia Wilkinson Peattie (1862–1935) was an American journalist, novelist, poet, short story writer, and playwright. At the time she wrote this story, she was living in Omaha, Nebraska, where she and her husband worked for the Omaha Herald.[1] *Peattie was likely the reporter who interviewed Louise Armaindo in Omaha in January 1889.[2] Although the story is a thinly disguised fictional representation of Louise and her husband, Norman Stewart (whom she called Charlie), it authentically captures her life. The ending, however, is entirely fictional.*

The grandfather of Louise Viellard Sainte-Foix had been an officer in the army of Napoleon I. Her father was a Canadian farmer, more renowned for his feats of strength than for his farming. Her mother was a woman whom Louise could never revere too deeply.

"My mother," she used to say, in the midst of those brilliant days when she was making more money than any other woman in the United States, "was the best and the noblest woman in the world. I have seen her lift 900 pounds in one hand." If this motherly quality failed to impress the listener, Louise would straighten her agile shoulders, and cry in shrill patois:

"She was even greater than that! She could throw a grown man over her shoulder. There was a mother for you! Which of you has such another?"

The world is a curious thing. It appears to have no actual qualities. It is only what each person imagines it to be. It is as changeable as the mirage in that mysterious California valley where none may live and keep their reason.

To the scholar, the world consists of books. The epochs of the past are made by writers. To the scientist the whole universe is but an oyster that he must open; a tailor thinks of it as a place where men live to be clothed. The affectional child-bearing woman finds nothing in it that the adventuress would recognize; and the clergyman and the clown may live within two doors of each other and never have a thought in common – beyond the universal animal impulses.

Louise Vieillard Sainte-Foix took a not undignified view of the world. She believed it to consist of force. She was nearer right, perhaps, than any of the rest. She gaged the importance of each person by the physical force that he or she possessed. As a baby, she had been the marvel of all the mothers in the hamlet. At an age when other children lie upon their backs, softly pillowed, Louise was sitting up, with her head fairly well balanced between her strong shoulders. The games she enjoyed, as she grew older, were not the womanly ones of housekeeping and doll tending, such as her playmates indulged in. They were games in which skill and strength were required. She was of no use whatever to her mother. If she was made to wash the dishes, she was sure to break several in the process. Everything that she touched, she broke or tore by her wanton exhibition of strength. Her only ambition seemed to be to discover something that could resist her. To find such a thing pleased her well, and she would set herself with renewed industry to the development of her young muscles.

When she had reached the age of sixteen she was full-grown, and even her father no longer found it possible to throw her. She could dive almost as well as her brother, who soon after left home to profit by his abilities, and who has since become noted for his feats under water. But there is no need to advertise the accomplishment of Jacques Sainte-Foix. What he can do is known to everyone.

So idle and so ill-natured was Louise that her mother no longer essayed to keep her in the house, or to teach her any of the things that women are supposed to know. Even the offer of finery could not tempt her to take to feminine occupations, for Louise was vain of nothing but her ability to throw quoits, to run and jump, to wrestle and swing clubs.

One night the amber lights faded from the St Lawrence, and the night closed in without bringing Louise home. When morning came she was still absent. Before a week had passed, her not very anxious parents learned that she was at a gymnasium at Montreal. When they heard a little later that she had left there, they still did not worry.

"If Louise cannot take care of herself there is no one that can," the mother would say to her neighbors. To tell the truth, there was plenty to worry about at home. The farm was heavily encumbered. M. Sainte-Foix became ill with what the doctors termed a decay of muscular force. It was the result of having once been very strong. Mme. Sainte Foix, therefore, preferred to worry about matters at home. Louise had never been much of a daughter, anyhow. The mother was quite unconscious of the pride that Louise felt in her, and would not have understood it had she known of it. Nothing was heard from Jacques, who might perhaps have helped them had he known of their distresses. But one day a letter came from Louise. It contained more money than the good farmer folk had ever made in any five years of their life. With it came the information that she was in Boston, walking. Monsieur could not be made to understand how walking could earn a sum like that for one. He was a simple old man, and Louise's statement that she had won first money puzzled him. Both father and mother had some doubts as to the truth of the assertion, and they even went so far as to wonder if the money had not been obtained by regrettable means.

But they kept it.

As time went on these letters became frequent, and they always contained money. Almost everyone was sent from a different city. M. and Mme. Sainte-Foix never had any thought of replying to them. True, there may have been some excuse for them in the fact that they could not write – at least, not much. But they boasted a good deal of the wealth of their daughter, whom they imagined to be living in magnificence.

Now, the truth about Louise was – but it is a long story, and cannot be told in a sentence. To begin with, she was never called Louise. She

was always called Miss Vieillard. Indeed, so famous had she become
that the bills that announced her performances, termed her simply Vieillard. It is only the great that are allowed to go without titles. Vieillard
was not alone distinguished as a pedestrienne. She had a national reputation as a lifter of heavy weights, and she had beaten the record in
roller-skating. This latter distinction, however, she always apologized
for. She was ashamed of it. She preferred to do something in which her
wonderful endurance could be shown. That was why she took to bicy-
cle-riding; and she may be said to have invented the six-day race.

When, half-fainting, sore, hungry, and dazed, Vieillard was carried at
10 o'clock from her saddle after hard riding for eight hours, she was hap-
piest. To lie there and be rubbed down by her serving maid, while the
plaudits of the arena rung in her ears, was delicious. What if there were
throbs of pain that made her leap spasmodically into the air? What if
the night was feverish? What if the next morning brought a renewal of
anguish? Did it not also bring fresh glory? To walk down the street and
hear one well-known sport say to another:

"There goes a woman who has broken the record," was a delight
that thrilled. The boys showed no jealousy. For one thing, it was
worthwhile to be the friend of Vieillard. No professional in the country
made more money, and of all those prodigal people, she was the most
prodigal. Though she never wore diamonds herself, she dispensed
them with princely freedom. True, there were times when she was entirely out of money, almost ragged and not very sure of her dinner.
But these times were soon forgotten, and the next money was spent
with the same recklessness.

So the years passed on. The clean bicycle track, the arena of faces,
mistily swimming before the eye, the blue tights, with their trimmings of
gold; the rollicking friends, the thirst for victory, were the components
of Vieillard's life. To be sure, her temper was still bad when she was
vexed; but, on the other hand, her fierce friendship was well worth having. Animals, as well as men, felt her powerful magnetism. When, for a
time, she led a precarious existence in the trapeze of the Great National
Exposition, she made friends with the most ferocious beasts in the

menagerie. They told a story to the effect that one night when she was suffering with neuralgia, she took a lion's whelp and held it to her aching face for warmth.

One day, at the beginning of a great race, Vieillard entered the ring of the racing Coliseum jauntily, and met her fate. The boys – otherwise her competitors – stood together talking. With them was a lad five years younger than Vieillard. For it is unnecessary to say that a long period of years had passed, and that it was now fifteen years since Louise had hurried away from the little French hamlet toward Montreal. The young man had an infantile face and the muscles of a girl. The bow with which he acknowledged his introduction to Vieillard had in it a touch of courtliness that was entirely new to the bicyclist. That day, as she spun around the track, dearer to her than the pleasant cry of "Tally Vieillard," was the applause of the pale young man, whom she watched out of the corner of her eye.

When the afternoon and evening had passed, and the attendants had lifted Vieillard from her saddle and carried her to her room, she found a bunch of roses awaiting her. To them was attached the card of Charles Stuart. It was a bewildering moment for Louise. Never before had any one seen fit to pay her a compliment of the sort. The heart of Louise had never been touched before. No one indeed had ever suspected her of having any sentimentality. She had simply been considered one of the fellows. To arouse the affections of a woman like Vieillard is no light matter. The man who had had the temerity to do it soon learned that. In a month Vieillard was wearing a ring on her finger and Charlie Stuart admitted that he was married. Louise made light of the affair.

"What good is Charlie?" she would say to her friends in broken English, and with deprecating accents, "I shall have to feed him!" But she was secretly puffed up with pride. To have Charlie take her out for a walk, clad in the new fur-lined overcoat she had purchased him, swinging a natty cane, and bestowing a few careless words upon her between the puffs of his cigar, was a happiness such as she had never known. She kept him in perfumes, in the daintiest gloves, and in wines. Her friends warned her that she was working too hard.

"Another year like the present one, and you will be laid out, Louise, old girl," said one of her fellow-sportsmen. But the truth was that Charlie was an expensive luxury.

"My husband," she said to a reporter, "is a gentleman. He is of the house of Stuart. You know the record of the Stuarts of Scotland!"

At another time she said:

"Parnell of England is the uncle of my Charlie."

As for Charlie, he really believed that he had married the most brilliant and delightful woman in the world. He was never tired of talking about her fascinations.

"I have seen that woman," he would say, "thrown from her saddle against a brick wall. I have seen her stagger up, get into her saddle, with the blood running from her mouth and a cut in her head, and win the race. Another time I saw her thrown seven feet from a gallery. She hit on her head and got up bleeding. I kept my eye on the time-piece, and in four seconds she had got up the stairs and in her saddle. Another time that girl kept on her wheel eighteen hours. She never got off one minute. I gave her some milk and bread now and then running alongside. We bagged $1,000 that time, and had the satisfaction of breaking the record in the bargain." Louise had trouble in keeping trained down to racing condition as she neared thirty. A race caused her much more suffering on that account. But though she might lie weeping in bed, the sound of Charlie's voice in the adjoining room, as he related these adventures, would cause a flattered smile to break over her face.

They traveled together from New York to Denver, and from Minneapolis to New Orleans. The endurance of the woman was wonderful. Never before had anyone been known to run so many races in so short a space of time. But she made no complaints. If she could keep Charlie in money she was satisfied. She never confessed to herself what others saw, and what she must have realized, that Charlie carefully avoided spending any more time with her than he could help, and that, though he accompanied her cheerfully enough on all her travels, it was more to have the excitement of the sporting atmosphere than to share in his wife's company. Charlie had heard anecdotes about her temper that warned him that it was best for him to be amiable, and he showed a docility that was lamblike.

They were at Louisville when Vieillard discovered that Charlie of the house of Stuart was spending the money she gave him in some mysterious way. Elegant as were his clothes, choice as were his wines, flashing as were his jewels, they could not account for his reckless expenditure.

She overheard a jest that put her on the right track.

That night, when the race was well under way, she feigned a sudden sickness and left the ring. Charlie was nowhere to be seen. She dressed hastily and went out on the street. The fact that 2,000 people were waiting for her return made no difference. She had forgotten all about them. As she walked along the street leading from the building where the racing was, she heard a voice she knew. It had a different accent than she was accustomed to, but she knew it only too well. It was Charlie's.

He was walking along slowly, his arm linked in that of a young girl, his head bent over her, his voice full of affectionate insinuation. The girl was slight and graceful, and she was dressed with that attractive bastard elegance that holds the eye in the way that all good imitations do. Vieillard gave a downward glance at her own outlandish dress. She had taken to wearing gay dresses of silk and plush lately, thinking that she would be a better mate for Charlie, so attired. But she was conscious now of the fact that she did not wear them well. A light snow was beginning to fall and Vieillard felt an angry impatience with it for hiding the couple before her from her sight. She could only see them dimly, but she felt that she must follow them till she found their destination. Just as they were turning into a dark quiet house, at the end of a by-street, Vieillard recollected the waiting crowd she had left behind her. Till this moment she had been borne along by such a mad and unreasoning rage that she had thought of nothing but the cause of her fury. Now a sort of despair settled down upon her with a terrible leaden coldness. She almost fell there in the snow from sheer sickness of heart. In all her intrepid life she had never felt anything like it. But it was this sensation that brought back her sanity and caused her to remember the waiting crowd. She ran back to the building wildly, unbuttoning her cloak as she went. In a few moments her racing costume was on again and she was back in the arena. The audience gave a cheering shout. They supposed that she had forced herself to appear after succumbing to temporary exhaustion. She had been gone nearly an hour, and her competitors had distanced her beyond all recovery. But she rejoiced in the spur that her disadvantage gave her. She leaped to her seat with frenzied impatience. Then with head bent nearly to the handle, muscles tense, eyes staring, she drove the wheel around the track with a velocity that amazed and almost dismayed the spectators. Her competitors fell behind her pace, and the building shook with applause.

When at last it was over, the spectators expected to see her drop from her seat. But she got off alone and looked around. Charlie, true to his policy of devotion, was waiting to help her to her room. She nodded a good-night to the boys and went out with him. The next morning Charlie had a painful limp which he failed to account for to the satisfaction of her friends. His jaunty air had deserted him, and he looked as if he had seen some terrible sight overnight. Oddly enough, that limp never left him. His fine, gentleman airs gave place to a sullen quiet, and he seldom lifted his eyes from the ground. The day they left Louisville there was a good deal of chat about a curious murder, but even that could not arouse Charlie from his apathy.

A young girl, a stranger in the city, had taken a room in an apartment house, and a week from the time she took it was found dead. She was in her nightgown and lay upon the floor with her neck broken. After a careful examination the coroner gave a curious verdict of death to the effect that she had been thrown after the manner of a wrestler. Nothing was found by which the murderer could be traced. Nothing, in deed, was found in the room which did not belong to the dead girl, except a blue silk garter with a silver clasp – or at least, if this had been hers, she had lost its mate, for the most diligent search failed to reveal it.

All this has nothing to do with Vieillard. She died the next year of quick consumption, caused, the doctors said, by over exertion. And when she died it was found that she had one thing in common with the murdered girl. It was a blue silk garter with a silver clasp.

Notes

INTRODUCTION

1 Jack Kofoed, "Thrills in Sports," *New York Evening Post*, 19 March 1931, 16.

2 Frank G. Menke, "Louise Armaindo One of Greatest Women Athletes," *Boise Idaho Statesman*, 15 August 1922, 6.

3 Menke, *Encyclopedia of Sports*. Menke published revised and expanded versions of his book until 1953, and it continued to be updated after his death in 1954. The sixth revised edition was published in 1978.

4 "Greatest Woman Athlete," *Philadelphia Inquirer*, 4 April 1938, 15.

5 For example, the chapter about Louise Armaindo in Marthaler, *À tire-d'elles* (2016) is based almost entirely on inaccurate information found on a website called *Le petit braquet* (http://www.lepetitbraquet.fr/chron70_louise_armaindo.html).

6 Massicotte, *Athlètes Canadiens-Français*, 209–15.

7 Janson, *Dictionnaire des grands oubliés du sport*.

8 Hall, *Immodest and Sensational*, 12; Hall, *Girl and the Game*, 21–3. See also Macy, *Wheels of Change*, 58–67.

9 Ritchie, *Quest for Speed*, 124.

10 Smith, *Social History of the Bicycle*.

11 Representations of all twenty-five advertising cards can be found in Ben Crane, "Bicycles and Trick Riders," accessed 13 January 2018, http://www.tradecards.com/articles/tr/.

12 Park, "Contesting the Norm."

13 For more on female baseball, see Shattuck, *Bloomer Girls*.

14 See Todd, "Bring on the Amazons"; and Chapman and Vertinsky, *Venus with Biceps*, for more about female strongwomen. About women's boxing, see Smith, *History of Women's Boxing*; Gems and Pfister, "Women Boxers"; and Pfister and Gems, "Shady Past."

15 Adams and Keene, *Women of the American Circus*, 16.

16 See, for example, Algeo, *Pedestrianism*; Sears, *Running through the Ages*; and Hall, *Pedestriennes*.

17 See Hadland and Lessing, *Bicycle Design*, 1–36; Herlihy, *Bicycle*, 15–52.

18 Hadland and Lessing, *Bicycle Design*, 37–71; Herlihy, *Bicycle*, 75–126; Gant and Hoffman, *Wheel Fever*, 1–24.

19 Goddard, *Velocipede*, 859. See also Herlihy, *Bicycle*, 138–9.

20 Bottomley, *Velocipede*, 77.

21 Norcliffe, *Ride to Modernity*, 29–31; Humber, *Freewheeling*, 27–33.

22 "Notes and Comments," *Toronto Globe*, 25 March 1869, 2.

23 "Notes and Comments," *Toronto Globe*, 17 April 1869, 2.

24 "Courses de Vélocipèdes (Dames)," *Le Monde illustré*, 21 November 1868, 327.

25 "Velocipede Race in Paris—Sunday Afternoon," *Harper's Weekly*, 19 December 1868, 812.

26 Jacques, *Manuel du vélocipède*, 93–4. For an interesting discussion about the velocipede and women's attire in the 1860s, see Cohn, "Wheelwomen," 54–78.

27 For more about early women velocipedists racing in France, see Dauncey, *French Cycling*, 34–42; and Kobayashi, *Histoire du vélocipède*, 267–9, 292–308, 381.

28 "A Velocipede Race at Jersey City," *New York Times*, 2 May 1869, 8.

29 "The Furore. The Velocipede Fever Increases – A Lady in the Bicycle Saddle," *Boston Post*, 11 March 1869, 3.

30 See reports in the *Daily Milwaukee News*, 16–25 April 1869.

31 See, for example, Mackintosh and Norcliffe, "Men, Women and the Bicycle."

32 Pratt, *American Bicycler*, 31.

33 Norcliffe, *Ride to Modernity*, 190. See also Norcliffe, "Associations, Modernity and the Insider-Citizens of a Victorian Highwheel Bicycle Club"; Kossuth and Wamsley, "Cycles of Manhood."

34 Guroff, *Mechanical Horse*, 35. Francis Willard, suffragist, educator, and temperance advocate, wrote a delightful little book, *A Wheel within a Wheel*, about learning to ride a safety bicycle, and why other women should do the same. She mentioned Bertha von Hillern, claiming she gave exhibitions of her skill in riding a bicycle, probably around 1880. At the time, this could only have been a high wheel, and although there is some evidence that von Hillern rode the machine, there is no indication she raced one. What is interesting is that Willard claims that von Hillern was "thought by some to be a sort of semi-monster," and she herself would "certainly have felt compromised . . . by going to see her ride" (see Willard, *Wheel*, 13).

35 Norcliffe, *Ride to Modernity*, 270n19.

36 Oddy, "Bicycles," 60.

37 Wilcox, "The Bicycle, and Riding It," 628–9.

38 See Herlihy, *Bicycle*, 215–16 for a description and photo of this complicated design.

39 Hallenbeck, *Claiming the Bicycle*, 152.

40 Williams, *Contemporary History of Women's Sport*, 24.

41 Ritchie, "League of American Wheelmen," 12.

42 Finison, *Boston's Cycling Craze*, 106.

43 Ritchie, "League of American Wheelmen," 12.

44 According to cycling historian Andrew Ritchie, the LAW, which became the League of American Bicyclists, did not formally repeal the coloured ban until 1999.

45 See Finison, *Boston's Cycling Craze*, especially 5–42, for a thorough description and analysis of the Kittie Knox incident.

46 For more about Taylor and his remarkable struggle, see Ritchie, *Major Taylor*; and Balf, *Major*.

47 The appellation comes from Claude Marthaler's chapter (35–9) about Louise Armaindo in *À tire-d'elles*.

CHAPTER ONE

1 According to the *Historic Pennsylvania and New Jersey, Church and Town Records, 1708–1985*, the marriage took place on 21 April 1888 in Camden, New Jersey, in the Union Methodist Episcopal Church.

2 To date I have found only four newspaper interviews that Louise had given between 1879 and 1900: "Limber Legs," *Sedalia (MO) Weekly Bazoo*, 7 October 1879; "Louisa and Her Legs," *Milwaukee Daily Journal*, 21 June 1883; "Louise Armaindo," *San Antonio Light*, 10 February 1885, 1; "Athletic Louise Armaindo," *Omaha Herald*, 11 January 1889, 5.

3 "Mlle. Louise Armaindo," *New York Clipper*, 8 September 1883, 402. With some updating, this article appeared again as "The Champion Bicyclists," *National Police Gazette*, 10 May 1884, 6. It also appeared in the *Springfield Wheeler's Gazette*, February 1885, 151.

4 "The Bicycle Contest," *Chicago Inter Ocean*, 25 May 1883, 6.

5 See appendix 1 for further information about Louise Armaindo's background.

6 "Radfahren," *Allgemeine Sport-Zeitung*, 12 December 1886, 989: "Nache dem Tode ihrer Mütter verliess Louise Canada und ging nach Chicago in eine Mädchenschule." After the death of her mother, Louise left Canada and went to a girls' school in Chicago.

7 "Athletic Louise Armaindo," *Omaha Herald*, 11 January 1889, 5.

8 "Epse Stuart Louise Brisebois," in *Quebec, Canada, Vital and Church Records (Drouin Collection), 1621–1968*.

9 *Quebec, Vital and Church Records (Drouin Collection), 1621–1967*, Ste-Anne-de-Bellevue, Ste-Anne, 1847–1862, 135.

10 Library and Archives Canada, *Census Returns for 1861*, roll C-1285-1286.

11 Library and Archives Canada, *Census of Canada*, 1871, roll C-10051, family no. 176, p. 46.

12 "The Pedestrian Craze," *Chicago Inter Ocean*, 19 March 1879, 8.

13 Brady, *Showman*, 227.

14 For more about Joseph Montferrand, see Goyer and Hamelin, "Montferrand"; Monteiro, "Histoire de Montferrand"; and Finnigan, "Joseph Montferrand."

15 "Athletic Louise Armaindo," *Omaha Herald*, 11 January 1889, 5.

16 Miller, *City of the Century*, 188.

17 McQuillan, "French-Canadian Communities"; Charles Balesi, "French and French Canadians," *Encyclopedia of Chicago*, accessed 30 January 2018, http://www.encyclopedia.chicagohistory.org/pages/488.html.

18 U.S. Bureau of Census, *Historical Statistics*, 134.

19 Meyerowitz, *Women Adrift*, xix, 145n3.

20 U.S. Bureau of the Census, *Statistics of Women at Work*, 39.

21 For an interesting discussion of early iron jaw circus performers, see Tait, *Circus Bodies*, 40–8.

22 Slout, *Olympians of the Sawdust Circle*, 75.

23 "Barnum's Bonanza," *St. Louis Post-Dispatch*, 22 August 1877, 4.

24 Tait, *Circus Bodies*, 38.

25 Brady, *Showman*, 227.

26 "Limber Legs," *Sedalia (MO) Weekly Bazoo*, 7 October 1879, n.p.

27 Willoughby, *Super-Athletes*, 577.

28 "Racing at Madison Square Garden," *New York Tribune*, 13 February 1889, 2.

29 Information about the Chicago Athenæum comes from Andreas, *History of Chicago*, 3:416–17; also from "The Atheneum," *Chicago Inter Ocean*, 23 March 1878, 8.

30 For a description of how pedestrianism worked as a sport, see Vincent, *Mudville's Revenge*, 30–57.

31 See various reports: "Here's Fun," *Chicago Sunday Times*, 30 January 1876, 10; "Tramp, Tramp, Tramp," *Chicago Inter Ocean*, 3 February 1876, 8; "Nony a Weary Foot," *Chicago Inter Ocean*, 4 February 1876; "Nearing the Goal," *Chicago Inter Ocean*, 5 February 1876, 12; "Track and Turf," *Chicago Sunday Times*, 6 February 1876, 3; "Tired-Out Trampers," *Chicago Inter Ocean*, 7 February 1876, 7; "Those Female Walkists," *Chicago Inter Ocean*, 10 February 1876, 3.

32 See "City Brevities," *Chicago Inter Ocean*, 15 March 1876, 8; "Those Suffering Pedestrians," *Chicago Inter Ocean*, 16 March 1876, 2; "City Brevities," *Chicago Inter Ocean*, 17 March 1876, 5; "City Brevities," *Chicago Inter Ocean*, 21 March 1876, 8.

33 John H. Wallace, *Wallace's Monthly, An Illustrated Magazine Devoted to Domesticated Animal Nature*, vol. 2 (B. Singerly Publisher, 1876): 384, 546, 562.

34 McNulty and Radcliffe, *Canadian Athletics 1839–1992*, 10.

35 *Gazette and Directory of the County of Ontario*, 60.

36 1871, 1881, 1891, and 1901 Census of Canada.

37 *Soundex Index to Naturalization Petitions for the United States District and Circuit Courts, Northern District of Illinois and Immigration and Naturalization Service District 9, 1840–1950*, Microfilm serial M1285, Microfilm roll 49, National Archives and Records Administration, Washington, DC.

38 Around this time, another young Canadian woman, also identified as Louisa Brisbois, was likely prostituting in Chicago and reportedly tried to end her life through several suicide attempts ("City Brevities," *Chicago Inter Ocean*, 8 August 1876, 8; "Mistakes, Morals, and Morphine," *Chicago Inter Ocean*, 13 May 1878, 3). When she was seventeen, this particular Louisa Brisbois gave birth on 31 March 1880 in Chicago to a son fathered by one John St George Sever (Illinois, Cook County Birth Certificates, 1878–1922). Although this Louisa was not Louise Armaindo, it is a strange coincidence.

39 "The Pedestrian Craze," *Chicago Inter Ocean*, 19 March 1879, 8.

40 "Limber Legs," *Sedalia (MO) Weekly Bazoo*, 7 October 1879, n.p. In fact, there are only occasional references to female pedestrian contests in Montreal and Toronto. See Hall, *Girl and the Game*, 19–21.

41 See Algeo, *Pedestrianism* for more information and history.

42 "Six Day Legs," *St. Louis Post-Dispatch*, 4 August 1879, 1.

43 See Kofoed, *Thrills in Sport*, 11–14, who describes in vivid detail a match between Armaindo, Carrie Howard, and Nellie Worrell in St Louis, but does not provide a date. According to him, Louise beat the two pedestriennes by seven miles. See also Frank Menke's account in *Encyclopedia of Sports* mentioning a similar race in St Louis between Armaindo and Carrie Howard of Buffalo and Nellie Warril (*sic*) of Rochester.

44 "Louise Armaindo," *San Antonio Light,* 10 February 1885, 1.

45 "Limber Legs," *Sedalia (MO) Weekly Bazoo*, 7 October 1879, n.p.

46 *Palmyra (MO) Spectator*, 21 November 1879, 1.

47 See reports in *Quincy (IL) Daily Herald* on 15, 21, 25, 27 November and 10, 12, 21 December 1879.

48 *Burlington (IA) Daily Hawk Eye*, 23 December 1879, n.p.

49 "M'lle Armaindo's Walk Last Night – A Challenge," *Springfield Daily Illinois State Register*, 16 May 1880, 4.

50 "Local Intelligence," *Aurora (ON) Banner*, 5 November 1880, n.p.

51 "Pedestrianism," *The Spirit of the Times*, 5 December 1880, 450.

CHAPTER TWO

1 "Elsa Von Blumen," *Wheeling (WV) Register*, 22 January 1880, 4; "Elsa Von Blumen," *Auburn (WV) Bulletin*, 22 February 1887, n.p.; *1870 United States Federal Census*.

2 *US Civil War Pension Index: General Index to Pension Files 1864–1834*, roll #T288_325.

3 "Bert Miller's Career Ended," *Watertown (NY) Times*, 16 February 1892, 2.

4 Others have stated that her real name was Maggie Von Gross, but this is incorrect.

5 "Miss Von Berg's Walk," *Syracuse (NY) Daily Standard*, 23 August 1878.

6 "Beating a Pedestrian," *Oswego (NY) Morning Herald*, 27 March 1879, n.p.

7 "Fashionable Event," *Canton (NY) Daily Repository*, 28 November 1879, n.p.

8 "Walking Match," *Wheeling (WV) Register*, 3 February 1880, 4.

9 "Bertha von Hillern," *Cincinnati Volksfreund*, 26 November 1879, 3.

10 See reports in the *Boston Daily Globe*, 18–27 December 1976.

11 "Bertha Von Hillern," *Washington (DC) Daily Critic*, 14 January 1878, 4.

12 "Miss Bertha Von Hillern; Washington," *Lowell (MA) Daily Citizen and News*, 1 February 1878, 2.

13 For more information, see Todd, *Physical Culture*, 175–208.

14 "The Popular Scientific Lecture on Physical Training and Bertha von Hillern," *Lowell (MA) Daily Citizen and News*, 30 October 1877, 3. For a description of the Butler Health Lift and its importance to women, see Todd, *Physical Culture*, 189–98.

15 For example, see "Bertha von Hillern on Walking," *The Woman's Jour-nal*, 15 April 1882, 118–19; "Bertha von Hillern on Physical Exercise," *Boston Daily Globe*, 1 October 1882, 3. Von Hillern studied with land-scape artist William Hunt in Boston. She and fellow artist Maria Beckett hiked and painted the forests of Virginia's Shenandoah Valley, and eventu-ally bought a summer home in the region. Von Hillern always exercised regularly by walking and hiking out-of-doors, and was a fervent advocate for girls and women to have every opportunity to lead healthier lives. Her art sold well allowing for a life of painting and travel. Around 1890 she met the author and journalist Emma Howard Wright, and they were constant companions until Wright's death in 1935. Bertha von Hillern died in Staunton, Virginia on 19 September 1939 at age eighty-two.

16 Mary Tryphena Curtis Lipsey's background is documented through records available at ancestry.ca. Her son Allen was raised by his grand-parents in Ontario and his surname changed to Curtis. At some point Marshall and Thomas Lipsey were divorced, and in 1880 he married Elizabeth Higgins. Tryphena Lipsey (under her stage name of Mary Marshall) was married again in 1882 to Henry Cortez Hager, who was considerably younger and had also been a pedestrian. In 1900 they were farming in Houghton County, Michigan, and Marshall's son Allen Curtis, now in his twenties, was living with them. Her other son James died early in 1907 at age forty-five. Their mother, Mary T. Hager, died of a stroke on 11 September 1911 at age seventy.

17 "Madame Anderson's Rival," *Washington Post*, 21 January 1879, 1.

18 "Sure of Success," *Washington Post*, 23 January 1879, 1.

19 There are several secondary accounts of Madame Anderson's walk. See, for example, Shaulis, "Pedestriennes, Marathoners, Ultramarathoners"; Shaulis, "Pedestriennes"; Hall, *Pedestriennes*; and Lewis, "Ladies Walked." The best sources are newspaper accounts especially those in the *Brooklyn Daily Eagle* between 16 December 1878 and 17 January 1879. For access, see Brooklyn Public Library, http://bklyn.newspapers.com/.

20 For accounts of the pedestrian craze, see "The Mania for Walking," *New York Times*, 2 February 1879, 2; "Pedestrianism Gone Mad," *New York Times*, 14 February 1879, 5; "Walking in Six Cities," *New York Times*, 16 February 1879, 2; "The Pedestrian Mania Increasing –

Walkers Leaving and Others Beginning," *New York Herald*, 18 February 1879, 5.

21 "May Marshall's Feat," *Washington Post*, 19 February 1879, 1.

22 James, *Practical Training*, 31. Also included were Cora Cushing, Mary Marshall, Fannie Edwards, Bertha von Berg, Fanny Rich, Bella Kilbury, Madame Tobias, and Madame Franklin.

23 "In the Tents," *San Francisco Chronicle*, 20 July 1879, 8.

24 *Quebec, Vital and Church Records (Drouin Collection), 1621–1968*, Basilique Notre-Dame, Montréal, Québec, 1859, 281. I am indebted to Alain Lachapelle for helping sort out Exilda Lachapelle's background; see his article "Marcher pour survivre."

25 "The Great Walk," *Rockford (IL) Daily Register*, 29 June 1878, n.p.

26 See Shaulis, "Enduring a Life of Hardship."

27 In a short article about Exilda Lachapelle in the *New York Clipper* on 29 June 1978 (p. 3), it said that she had been before the public as a pedestrian for four years, but in the United States for eight months. This would mean that she arrived in the United States in October 1877.

28 "Other Sports: Pedestrianism," *Chicago Daily Tribune*, 20 January 1878, 7.

29 "One Hundred Miles," *Madison Democrat*, 16 June 1878, 4.

30 *Rockford (IL) Daily Register*, 30 September 1878, 3.

31 See reports of her walk entitled "Pedestrianism" in the *Chicago Daily Tribune* between 21 January and 23 February 1879.

32 *Chicago Daily Tribune*, 24 February 1879, 4.

33 See Algeo, *Pedestrianism*, especially 185–96.

34 "Walking Matches – Brutal Torture of Women," *Chicago Daily Tribune*, 5 March 1879, 9.

35 "The Walking Torture," *New York Times*, 4 May 1879, 6.

36 "The Woman's Walk," *New York Times*, 14 December 1879, 6.

37 "Walking Matches – Brutal Torture of Women," *Chicago Daily Tribune*, 5 March 1879, 9.

38 See "The Women's Walking Match," *New York Times*, 1 April 1879, 2; "War among the Walkers," *Chicago Inter Ocean*, 8 April 1879, 6; "The Pretty Pedestrians," *National Police Gazette*, 12 April 1879, 11.

39 "The Climax of the Tramp Absurdity," *National Police Gazette*, 12 April 1879, 2.

40 "Walking Notes," *Philadelphia Inquirer*, 29 March 1879, 3.

41 For a lively account of these races and the individuals involved, see Hall, *Pedestriennes*, 167–83.

42 Sears, *Running through the Ages*, 134.

43 "The Women Pedestrians," *New York Times*, 15 December 1879, 8.

44 "Miss Howard Wins Belt," *New York Times*, 21 December 1879, 5.

45 "The Board of Aldermen," *New York Times*, 24 December 1879, 3.

46 Exilda Lachapelle and her husband, William Derose, opened a saloon in San Francisco, while she continued to participate in walking matches primarily against male pedestrians. Their marriage was always difficult, and in 1879 she filed for divorce from Derose on the grounds of cruelty and unfaithfulness. She stuck with him for several more years, but finally, tired of his escapades and philandering, divorced him and returned to Chicago. In 1891 Derose was shot to death by his mistress in a drunken row. In Chicago, Exilda continued to enter walking races against both men and women. She married hotelier Austin R.A. Brice in 1886, and together they had two sons – Reginald in 1889 and Byron in 1894. Fifty years later, they were still married and living in San Antonio, Texas. Less than a year after their fiftieth anniversary, on 9 April 1937, seventy-eight-year-old Exilda Lachapelle Brice succumbed to cancer ("San Antonio Pair Married 50 Years," *San Antonio Express*, 28 November 1936).

47 "The Ladies' Walk," *San Francisco Daily Alta California*, 2 May 1880, 1; "The War of Roses," *San Francisco Chronicle*, 6 May 1880, 3; "Tramp, Tramp, Tramp," *Daily Alta California*, 8 May 1880, 1; "Belt Hunters," *San Francisco Chronicle*, 11 May 1880, 3.

48 Amy Howard's maiden name was Emma Dolan. She was born in Brooklyn in 1862, and married Frank Howard, a pedestrian, in 1878 when she was only sixteen. After her last race in Baltimore in June 1884, she performed comic skits in vaudeville theatres along with her husband and sister. Tragically, she was only twenty-three when she died in childbirth in Brooklyn on 4 October 1885. For more information about her achievements as a pedestrienne, see Sears, *Running through the Ages*, 134–7.

49 Vincent, *Mudville's Revenge*, 53.

CHAPTER THREE

1 "The Lady Contestants," *San Francisco Chronicle*, 8 October 1879, 3.

2 Bertha von Berg, whose real name was Margaret Catherine "Maggie" Gangross, married George Linden Russ in 1878 and eventually had four children. The couple lived for many years in Palestine, Texas, where George worked as a railway conductor. Margaret Russ was sixty-five when she died on 18 March 1923, precisely one hour after the death of her husband ("Wife Expires Hour after Death of Husband," *Dallas Morning News*, 20 March 1923, 7).

3 "Legs and Wheels," *San Francisco Daily Alta California*, 1 December 1879, 1; "Ladies' Bicycle Race," *Bicycling World*, 27 December 1879, 53.

4 "The Female Bicyclist," *Eureka (NV) Daily Sentinel*, 4 May 1880, n.p.

5 "Horse vs Bicycle," *Bicycling World*, 4 September 1880, 365.

6 "Brief Notes," *Sacramento Daily Record-Union*, 9 August 1880, 2.

7 *National Police Gazette*, 16 October 1880, 4.

8 "Personal," *Bicycling World*, 17 December 1880, 88.

9 Herlihy, *Bicycle*, 97–9.

10 "Female Muscle against Horse Flesh," *National Police Gazette*, 28 June 1879, 2.

11 *Madison Wisconsin State Journal*, 20 September 1881, 4. For an interesting interpretation of Elsa von Blumen's races against horses, see also Ritchie, "Seeing the Past."

12 "Elsa von Blumen," *Bicycling World*, 11 November 1881, 11.

13 "Elsa von Blumen," *Bicycling World*, 11 November 1881, 11.

14 "Racing Notes," *Bicycling World*, 18 November 1881, 17.

15 "Atheneum Athletes," *Chicago Inter Ocean*, 21 April 1881, 2.

16 "Editorial Spokes," *Bicycling World*, 2 December 1881, 38.

17 "Chicago," *Bicycling World*, 28 October 1881, 302.

18 "Sporting Matters," *Chicago Inter Ocean*, 24 December 1881, 2.

19 "Elsa von Blumen," *Bicycling World*, 16 December 1881, 65–6.

20 *Bicycling World*, Special Section, 4 May 1883, 9–13. It provides a complete record for 1882 of all races held in the United States and Canada. See also Wells, "Ordinary Women," for accounts of Louise Armaindo's races during this period.

21 "Professional Challenge," *Bicycling World*, 17 February 1882, 178; "Challenge Answered," *Bicycling World*, 24 February 1882, 190; "More Challenges," *Bicycling World*, 31 March 1882, 249; "Prince vs Mlle Armaindo," *Bicycling World*, 14 April 1882, 278.

22 "Bicycling," *Toronto Globe*, 31 March 1882, 8, and 1 April 1882, 16.

23 "The Bicycle Tournament," *Montreal Gazette*, 17 April 1882, 8.

24 "Races," *Bicycling World*, 5 May 1882, 309; "Bicycling in Boston," *Spirit of the Times (New York)*, 6 May 1882, 376.

25 "Prince vs Armaindo," *Bicycling World*, 2 June 1882, 362.

26 *Bicycling World*, 21 April 1882, 288.

27 *De Ruyter (NY) New Era*, 28 March 1882, n.p.

28 "Philadelphia, 17–22 July," *Bicycling World*, 4 August 1882, 472.

29 "Racing on Bicycles," *New York Tribune*, 7 August 1882, 8.

30 "Morgan Wins the Bicycle Race," *New York Tribune*, 11 August 1882, 3.

31 "The Bicycle Contest," *New York Truth*, 6 August 1882, 1.

32 "Coney Island, NY, 13 August," *Bicycling World*, 25 August 1882, 507–8.

33 "Elsa Von Blumen," *Auburn (NY) Bulletin*, 22 February 1887, n.p.

34 "Athletic," *New York Clipper*, 1 January 1881, 822.

35 The author has a photocopy of the scrapbook. Lizzie Baymer Scrapbook, Nevada Historical Society, 1650 N Virginia Street, Reno, NV, 89503. For further information, see Sorensen, "Cycling Seamstress."

CHAPTER FOUR

1 Wells, "Ordinary Women," 5.

2 "A Bicycle Contest," *New York Times*, 3 September 1882, 8.

3 For example, see "Heel and Toe," *Sedalia (MO) Daily Democrat*, 5 October 1879, 1; "Rifle Practice," *Milwaukee Sentinel*, 2 January 1883, 6; "Currente Calamo," *Bicycling World*, 17 August 1883, 182; "Elements of Strength," *Denver Rocky Mountain News*, 24 November 1884, 2.

4 *New York Sunday Courier*, 24 October 1882. Reprinted in "Notes by the Way," *Wheel Trade Review*, 14 June 1900, 11.

5 "Sporting News," *Rockford (IL) Daily Register*, 28 May 1883, 4.

6   "The Bicycle Contest," *Chicago Inter Ocean*, 25 May 1883, 6.

7   "Bicycle Tournament," *Springfield Daily Illinois State Register*, 27 May 1883, 4.

8   "Bicyclists at Their Best," *Milwaukee Sentinel*, 16 June 1883, 5.

9   *Globe Arizona Silver Belt*, 2 June 1883, 2.

10 "Bicyclists at Their Best," *Milwaukee Sentinel*, 16 June 1883, 5; "Armaindo's Medals," *Springfield Daily Illinois State Register*, 11 July 1883, 3. Louise is wearing some of her medals and badges in Figure 3.4.

11 "Challenge," *Bicycling World*, 15 June 1883, 68.

12 "Riding the Bicycle," *Janesville (WI) Daily Gazette*, 7 June 1883, 4.

13 "The Champion Bicyclists," *National Police Gazette*, 10 May 1884, 6; "John S. Prince," *Springfield Wheelmen's Gazette*, March 1885, 166.

14 *US Federal Census*, 1900, Newark Ward 6, Essex, NJ, Enumeration District 0056, roll 963, p. 11A, FHL Microfilm 1240963.

15 "A Champion of Ireland," *National Police Gazette*, 10 February 1883, 12; "On the Wheel," *Milwaukee Sentinel*, 18 June 1883, 2.

16 "Louisa and Her Legs," *Milwaukee Daily Journal*, 21 June 1883, n.p.

17 "Louisa and Her Legs," *Milwaukee Daily Journal*, 21 June 1883, n.p.

18 "Bicyclists at Their Best," *Milwaukee Sentinel*, 16 June 1883, 5.

19 "The Bicyclists," *Milwaukee Sentinel*, 22 June 1883, 4.

20 "Racing News," *Bicycling World*, 6 July 1883, 104.

21 "Local Events," *Milwaukee Sentinel*, 1 July 1883, 3.

22 "The Lady Bicyclists," *Washington (DC) Evening Star*, 26 December 1883, 6.

23 "Miss Wallace and Madam Armaindo," *Chicago Tribune*, 2 July 1883, 8.

24 "Bicycles, Women on the Wheel," *Chicago Tribune*, 4 July 1883, 8.

25 "The Wheel, Armaindo Beats the Record," *Chicago Inter Ocean*, 5 July 1883, 6.

26 "An Unequalled Success," *Lawrence (KS) Western Home Journal*, 9 August 1883, 1.

27 "An Unequalled Success," *Lawrence (KS) Western Home Journal*, 9 August 1883, 1.

28 "Oak Ridge Park," *Springfield Daily Illinois State Register*, 13 July 1883, 3.

29 "No Race Yesterday," *Daily Illinois State Register,* 14 July 1883, 3.

30 "Currente Calamo," *Bicycling World*, 17 August 1883, 182.

31 "Minor Mention," *Daily Illinois State Register*, 27 July 1883, 3.

32 "Local Miscellany," *Quincy (IL) Daily Whig*, 15 August 1883, 8.

33 *Leavenworth (KS) Times*, 7 September 1883 cited in Lewis, "Beautiful Bismark."

34 "The Bismark Fair," *Lawrence (KS) Gazette*, 13 September 1883, 1.

35 "The Bicycle Race," *Emporia (KS) Weekly News*, 13 September 1883, n.p.; "Last Day of the Fair," *Sterling (IL) Gazette*, 22 September 1883, n.p.

36 "Racing News," *Bicycling World*, 16 November 1883, 22.

37 On the origins of bicycle racing in the United States, see Ritchie, *Quest for Speed*, 111–50.

38 "Mlle. Louise Armaindo," *New York Clipper*, 8 September 1883, 402.

39 *Milwaukee Sentinel*, 24 December 1883, 3.

CHAPTER FIVE

1 "Fred Engelhardt," *San Francisco Daily Alta California*, 1 January 1884, 5.

2 There is confusion over Henry W. Higham's birthdate. Some sources indicate 17 September 1851 and others have it as 24 January 1855. There is also contradictory information on Higham's death certificate (*Virginia Death Records, 1912–2014* for Henry W. Higham).

3 For reports of Higham's races in the UK, see *Six Day Cycle Race*, accessed 15 January 2018, http://www.sixday.org.uk/html/the_beginnings.html.

4 Park, in "Contesting the Norm," questions this assertion, but does not say why (see p. 740).

5 "Fred Engelhardt," *San Francisco Daily Alta California*, 1 January 1884, 5.

6 *Bicycling World*, 23 November 1883, 34; "The Wheel," *Sporting Life*, 28 November 1883, 6.

7 Advertisement, *Salt Lake Daily Herald*, 23 December 1883, 8.

8 Advertisement, *Rocky Mountain News*, 1 December 1883; "Modern Olympia," *Rocky Mountain News*, 3 December 1883, 2.

9 "The Champions at the Pavilion," *Salt Lake Daily Herald*, 25 December 1883, 8.

10 "Muscle on Wheels," *Daily Alta California*, 6 January 1884, 1.

11 "A Dude on Wheels,"*Daily Alta California*, 2 February 1884, 8.

12 "Local Intelligence," *Sacramento Daily Union*, 28 February 1884, 2

13 "Local Intelligence," *Sacramento Daily Union*, 22 May 1884, 2.

14 "The Bicycle Races," *Daily Alta California*, 23 February 1884, 1; "Racing News," *Bicycling World*, 7 March 1884, 220.

15 The exact date of Rollinson's release was 23 March 1885 (telephone conversation with Jim Brown, operation manager, Folsom Prison Museum, 16 August 2014).

16 In early June 1886 Rollinson left San Francisco on a steamship bound for Hawaii and eventually Australia. He was accompanied by a Mr Riddell, who owned a bicycle firm in San Francisco, and the well-known trick rider W.S. Maltby (see Maltby, *Trick Cycling in Many Lands*, especially chapters 1 and 2). Rollinson's plan was to compete in races in Australia and also join Maltby in double-act performances of trick or fancy riding. They arrived in Sydney in July, and set about booking performances and races. After a few weeks, and much to everyone's surprise, "Rolly" (as Maltby called him) announced that he had married an Australian woman, Louisa E. Barton. Maltby continued on his world tour, whereas Rollinson remained in Australia, apparently happily married. He continued to earn a living through performances in both Australia and New Zealand by touring with a minstrel show. On the death of his father in April 1891, Rollinson and his wife went to England, where for several years he toured and performed as the "World's Comic Bicycle Wonder." Sadly, Rollinson died on 26 January 1894 at thirty-six years of age and was buried in Norwood Cemetery, London. The cause and circumstances of his death are unknown. In his will he left his effects and £20 to his widow.

17 The Mechanics' Institute Pavilion was destroyed by fire on 18 April 1906 during the San Francisco earthquake.

18 "Horse against Bicycle," *Daily Alta California*, 15 April 1884, 8.

19 "Horse against Bicycle," *Daily Alta California*, 15 April 1884, 8.

20 "The Bicycles Ahead," *Daily Alta California*, 16 April 1884, 8.

21 "The Bicycles Ahead," *Daily Alta California*, 16 April 1884, 8.

22 "The Wonderful Riders of the Flying Wheels Who Have Beaten Man and Beast," *National Police Gazette*, 10 May 1884, 6.

23 See Reel, *National Police Gazette*, and Chudacoff, *Age of the Bachelor*, 187–210. For more about sports coverage in the *National Police Gazette*, see Betts, "Sporting Journalism," and Welky, "Culture, Media and Sport."

24 Reel, *National Police Gazette*, 144.

25 See *National Police Gazette*, 6 August 1881, 13 (Howard) and 2 September 1882, 5 (von Blumen). For Stanley, see 26 January 1889, 13; 2 March 1889, 1; 27 April 1889, 7, 13; and 28 April 1894, 6, 13.

26 "Racing News," *Bicycling World*, 6 June 1884, 83. Every attempt was made to check the *Aurora (ON) Banner* in 1884 for further information, but unfortunately the newspaper has not survived for that year.

27 From reports in the *Springfield Daily Illinois State Register*, 20 June–21 July 1884.

28 *Springfield Wheelmen's Gazette* 2, no. 3 (July 1884), 38.

29 *Springfield Wheelmen's Gazette* 2, no. 2 (June 1884), n.p.

30 "The Poetry of It," *Canadian Wheelman* 2, no. 1 (October 1884): 7.

31 "Bicycle vs. Horse," *Elkhart (IN) Daily Review*, 25 August 1884, 4.

32 From reports in the *St. Louis (MO) Globe-Democrat*, 6–15 September 1884.

33 "Wheel Tracks," *Canadian Wheelman* 2, no. 2 (November 1884): 22.

34 "Reminiscences of Professional Days," *Bearings* 8, no. 21 (22 December 1893): n.p.

35 From reports in the *Kansas City Star*, 8, 10, and 11 November 1884, in addition to "Elements of Strength," *Denver Rocky Mountain News*, 24 November 1884, 3.

36 "Racing News," *Bicycling World*, 12 September 1884, 322.

37 "Racing News," *Bicycling World*, 5 December 1884, 77.

38 "Von Blumen Elsa," *Auburn (NY) News-Bulletin-Auburnian*, 19 February 1885, 1.

39 "On the Wheel," *Boston Daily Globe*, 14 December 1884, 5.

CHAPTER SIX

1 "The Great Bicycle Contest," *Memphis Daily Appeal*, 9 January 1885, 4.
2 "Grand Finish," *Memphis Daily Appeal*, 11 January 1885, 4.
3 "Texas Siftings," *Springfield Wheelmen's Gazette* 2, no. 11 (March 1885): 176.
4 "Louise Armaindo," *San Antonio Light*, 10 February 1885, 1.
5 "Louise Armaindo," *San Antonio Light*, 10 February 1885, 1.
6 *Sporting and Theatrical Journal* 4, no. 4 (16 August 1884): 218.
7 "Fourth of July," *Montrose (PA) Democrat*, 11 July 1884, n.p.
8 Woodson, "Troubled Life," 18.
9 In addition to Woodson's extensive article in *True West*, see also "Queen of the Bicycle," *Springfield Wheelmen's Gazette* 2, no. 2 (April 1885): 203. Annie Sylvester's life was never easy and she experienced considerably tragedy. She died in California on 13 September 1938 at age seventy-four.
10 McCullough, *Old Wheelways*, 55. See pages 40–3 for an explanation of the complicated relationship between the LAW *Bulletin* and *Bicycling World*.
11 "Mlle. Louise Armaindo," *Springfield Wheelmen's Gazette* 2, no. 10 (February 1885): 151.
12 "Exotics," *Bicycling World*, 6 February 1885, 224.
13 Higham arrived in the United States from England in 1882 and settled in Washington, DC, with his wife and five children. Tragically, a couple of weeks after giving birth to their sixth child in May 1886, Harriet Higham died of burns suffered in a house fire. Higham opened a bicycle shop in Washington, where he sold new bikes, tires, and sundries. By 1890 the shop had two locations, and Higham had also married again. Eventually, he sold his business and moved with his wife Margaret to Newington, Virginia, where he had a farm. Higham passed away on 20 March 1926 at age seventy-four, and was buried in the church cemetery in Pohick, Virginia.
14 Hadland and Lessing, *Bicycle Design*, 115.
15 Advertisement in *Vinita (OK) Indian Chieftain*, 10 September 1885, 2.
16 "Bicycle Spokes," *Chicago Inter Ocean*, 8 November 1885, 3.

17 Woodside continued to race well into the 1880s, both in America and Europe, winning championships at both short and long distances. Unfortunately, he died of yellow fever on 18 May 1890 in Rio de Janeiro, where he was managing a sporting enterprise. He was only twenty-nine years of age, and his remains were interred in Brazil ("William M. Woodside," *Hartford Connecticut Courant*, 8 July 1890, 5).

18 Prial, *Best American and English*, 12.

19 "A Wheelman's Challenge," *St. Paul Daily Globe*, 2 January 1886, 3.

20 "Sporting News and Gossip," *Springfield Republican*, 27 December 1885, 6.

21 "The Wheel," *Sporting Life*, 27 January 1886, 8.

22 "Decadence of Roller Rinks," *St. Paul Daily Globe*, 2 January 1886, 3; Hage, "Games People Played," 326–7.

23 "Minneapolis Sports," *St. Paul Daily Globe*, 4 January 1886, 3; "History of Six-Day Races," *Minneapolis Journal*, 19 December 1903, 8.

24 "Minneapolis Sports," *St. Paul Daily Globe*, 1 March 1886, 3.

25 As it turned out, Cardiff scored a win over Rooke and Wilson, and a draw against Mitchell. In the bout with Wilson, for the Northwest Heavyweight Championship, Wilson went down six times before Cardiff knocked him out for good. Cardiff boxed professionally until 1892, meeting all the contemporary heavyweights, and ended his career with a record of 25 wins (11 KOs), 6 losses, and 8 draws. He died in a mental asylum in Salem, Oregon, in 1917. See "Patsy Cardiff," BoxRec, accessed 19 February 2018, http://boxrec.com/en/boxer/32590.

26 "Faribault Matters," *St. Paul Daily Globe*, 6 March 1886, 5; "Snyder the Winner," *St. Paul Daily Globe*, 7 March 1886, 1.

27 "T.W. Eck," *Bicycling World*, 4 June 1886, 148.

28 "Enterprising Wheelmen," *Springfield Republican*, 20 September 1886, 5; "The 24-hour Tandem Race," *Boston Daily Globe*, 21 October 1886, 3.

29 "The Rapid Wheel," *Auburn (NY) Sunday Dispatch*, 31 October 1886, n.p.

30 "It Is Three-Cornered," *St. Paul Daily Globe*, 20 December 1886, 1.

31 "The Bicycle Race," *St. Paul Daily Globe*, 21 December 1886, 3.

32 "Schock's Great Ride," *Minneapolis Star Tribune*, 26 December 1886, 6.

33 "Reminiscences of Professional Days," *Bearings* 8, no. 21 (22 December 1893): n.p.

34 "Scraps of Sports," *St. Paul Daily Globe*, 26 February 1887, 1.

35 "Armaindo Beaten," *St. Paul Daily Globe*, 6 March 1887, 2; "The Minneapolis Walking Match," *St. Paul Daily Globe*, 23 March 1887, 5.

36 "Society in Home Circles," *Omaha Daily Bee*, 17 July 1887, 10. See also "ECK, Thomas W.; 31; md. Jennie Z. CARLISLE; 18; Jul 1887 p 448," *Omaha Area Marriages*, accessed 31 January 2018, http://omaha marriages.wordpress.com/e-em/.

37 "Not an Enlopement," *St. Paul Daily Globe*, 20 July 1887, 4.

38 "She's Still Heart Whole," *St. Paul Daily Globe*, 23 July 1887, 1.

39 "Here and There," *Bicycling World*, 4 November 1887, 6.

40 Ritchie, *Quest for Speed*, 145.

41 Buck Peacock, "Stillman G. Whittaker, Highwheel Champion, Part 1," 1997, accessed 31 January 2018, http://www.oldbike.com/Whittaker. html.

42 "The Bicycle Race," *Philadelphia Inquirer*, 23 February 1888, 3.

43 "Louise Armaindo Beaten," *Philadelphia Times*, 25 March 1888, 1.

44 "Here & There," *Bicycling World and L.A.W. Bulletin*, 30 March 1888, 362.

45 *Historic Pennsylvania and New Jersey, Church and Town Records, 1708–1985*, reel 1090, Historical Society of Pennsylvania, Philadelphia, PA.

46 Image no. 298388, *United States Federal Census, 1870*, Camden North Ward, Camden, NJ.

47 "Divorce Granted," *Rochester (NY) Democrat and Chronicle*, 12 February 1887, 5. Emery Ellsworth Beardsley (1863–1948) was married six more times after he and Caroline were divorced. He also spent time in Auburn (New York) state prison in the early 1920s.

48 "For our dead heroes! Grand entertainment for the benefit of the Soldiers' and Sailors' Monument Fund at the New York State Arsenal," 1885, Rochester Public Library Historic Monographs Collection.

49 "Female Cyclists," *Wilkes-Barre (PA) Sunday Leader*, 10 June 1888, 3.

50 "Ladies on the Wheel," *Toronto Globe*, 12 September 1888, 3, and 13 September 1888, 4.

51 "She Went Willingly," *St. Paul Daily Globe*, 6 October 1888, 3.

52 "Running Off with His Wife," *New York Times*, 6 October 1888, 5.

53 "Mlle Armaindo's Challenge," *Chicago Inter Ocean*, 5 August 1888, 2.

54 "A Lady Champion," *Chicago Inter Ocean*, 26 August 1888, Part 2, 12.

CHAPTER SEVEN

1 Prince stopped racing bicycles in 1886 when he started to design and construct bicycle velodromes. At the turn of the century he embraced the motorcycle and began enlarging his velodromes to accommodate motorcycles. When these machines gave way to automobiles, Prince built board track speedways for racing cars. With his English mannerisms, impeccable dress, and trademark Derby hat, Prince was highly respected for his contributions to racing. He passed away at his home in Los Angeles on 7 October 1927 at sixty-eight years of age (Ball, "John Shillington 'Jack' Prince").

2 "Will Louise Be a Starter," *Omaha Herald*, 30 December 1888, 5.

3 "Athletic Louise Armaindo," *Omaha Herald*, 11 January 1889, 5.

4 "Athletic Louise Armaindo," *Omaha Herald*, 11 January 1889, 5.

5 Bloomfield, *Impertinences*, 7.

6 "Women on the Wheel," *Pittsburgh Press*, 26 November 1888, 8.

7 Hilda Suallor's name was often misspelled as Snallor, Shallor, and even Swallow.

8 "The Female Bicyclists," *Pittsburgh Post-Gazette*, 27 November 1888, 8.

9 Reports of the race were gathered from the *Pittsburgh Post-Gazette* and the *Pittsburgh Press*, 27 November to 3 December 1888.

10 "Away on Business," *Pittsburgh Press*, 4 December 1888, 2.

11 *Pittsburgh Press*, 18 December 1888, 5; "Pending Legal Advice," *Pittsburgh Press*, 21 December 1888, 2.

12 "Women on Bicycles," *St. Louis Republic*, 26 December 1888, 3.

13 "Fair Bicyclists," *New York Herald*, 26 December 1888, 6.

14 "Five Fair Riders," *Pittsburgh Dispatch*, 1 January 1889, 6.

15 "Hattie Is a Winner," *Pittsburgh Dispatch*, 6 January 1889, 6.

16 "When Wheels Begin to Whirl," *Omaha Herald*, 1 January 1889, 5.

17 "Wheel Gossip," *Wheel and Cycling Trade Review*, 4 January 1889, 371.

18 "Lottie Stanley," *National Police Gazette*, 26 January 1889, 3

19 "Here & There," *Bicycling World and L.A.W. Bulletin*, 21 December 1888, 119.

20 "Here & There," *Bicycling World and L.A.W. Bulletin*, 1 February 1889, 218.

21 "News and Comment," *Bicycling World and L.A.W. Bulletin*, 8 February 1889, 239.

22 "Here & There," *Bicycling World and L.A.W. Bulletin*, 15 February 1889, 252.

23 "Wheeling around the Garden," *New York Tribune*, 14 February 1889, 2.

24 "Astride the Silent Steed," *New York Herald*, 13 February 1889, 10.

25 "Stanley Wins the Race," *New York Times*, 17 February 1889, 2.

26 "Only Two of the Sick," *New York Times*, 18 February 1889, 8.

27 "Only Two of the Sick," *New York Times*, 18 February 1889, 8. This information was also reported in several other newspapers.

28 "The Riders May Turn Walkers," *New York Tribune*, 19 February 1889, 3.

29 "The Ladies Tournament," *New York Clipper*, 23 February 1889, 804.

30 Throughout her competitive career, Elsa von Blumen's life was intertwined with her long-time manager Bert Miller, whose real name was William H. Rosevelt (also spelled as Roosevelt). He was married with two children, but his wife Cornelia died in 1877, a couple of years before he met Elsa. Around 1880 he married Mary Raveret, whom Elsa certainly would have known. Later articles about Elsa suggest she had married Bert/William, which was not true. Perhaps she perpetuated the falsehood herself to erase the unfortunate marriage to Beardsley. William Rosevelt had three brothers, the youngest being Isaac L. Rosevelt, born in 1845. These particular Rosevelts were distant cousins of the more famous Roosevelts, notably Theodore. William Rosevelt (Bert Miller) died of heart disease on 13 February 1892 in Utica, New York. A couple of months later, on 19 April 1892, Elsa married William's brother Isaac. The wedding took place in St Paul's Rectory in Fort Erie, Ontario, located on the Niagara River directly across from Buffalo. Now aged thirty-two and a spinster, she was married under the name of "Flora Kiner"; Isaac was a forty-seven-year-old widower. Nine months

later, on 26 January 1893, their son Claude was born. By 1901 the
family was living in Troy, New York, on the Hudson River, where Isaac
worked as a lockmaster. He died in 1913 at sixty-eight, and Elsa moved
back to Rochester, New York. She was seventy-six when she died on
3 June 1935 and was buried in Riverside Cemetery in Rochester.

31 "Sutton Secures the Stakes," *Omaha Herald*, 24 March 1889, 7.

32 "Athletic Louise Armaindo," *Omaha Herald*, 15 March 1889, 5.

33 "In the Soup," *Omaha Herald*, 22 March 1889, 4.

34 "Women astride the Wheel," *Omaha Herald*, 24 March 1889, 4.

35 "Here & There," *Bicycling World and L.A.W. Bulletin*, 19 April 1889,
    515.

36 "The Seven Sweet Swifts," *Chicago Inter Ocean*, 14 April 1889, 22.

37 After this episode, no further reports of Louise and Norman being
    together were found, and it is possible they went their separate ways.
    By 1897 Stewart lived in Alma, a small mining town of about three hun-
    dred residents, situated high in the mountains of northwest Colorado.
    It was famous for rhodochrosite, a rose-coloured mineral used for jew-
    ellery. For the next few years, he was involved in mining by working
    several claims and supervising others. In April 1899 teenager Cora June
    Soash arrived in Alma with her family from Indiana because her father
    leased a hotel throughout the summer. He then stayed in Alma and be-
    came involved in various mining interests. On 23 July 1900 Norman B.
    Stewart (then thirty-three) and Cora J. Soash (now sixteen) were mar-
    ried. I think we can safely assume that Louise Armaindo knew nothing
    of Stewart's whereabouts at this time, and was unaware of his second
    marriage. It also seems that Norman and Louise were never officially di-
    vorced, although on the June 1900 US federal census Stewart's marital
    status was listed as "single." Since Louise was dead by early September,
    it was irrelevant. The Stewarts stayed in Alma while Norman pursued
    several mining ventures until the spring of 1905 when he became seri-
    ously ill and was sent to the hospital in Denver for a couple of months.
    He sold his mining interests in Alma, moved to Idaho and eventually to
    Reno, Nevada, supporting his family as a carpenter and painter. They
    had a daughter, Francis, probably in 1909, and a son, Harry, in 1912.
    By 1920 the family was living in Los Angeles, where Norman remained
    until his death in 1937 at age seventy-one.

38 Lulu Hart seems to disappear after the race in West Virginia. Lulu
    Gordon reappears in the next chapter, but as Frankie Nelson.

39 "Six Day Lady Bicyclists," *New York Herald*, 13 May 1889, 10.

40 "Morgan-Oaks," *Bicycling World and L.A.W. Bulletin*, 28 June 1889,
    244. However, no official marriage certificate was found, except that
    Morgan was married again in 1895 to Elizabeth C. Stilger (*New Jersey,
    Marriage Records, 1670–1965*). Often referred to as "Senator Morgan,"
    he earned the nickname when a Pennsylvania senator failed to arrive
    on time for a speaking engagement at a county fair and Morgan was en-
    listed to entertain the crowd, which he did with a spellbinding address.
    After retiring from racing, he turned his attention to cycle journalism
    and to promoting bicycle and eventually automobile races. He wrote
    regularly for newspapers, and for a brief period in 1894 was editor of
    American Wheelman; later he became a correspondent for *Automobile
    Magazine*. He died in his early eighties in 1941 in Newark, New Jersey.

41 "Off for Europe," *St. Paul Daily Globe*, 9 August 1889, 5.

42 "Fast Bicycle Riders," *Daily Alta California*, 22 October 1889, 3.

43 "The Bicycle Race," *Daily Alta California*, 28 October 1889, 3.

44 See the discussion in chapter 8 concerning the use of stimulants and
    drugs in professional cycling at this time.

45 "Lady Cyclists at Leicester," *Sheffield Daily Telegraph*, 23 September
    1889, 8. See also a report sent by cable from Leicester and published in
    several American papers (e.g., "England Captured," *Omaha Daily Bee*,
    23 September 1889, 1).

46 *Northampton Mercury*, 28 September 1889, n.p., and *Supplement to
    the Northampton Mercury*, 5 October 1889, 10.

47 "Lady Cyclists at Long Eaton," *Sheffield and Rotherham Independent*,
    9 October 1889, 8.

48 "Omaha Wheel Notes," *Omaha Daily Bee*, 13 October 1889, 9.

49 See reports of this race at *Six Day Cycle Race*, accessed 15 January
    2018, http://www.sixday.org.uk/html/1889_sunderland.html.

50 For more about the role of cycling in New Delaval, East Northumber-
    land, see Metcalfe, *Leisure and Recreation in a Victorian Mining Com-
    munity*, 120–3. He also mentions the women's visit to the New Delaval
    Amateur Bicycle Club, but has the date as May 1889, which is incorrect.

51 For a full report of the race and a photo of the Artillery Drill Hall in

Sheffield, see *Six Day Cycle Race*, accessed 15 January 2018, http://
www.sixday.org.uk/html/1889_sheffield.html.

52 "General Sport Notes," *Buffalo Courier*, 31 March 1890, 3.

53 For example, a search of several journals in the Bibliothèque nationale
de France, such as *Le véloce-sport (Journal officiel de l'Union Vélocipédique de France)*, produced no reports of the American riders in France.

54 "Our Cablegrams," *National Police Gazette*, 22 March 1890, 14.

55 "The Runners Are Ahead," *Chicago Inter Ocean*, 25 June 1890, 3 is the
only report found.

56 See reports in the *St. Joseph Herald* from 5 to 16 June 1890.

CHAPTER EIGHT

1 "Ladies Who Ride Wheels," *Chicago Inter Ocean*, 15 June 1890, 9.

2 Hadland and Lessing, *Bicycle Design*, 156.

3 Regarding the popularity of the safety bicycle, see Neejer, "The Bicycle
Girls," 42–53; Gant and Hoffman, *Wheel Fever*, 121–37; Finison,
Boston's Cycling Craze, 5–42, 43–68; and Friss, *Cycling City*, 161–85.
On the social construction of the safety bicycle, see also Bijker, *Of
Bicycles*, 18–100.

4 Gant and Hoffman, *Wheel Fever*, 63.

5 Cited in Ritchie, *Quest for Speed*, 218.

6 In October 1891 a highly successful men's professional high-wheel race
took place in Madison Square Garden because the track was built for
ordinaries, and the board floor was too dangerous for safeties. See "Off
on Their Long Ride," *New York Sun*, 19 October 1891, 5.

7 "In Bloomers," *St. Louis Post-Dispatch*, 30 August 1894, 1; "Miss
Walden," *St. Louis Post-Dispatch*, 2 September 1894, 15.

8 Ward, *Bicycling for Ladies*, 78–9.

9 "They Say They Will Ride," *Omaha World-Herald*, 12 September
1895, 8.

10 Nejeer, "The Bicycle Girls," 36.

11 "Now They're Off," *St. Paul Daily Globe*, 6 May 1891, 5.

12 "Starters Assured," *St. Paul Daily Globe*, 12 April 1891, 6.

13 For accounts of this race, see the *St. Paul Daily Globe*, from 26 April to
17 May 1891. Also, this was May Allen's last race for several years

because she and her husband, Harry Jeffs, had a daughter (Henrietta) in December 1892. She returned to racing during the summer of 1895.

14 "Commentaries," *Sporting Life*, 24 September 1892, 6.

15 "Cycling," *Sporting Life*, 4 February 1893, 11.

16 For a description of the geared ordinary and its relation to the safety bicycle, see "The Geared Ordinary," *Bearings Trade Supplement*, 23 December 1892, n.p.

17 "'Beauty Baldwin' the Winner," *Referee and Cycling Trade Journal (Supplement)*, 26 May 1893, 1.

18 See report in "Sport Queries Answered," *Chicago Inter Ocean*, 5 February 1894, 8 where it stated that Louise was in Chicago during the fair, but it cannot be ascertained where she is now.

19 "Like a River of Fire," *Chicago Daily Tribune*, 11 August 1893, 3.

20 "Sporting Notes," *Chicago Inter Ocean*, 9 February 1894, 8.

21 Library and Archives Canada, Department of Militia and Defense Fonds, R180-41-8-E, file no. A13706, MIKAN no. 3766105.

22 "Bicyclists," *Minneapolis Penny Press*, 6 January 1895, 8.

23 *Brooklyn Daily Standard Union*, 11 April 1895, 8. The same challenge appeared in the *National Police Gazette* on 27 April 1895, in *Bearings* on 3 May 1895, and in other newspapers as well.

24 "Miss Armindo [*sic*] Can't Race," *Rochester Democrat and Chronicle*, 23 June 1895, 15.

25 "She's a Champion," *Rochester Democrat and Chronicle*, 22 July 1895, 11.

26 "Women's Bicycle Races," *Courier-Journal (Louisville, Kentucky)*, 23 September 1894, 13.

27 "Objects to Ladies' Races," *Referee and Cycling Trade Journal*, 21 September 1894, 635.

28 "Bicycle Races for Women," *Pneumatic: A Monthly Journal of Cycling Literature and Trade News* (June 1895): n.p. About early women's baseball, see Shattuck, *Bloomer Girls*.

29 "Women's Bicycle Races," *Courier-Journal (Louisville, Kentucky)*, 23 September 1894, 13.

30 "By-Laws," *L.A.W. Bulletin and Good Roads*, 21 April 1895, 33.

31 "Wheelmen Combine," *New York Sun*, 28 July 1894, 5; "Wheelmen Who Want Protection," *New York Sun*, 30 July 1894, 6.

32 "Five Swift Girls," *St. Paul Daily Globe*, 7 July 1895, 6.

33 "Helen the Victor," *St. Paul Daily Globe*, 14 July 1895, 5.

34 See extensive reports in the *St. Paul Daily Globe* between 18 and 25 August 1895.

35 Compare this to the men's twenty-five-mile record in 1893, set by L.S. Meintjes, of one hour, four minutes, and thirty-four seconds.

36 "Won It by a Length," *Minneapolis Star Tribune*, 6 September 1895, 1.

37 "They Say They Will Ride," *Omaha World-Herald*, 12 September 1895, 8.

38 See reports in the *Omaha Daily Bee* between 13 and 24 September 1895.

39 "That 'Ladies Bicycle Race,'" *Bearings*, 26 December 1895, 8.

40 See reports primarily in the *New York Sun* between 6 and 14 January 1896.

41 "Extraordinary Vital Invigoration by Supplied Blood," *Modern Medical Science* 8, no. 8 (February 1896): 96–8.

42 "From the Female Champion," *Modern Medical Science* 8, no. 9 (March 1896): 134–5.

43 For a nuanced discussion of early doping in sport, see Dimeo, *A History of Drug Use in Sport*, 18–32.

44 "The Use of Stimulants by Athletes," *New York Times*, 1 December 1895, 16.

45 "Bicycle Dealers Remove Exhibits," *San Francisco Chronicle*, 14 March 1896, 8.

46 See Simpson, "Capitalising on Curiosity."

47 "Million and a Quarter," *Salt Lake Herald*, 22 March 1896, 13. The number was most likely exaggerated. See also Epperson, *Peddling Bicycles to America*, 149–70.

48 See also Kinsey, "Stamina, Speed and Adventure." For a useful analysis of women's international cycle racing, especially during 1896–98, see Simpson, "Capitalising on Curiosity."

49 "Cycling. Ladies International Tournament," *London Times*, 19 November 1895, 7.

50 Simpson, "Capitalising on Curiosity," 53.

51 See Sheila Hanlon, "Ladies' Cycle Races at the Royal Aquarium: A Late Victorian Sporting Spectacle," 26 January 2015, http://www.sheilahan lon.com/?p=1556. For a variety of news reports, see "19th Century

Female Riders," *Six Day Cycle Race*, accessed 15 January 2018, http://sixday.org.uk/html/19c_female_riders.html.

52 Advertisement, *London Daily News*, 22 April 1896, 4.

53 "Great International Six Days' Ladies Bicycle Race," *Sporting Life*, 21 April 1896, 4; "Ladies' Cycling Race at the Royal Aquarium," *London Daily News*, 21 April 1896, 9; "Sport Vélocipédique," *Le Gaulois*, 24 April 1896, 4.

54 *London Evening Standard*, 27 April 1896, 8.

55 "The Movement for Side Paths," *Rochester Democrat and Chronicle*, 16 May 1896, 19. Frankie Nelson returned to the American racing circuit for the remainder of the 1896 season. Although she began her high-wheel racing career as Lulu Gordon, and then became Frankie Nelson before she switched to a safety, her real name was Louise Reisman. Her racing career ended in 1896 when she married Burney B. Bird, also a racer, and then became Louise Bird. From then on, Louise and Burney, who do not appear to have had children, can be traced up to the 1930 United States census, at which time they (both aged fifty-seven) were living in Los Angeles, California.

56 "Girls Will Ride," *St. Paul Daily Globe*, 3 April 1896, 5.

57 See *St. Paul Daily Globe*, 19 to 26 April 1896 for a detailed description of the race.

58 "Helen's Fast Gait," *St. Paul Daily Globe*, 28 April 1896, 5.

59 "Females on Bikes," *Manitoba Morning Free Press*, 9 June 1896, 5. See also reports in the *Winnipeg Tribune*, 10–15 June 1896.

60 "Tillie Is All Right," *Chicago Dispatch*, 5 May 1896. I am grateful to Roger Gilles for this reference. For much more about Tillie Anderson and many other early women safety racers, see his book *Women on the Move*.

61 "Riot," *Minneapolis Star Tribune*, 7 July 1896, 1.

62 Hayes, *Two-Wheeled World*, 54.

63 Burgwardt, *Buffalo's Bicycles*, 38.

64 Burgwardt, *Buffalo's Bicycles*, 64. There is also a photo of Tom Eck as a "pusher" at the start of a men's bicycle race at the Buffalo Athletic Field on 24 August 1897 (see p. 63).

65 "Fire Guts Hotel," *Buffalo Evening News*, 2 November 1896, 7.

66 "Leaped from a Window," *Buffalo Express*, 20 November 1897, 6.

67 *Reports of Cases Heard and Determined in the Appellate Division of
the Supreme Court of the State of New York*, vol. 37, 1899, 160–1.
Note that *Armaindo v. Ferguson* was used as a legal precedent
concerning the liability of hotel owners and innkeepers for many
years following.

EPILOGUE

1   Allen continued to race until 1906, at which point she moved with her
husband and daughter back to Pittsburgh. Sadly, she died on 16 January
1911 of tuberculosis at the young age of thirty-eight ("Woman Bicyclist
Dies on North Side," *Pittsburgh Press*, 18 January 1911, 5).

2   Gilles, *Women on the Move*.

3   Eck, *Points on Training*. See also "Tom Eck's Advice to Amateurs Looking for Championship Laurels," *New York Times*, 14 January 1894, 3.

4   Pridmore and Hurd, *Schwinn Bicycles*, 28.

5   *US Federal Census*, 1900, Minneapolis Ward 10, Hennepin, MN,
Enumeration District 0107, roll 769, p. 6B, FHL Microfilm 1240769.

6   "Trainer Tom Eck Missing," *Chicago Daily Tribune*, 21 January 1898, 3.

7   "Tom Eck in Paris," *Times-Democrat (New Orleans, Louisiana)*, 13
February 1898.

8   "With the Whirring Wheels," *Detroit Free Press*, 26 August 1900, 26;
"Fail in Business," *Minneapolis Journal*, 3 May 1901, 7.

9   "Tom Eck Sued for Divorce," *Minneapolis Star Tribune*, 26 October
1901, 8.

10 Harper, *How You Played the Game*, 95; "Our Halftone Photos,"
National Police Gazette, 20 September 1902, 5, 7; "Lottie Brandon,
the Brooklyn Girl, Who Loops the Loop in Fearless Fashion," *Brooklyn
Daily Eagle*, 25 November 1902, 19; "Girl Beats All Men in Thrilling
Loop-the-Loop Performance," *Chicago Tribune*, 30 November 1902, 30.

11 For a photograph of Eck and Stalter, see "Attractions at the Theatres,"
Courier-News (Bridgewater, NJ), 2 May 1911, 10.

12 *US Federal Census*, 1910, Acquackanonk, Passiac, NJ, Enumeration
District 0059, roll T624_904, p. 3A, FHL microfilm 1374917.

13 No marriage notice or certificate was found.

14 "Gossip About the Boxers," *Cincinnati (OH) Enquirer*, 19 October
    1914, 9.
15 David P. Currie, "Do You Remember –," *University of Chicago Maga-*
    zine, 1921, 337.
16 Twelfth Census of the United States, Buffalo General Hospital, Ward 15,
    Buffalo, Erie, NY, 1 June 1900.
17 See chapter 7, note 37 for more information about Norman Stewart.
18 "Information Bureau Open," *Police Gazette*, 15 August 1903, 11.
19 "Louise Brisebois Epse (épouse) Stuart," in *Quebec, Canada, Vital*
    and Church Records (Drouin Collection), 1621–1968. In September
    1900 Norman Stewart was in Alma, Colorado, with his new bride
    (see chapter 7, note 37).
20 Watkins, "Cemetery and Cultural Memory," 52.
21 See appendix 1 for more information pertaining to Louise Armaindo's
    background and possible descendants.

APPENDIX ONE

1 I wish to acknowledge the work of Nancy Mitchell in developing this information. She spent countless hours researching genealogies of the individuals discussed here. Without her assistance, this appendix would not
   have been possible.
2 "Mlle Louise Armaindo," *New York Clipper*, 8 September 1883, 402.
   This same article said that she was born "at St Anne, near Montreal,
   Canada."
3 *Quebec, Canada, Vital and Church Records (Drouin Collection),*
   1621–1968, Pierrefonds, Ste-Geneviève, 1855–1873, 74.
4 *Quebec, Canada, Vital and Church Records (Drouin Collection),*
   1621–1968, Pierrefonds, Ste-Geneviève, 1855–1873, 20.
5 *Quebec, Canada, Vital and Church Records (Drouin Collection),*
   1621–1968, Vaudreuil, St-Michel, 1852–1858, 285.
6 *Quebec, Canada, Vital and Church Records (Drouin Collection),*
   1621–1968, Montréal, Basilique Notre-Dame, 1879, 581.
7 Gilles Janson, email messages to author, 9 and 13 May 2016. See also
   Janson, "1810–1895: L'entrée des femmes," 16; and the chapter about

Louise Armaindo in Marthaler, *À tire-d'elles*, 35–9, which was contributed by Janson.

8   In the *Quebec, Canada, Vital and Church Records (Drouin Collection),
    1621–1968*, there is a record of the baptism in Saint-Clet parish of
    Aglaé Brisebois on 23 August 1863, born five days earlier of the legiti-
    mate marriage of Moeyse Brisebois and Adele Charlebois.

9   *Census of Canada*, 1871, Saint-Clet, Soulanges, QC, roll C-10053,
    family no. 6, p. 1.

10 *Census of Canada*, 1881, Saint-Clet, Soulanges, QC, roll C-13207,
    family no. 41, p. 9.

11 *Quebec, Canada, Vital and Church Records (Drouin Collection),
    1621–1968*, Montréal, Basilique Notre-Dame, 1885, 338.

12 *Census of Canada*, 1881, Ste Anne de Bellevue, Jacques Cartier, QC, roll
    C-13222, family no. 179, p. 36. Louise Armaindo is not here because
    by this point she is in the United States.

13 At a six-day race in Minneapolis in December 1886, one of Louise's
    trainers/attendants was "Ellen Armaindo," who could have been her
    sister Hélène.

14 In an interview Louise said that her brother was "one of the most suc-
    cessful divers in the world." The reporter also noted that Louise had
    "made great sacrifices to help her old father in business" ("Athletic
    Louise Armaindo," *Omaha Herald*, 11 January 1889, 5).

15 "Athletic Louise Armaindo," *Omaha Herald*, 15 March 1889, 5.

16 *Census of Canada*, 1911, 3 – Alfred, Prescott, ON, family no. 159,
    p. 18.

17 *Census of Canada*, 1901, Sainte-Anne-de-Bellevue (Town/Ville),
    Jacques-Cartier, QC, family no. 47, p. 5.

18 *Census of Canada*, 1901, Sainte-Anne-de-Bellevue (Town/Ville),
    Jacques-Cartier, QC, family no. 29, p. 3.

19 Library and Archives Canada, *Census of Canada*, 1921, Ste Anne de
    Bellevue (Town), Montreal (Jacques-Cartier-Lachine), QC, RG 31, folder
    no. 120; p. 10.

APPENDIX TWO

1 First published in *America: A Journal for Americans* 2, no. 74 (29 August 1889): 685–7. For more information about the author Elia Peattie, see Bloomfield, *Impertinences*. See also *Elia Peattie: An Uncommon Writer, An Uncommon Woman*, a digital archive based on the life and writings of Elia Peattie at http://plainshumanities.unl.edu/peattie/ep. biography.html.

2 "Athletic Louise Armaindo," *Omaha Herald*, 11 January 1889, 5.

BIBLIOGRAPHY

A NOTE ABOUT SOURCES

Searching for traces of Louise Armaindo and the other high-wheel racers discussed in this book was made possible through the digitization of archival newspapers in Canada, the United States, and Europe. Through the University of Alberta Libraries I was able to access major newspapers in both the United States and Canada. Comprehensive and free resources in the United States such as the Library of Congress *Chronicling America*, and a number of individual state newspaper collections, such as the *California Digital Newspaper Collection* or the *Old Fulton* NY *Post Cards* were invaluable. I also maintained subscriptions to several commercial newspaper archives, including Newpapers.com, Geneologybank.com, NewspaperArchive.com, and the British Newspaper Archive, and though they varied in quality and accessibility, they were worth the money spent. I have not provided a list of newspapers consulted because there are far too many, but the notes at the end of each chapter contain the citations to article titles, newspaper and journal titles, dates, and page numbers.

The use of online databases, and specifically comprehensive newspapers databases, has profoundly changed how historians conduct their research, and I am aware of the need for a critical methodology if we are to use these tools responsibly. For example, there is little comparison between the meticulous reading of a microfilmed version of an archival newspaper and the use of keyword searches of a digitized version of the same newspaper, especially those processed through optical character recognition. I have been conducting historical research long enough to have done my share of microfilm reading, and I have also been involved with projects where I started out reading the microfilm and ended up using a newly digitized form. Of course, there are many advantages to keyword searches, the main one being the less time it takes to find something specific. However, the central question is always whether the database can be trusted, and has the keyword search found everything relevant? Where possible I favoured digital newspaper databases where I could read a specific article in the context of a full page. Often, I scanned through the entire newspaper to locate what I needed, just as I would if it were a microfilm version.

The central task of this particular research project was to find the whereabouts of Louise Armaindo from the first newspaper occurrence (on 19 March 1879 in Chicago) until her death on 2 September 1900 in Montreal. Although using the keyword "Armaindo" produced many results, and almost all were relevant, it often took considerably more searching to find her. With very few gaps, I discovered where Louise was every month of her twelve-year competitive career. Not unexpectedly, newspaper reports of the same event or race were sometimes contradictory, and to gain a better perspective I used a triangulation approach of several accounts.

Finally, the references listed below contain the complete bibliographic information for short form versions cited in the notes to each chapter.

Adams, Katherine H., and Michael L. Keene. *Women of the American Circus, 1880–1940*. Jefferson, NC: McFarland, 2012.

Algeo, Matthew. *Pedestrianism: When Watching People Walk Was America's Favorite Spectator Sport*. Chicago: Chicago Review Press, 2014.

Andreas, Alfred T. *History of Chicago: From the Earliest Period to the Present Time*. Volume 3, *From the Fire of 1871 until 1885*. Chicago: A.T. Andreas Company, 1886.

Balf, Todd. *Major: A Black Athlete, a White Era, and the Fight to Be the World's Fastest Human Being*. New York: Crown Publishers, 2008.

Ball, Larry L. "John Shillington 'Jack' Prince." National Sprint Car Hall of Fame and Museum. Accessed 13 January 2018. https://www.sprintcarhof. com/FileGet.aspx?ID=51.

Betts, John R. "Sporting Journalism in Nineteenth Century America." *American Quarterly* 5, no. 1 (1953): 39–56.

Bijker, Wiebe. *Of Bicycles, Bakelites, and Bulbs: Toward a Theory of Sociotechnical Change.* Cambridge, MA: MIT Press, 1995.

Bloomfield, Susanne George. *Impertinences: Selected Writings of Elia Peattie, a Journalist in the Gilded Age.* Lincoln: University of Nebraska Press, 2005.

Bottomley, J. F. *The Velocipede: Its Past, Its Present, and Its Future.* London: Simpkin, Marshall & Co., 1869.

Brady, William A. *Showman.* New York: E.P. Dutton, 1937.

Burgwardt, Carl F. *Buffalo's Bicycles: Reflections on Buffalo's Colossal and Overlooked Bicycle Heritage.* Orchard Park, NY: Pedaling History Bicycle Museum, 2001.

Chapman, David L., and Patricia Vertinsky. *Venus with Biceps: A Pictorial History of Muscular Women.* Vancouver, BC: Arsenal Pulp Press, 2010.

Chudacoff, Howard P. *The Age of the Bachelor: Creating an American Subculture.* Princeton, NJ: Princeton University Press, 1999.

Cohn, Caitlin S. "Wheelwomen: Women's Dress in a Transatlantic Cycling Culture, 1868–1900." PhD diss., University of Minnesota, 2016.

Dauncey, Hugh. *French Cycling: A Social and Cultural History.* Liverpool, UK: Liverpool University Press, 2012.

Dimeo, Paul. *A History of Drug Use in Sport 1876–1976.* London: Routledge, 2007.

Eck, Thomas W. *Points on Training for Wheelmen.* Syracuse, NY: E.C. Stearns & Co., 1894.

Epperson, Bruce D. *Peddling Bicycles to America: The Rise of an Industry.* Jefferson, NC: McFarland & Company, 2010.

Finison, Lorenz J. *Boston's Cycling Craze, 1880–1900.* Amhurst: University of Massachusetts Press, 2014.

Finnigan, Joan. "Joseph Montferrand: The Giant of the Ottawa Valley." In *Giants of Canada's Ottawa Valley,* 12–33. Burnstown, ON: General Store Publishing, 1981.

Friss, Evan. *The Cycling City: Bicycles and Urban America in the 1890s.* Chicago: University of Chicago Press, 2015.

Gant, Jesse J., and Nicholas J. Hoffman. *Wheel Fever: How Wisconsin Became a Great Bicycling State.* Madison, WI: Wisconsin Historical Society Press, 2013.

Gazette and Directory of the County of Ontario for the Year 1876. Uxbridge, ON: J.A. Crawford, 1860.

Gems, Gerald, and Gertrud Pfister. "Women Boxers: Actress to Athletes – The Role of Vaudeville in Early Women's Boxing in the USA." *The International Journal of the History of Sport* 31, no. 15 (2014): 1909–24.

Gilles, Roger. *Women on the Move: The Forgotten Era of Women's Bicycle Racing.* Lincoln: University of Nebraska Press, forthcoming.

Goddard, J.T. *The Velocipede: Its History, Varieties, and Practice.* New York: Hurd and Houghton, 1869.

Goyer, Gérard, and Jean Hamelin. "Montferrand, Favre, Joseph." In *Dictionary of Canadian Biography*, vol. 9. University of Toronto/Université Laval, 2003. http://www.biographi.ca/en/bio/montferrand_joseph_9E.html.

Guroff, Margaret. *The Mechanical Horse: How the Bicycle Reshaped American Life.* Austin: University of Texas Press, 2016.

Hadland, Tony, and Hans-Erhard Lessing. *Bicycle Design: An Illustrated History.* Cambridge, MA: MIT Press, 2014.

Hage, George S. "Games People Played: Sports in Minnesota Daily Newspapers 1860–1890." *Minnesota History* (Winter 1891): 321–28. http://collections.mnhs.org/MNHistoryMagazine/articles/47/v47i08p321-328.pdf.

Hall, Harry. *The Pedestriennes: America's Forgotten Superstars.* Indianapolis, IN: Dog Ear Publishing, 2014.

Hall, M. Ann. *The Girl and the Game: A History of Women's Sport in Canada.* 2nd ed. Toronto: University of Toronto Press, 2016.

– *Immodest and Sensational: 150 Years of Canadian Women in Sport.* Toronto: James Lorimer, 2008.

Hallenbeck, Sarah. *Claiming the Bicycle: Women, Rhetoric, and Technology in Nineteenth-Century America.* Carbondale: Southern Illinois University Press, 2016.

Harper, William A. *How You Played the Game: The Life of Grantland Rice.* Columbia: University of Missouri Press, 1999.

Hayes, Kevin J. *The Two-Wheeled World of George B. Thayer.* Lincoln: University of Nebraska Press, 2015.

Herlihy, David V. *Bicycle: The History.* New Haven, CT: Yale University Press, 2004.

Humber, William. *Freewheeling: The Story of Bicycling in Canada.* Erin, ON: The Boston Mills Press, 1986.

Jacques, Le Grand. *Manuel du vélocipède.* Paris: Librairie du Petit Journal, 1869.

James, Ed. *Practical Training for Running, Walking, Rowing, Wrestling, Jumping and All Kinds of Athletic Feats.* New York: Ed. James, 1878.

Janson, Gilles. "1810–1895: L'entré des femmes dans l'arène sportive." *Cap-aux-Diamants: La revue d'histoire du Québec* 13 (Spring 2013): 11–16.

– ed. *Dictionnaire des grands oubliés du sport au Québec 1850–1950.* Québec: Septentrion, 2013.

Kinsey, Fiona. "Stamina, Speed and Adventure: Australian Women and Competitive Cycling in the 1890s." *International Journal of the History of Sport* 28, no. 10 (2011): 1375–78.

Kobayashi, Keizo. *Histoire du vélocipède de Drais à Michaux 1817–1870: Mythes et réalités.* Tokyo: Bicycle Culture Center, 1993.

Kofoed, Jack. *Thrills in Sport.* New York: Holborn House, 1932.

Kossuth, Robert S., and Kevin B. Wamsley. "Cycles of Manhood: Pedaling Respectability in Ontario's Forest City." *Sport History Review* 34, no. 2 (2003): 168–89.

Lachapelle, Alain. "Marcher pour survivre: le parcours extraordinaire d'Exilda Lachapelle." *Le Marin*, Bulletin no. 6 (August 2015), 11–14.

Lewis, Guy M. "The Ladies Walked and Walked." *Sports Illustrated*, 18 December 1967. https://www.si.com/vault/1967/12/18/610183/the-ladies-walked-and-walked.

Lewis, Jim L. "Beautiful Bismark: Bismark Grove, Lawrence, 1878–1900." *Kansas Historical Quarterly* 35, no. 3 (Autumn 1969): 225–56. http://www.kshs.org/p/kansas-historical-quarterly-beautiful-bismarck/13197.

Mackintosh, Phillip Gordon, and Glen Norcliffe. "Men, Women and the Bicycle: Gender and Social Geography of Cycling in the Late Nineteenth-Century." In *Cycling and Society*, edited by Dave Horton, Paul Rosen and Peter Cox, 153–77. Aldershot, UK: Ashgate 2007.

Macy, Sue. *Wheels of Change: How Women Rode the Bicycle to Freedom.* Washington, DC: National Geographic, 2011.

Maltby, W.S. *Trick Cycling in Many Lands: An Exhibition Tour of the World.* New York: Fless & Ridge Print Co., 1895.

Marthaler, Claude. *À tire-d'elles: Femmes, vélo et liberté.* Geneva: Éditions Slatkine, 2016.

Massicote, E.Z. *Athlètes Canadiens-Français: Recueil des exploits de force, d'endurance, d'agilité, des athlètes et des sportsmen de notre race, depuis le XVIIIe siècle,* 2nd ed. Montreal: Librairie Beauchemin, 1909.

McCullough, Robert L. *Old Wheelways: Traces of Bicycle History on the Land.* Cambridge, MA: MIT Press, 2015.

McNulty, Bill, and Ted Radcliffe, comp. *Canadian Athletics 1839–1992.* Published by authors, 1992.

McQuillan, D. Aidan. "French-Canadian Communities in the American Upper Midwest during the Nineteenth Century." *Cahiers de Géographie du Québec* 23, no. 58 (1979): 53–72.

Menke, Frank G. *Encyclopedia of Sports.* New York: Frank G. Menke, Inc., 1939.

Metcalfe, Alan. *Leisure and Recreation in a Victorian Mining Community.* London: Routledge, 2006.

Meyerowitz, Joanne J. *Women Adrift: Independent Wage Earners in Chicago, 1880–1930.* Chicago: University of Chicago Press, 1988.

Miller, Donald L. *City of the Century: The Epic of Chicago and the Making of America.* New York: Simon & Schuster, 1996.

Monteiro, George. "Histoire de Montferrand: L'Athlete Canadien and Joe Mufraw." *Journal of American Folklore* 73, no. 287 (1960): 24–34.

Neejer, Christine. "The Bicycle Girls: American Wheelwomen and Everyday Activism in the Late Nineteenth Century." PhD diss., Michigan State University, 2016.

Norcliffe, Glen. "Associations, Modernity and the Insider-Citizens of a Victorian Bicycle Club." *Journal of Historical Sociology* 19, no. 2 (2006): 121–50.

– *The Ride to Modernity: The Bicycle in Canada, 1869–1900.* Toronto: University of Toronto Press, 2001.

Oddy, Nicholas. "Bicycles." In *The Gendered Object,* edited by Pat Kirkham, 60–9. Manchester, UK: Manchester University Press, 1996.

Park, Roberta J. "Contesting the Norm: Women and Professional Sports in Late Nineteenth-Century America." *International Journal of the History of Sport* 29, no. 5 (2012): 730–49.

Peattie, Elia W. "Louise Vieillard Sainte-Foix." *America: A Journal for Americans* 2, no. 74 (1889): 685–87.

Pfister, Gertrud, and Gerald Gems. "The Shady Past of Female Boxers: What Case Studies in the USA Reveal." *Sport in Society* 20, no. 8 (2016): 998–1012.

Pratt, Charles E. *The American Bicycler: A Manual for the Observer, the Learner, and the Expert.* Boston, MA: Houghton, Osgood and Company, 1879.

Prial, Francis P. *The Best American and English Path and Road Cycle Records.* New York: W.N. Oliver & Co., 1885.

Pridmore, Jay, and Jim Hurd. *Schwinn Bicycles.* Osceola, WI: Motorbooks International, 1996.

Reel, Guy. *The National Police Gazette and the Making of the Modern American Man, 1879–1906.* New York: Palgrave MacMillan, 2006.

Ritchie, Andrew. "The League of American Wheelmen, Major Taylor and the 'Color Question' in the United States in the 1890s." In *Ethnicity, Sport, Identity: Struggles for Status,* edited by J.A. Mangan and Andrew Ritchie, 10–35. London: Routledge, 2004.

– *Major Taylor: The Extraordinary Career of a Champion Bicycle Racer.* Baltimore, MD: Johns Hopkins University Press, 1988.

– *Quest for Speed: A History of Early Bicycle Racing 1868–1903.* El Cerrito, CA: Andrew Ritchie, 2011.

– "Seeing the Past as the Present That It Once Was: A Response to Nancy Struna's 'Reframing the Direction of Change in the History of Sport' (*IJHS,* December 2001)." *International Journal of the History of Sport* 20, no. 3 (2003): 128–52.

Sears, Edward S. *Running through the Ages.* 2nd ed. Jefferson, NC: McFarland, 2015.

Shattuck, Debra A. *Bloomer Girls: Women Baseball Pioneers.* Urbana: University of Illinois Press, 2017.

Shaulis, Dahn. "Enduring a Life of Hardship, Exilda La Chapelle Was Not Afraid to Clear Her Own Path." Unpublished paper, 1995. http://www.thelizlibrary.org/undelete/woa/woa02-15.html.

– "Pedestriennes, Marathoners, Ultramarathoners, and Others: Two Centuries of Women's Endurance." *Women in Sport and Physical Activity
Journal* 5, no. 2 (1996): 1–27.

– "Pedestriennes: Newsworthy but Controversial Women in Sporting Entertainment." *Journal of Sport History* 26, no. 1 (1999): 29–50.

Simpson, Clare S. "Capitalising on Curiosity: Women's Professional Cycle
Racing in the Late-Nineteenth Century." In *Cycling and Society*, edited by
Dave Horton, Paul Rosen, and Peter Cox, 47–65. Aldershot, UK: Ashgate,
2007.

Slout, William L. *Olympians of the Sawdust Circle: A Biographical Dictio-
nary of the Nineteenth Century American Circus*. San Bernardino, CA:
Borgo Press, 2009. Also available online at http://www.circushistory.org/
Olympians/Olympians.htm.

Smith, Malissa. *A History of Women's Boxing*. Lanham, MD: Rowman &
Littlefield, 2014.

Smith, Robert A. *A Social History of the Bicycle*. New York: American
Heritage Press, 1972.

Sorensen, Sandra. "The Cycling Seamstress." *Nevada Magazine* (March/
April 2002): 16–17, 78.

Tait, Peta. *Circus Bodies: Cultural Identity in Aerial Performance*. London:
Routledge, 2005.

Todd, Jan. "Bring on the Amazons: An Evolutionary History." In *Picturing
the Modern Amazon*, edited by Joanna Frueh, Laurie Fierstein, and Judith
Stein, 48–61. New York: Rizzoli, 1999.

– *Physical Culture and the Body Beautiful: Purposive Exercise in the
Lives of American Women 1800–1875*. Macon, GA: Mercer University
Press, 1998.

U.S. Bureau of the Census. *Historical Statistics of the United States, Colonial
Times to 1970, Bicentennial Edition, Part 2*. Washington, DC: U.S. Bureau
of the Census, 1975.

– *Statistics of Women at Work: Based on Unpublished Information Derived
from the Schedules of the Twelfth Census (1900)*. Washington, DC: U.S.
Bureau of the Census, 1907.

Vincent, Ted. *Mudville's Revenge: The Rise and Fall of American Sport*. New
York: Seaview Books, 1981.

Ward, Maria E. *Bicycling for Ladies*. New York: Bretano's, 1896.

Watkins, Meredith G. "The Cemetery and Cultural Memory: Montreal, 1860–1900." *Urban History Review/Revue d'histoire urbaine* 21, no. 1 (2002): 52–62.

Welky, David B. "Culture, Media and Sport: The *National Police Gazette* and the Creation of an American Working-Class World." *Culture, Sport, Society* 1, no. 1 (1998): 78–100.

Wells, Michael S. "Ordinary Women: High-Wheeling Ladies in Nineteenth Century America." *The Wheelman* 43 (November 1993): 2–14.

Wilcox, Julius. "The Bicycle, and Riding It." *Lippincott's Magazine* 24 (November 1879): 623–29.

Willard, Frances E. *A Wheel within a Wheel*. New York: Revell, 1895.

Williams, Jean. *A Contemporary History of Women's Sport, Part One: Sporting Women, 1850–1960*. New York: Routledge, 2014.

Willoughby, David P. *The Super-Athletes*. New York: A.S. Barnes, 1970.

Woodson, Weldon D. "The Troubled Life of a Bicyclienne." *True West* (July–August 1972): 16–20, 39–42.

INDEX